Hannes Swoboda Arnold Klotz Lothar Fischmann (Hrsg.)

Wien erfahren
Ein Drehbuch für Wien

Experiencing Vienna
A Film-Script for Vienna

SpringerWienNewYork

Vorwort

1988 hatte ich die Ehre, als Wiener Stadtregierungsmitglied die Aufgaben eines Stadtrates für Stadtentwicklung und Stadtplanung zu übernehmen. Damals befand sich Wien an einem in der heutigen Konsequenz nicht absehbaren Wendepunkt. Jahrzehnte der europäischen und innerösterreichischen Randlage im Schatten des Eisernen Vorhanges hatten bis dahin zu einer langsamen, aber beständigen Abwanderung der Wiener Bevölkerung geführt.

Der Stadtentwicklungsplan aus dem Jahr 1984, auf den sich unsere Arbeit stützen sollte, sah eine Stabilisierung der Bevölkerungszahl bei rund 1,5 Millionen vor und ein Stadtforscher prognostizierte gar noch 1989 eine Zahl von 1,4 Millionen Menschen in Wien. Dementsprechend rückläufig war die Entwicklung im Wohnbau und bei Infrastrukturplanungen. Um dieser Abwärtsbewegung zu begegnen, waren allerdings bereits Mitte der achtziger Jahre Überlegungen angestellt worden, durch ein international beachtetes Großereignis wie eine Weltausstellung neue Impulse zu geben. „Brücken in die Zukunft" wollte Wien mit der damals noch im „Ostblock" unter kommunistischer Herrschaft befindlichen Schwesterstadt Budapest schlagen. Doch bereits 1989 wurde die gesamte Welt durch den positiven Schock der zu diesem Zeitpunkt völlig unvorhersehbaren Öffnung des Ostens, das plötzliche Verschwinden des Sowjetimperiums, das bis 60 Kilometer vor Wien gereicht hatte, erschüttert. Für Wien bedeutete das: Die Zukunft, in die wir Brücken schlagen wollten, war über Nacht Gegenwart geworden.

Und Wien begann wieder zu wachsen. Diese Periode des Wachstums, die wir zu Beginn als „Neue Gründerzeit" bezeichneten, durfte ich mit meinem Team, allen voran Planungsdirektor Arnold Klotz, mitgestalten. Wir hatten große Aufgaben zu bewältigen: Der

Foreword

1988 as a member of Vienna's City Council I had the honor of taking on the duties of City Councillor for Urban Development and Planning. Vienna was at a turning-point, the consequences of which could then not be foreseen in their present dimensions. Decades spent under the shadow of the Iron Curtain and hence in a situation of isolation both within Austria and in Europe as a whole had produced a slow but gradual exodus of the Viennese population. The 1984 Urban Development Plan on which we were to base our work foresaw a stabilization of the population at around 1.5 million and, as late as 1989, a demographer prophesied population figures of 1.4 million for Vienna. Given this demographic decline, progress in housing and infrastructure planning also lagged far behind. In order to counteract this downward trend, in the middle of the eighties consideration was given to the possibility of hosting a large-scale event at an international level, such as a World Exposition, to provide the city with new stimuli. Vienna wanted to build "Bridges into the Future" with its sister city Budapest – at that time still in the Eastern Bloc and under Communist rule. But then, in 1989, the whole world was shaken by the, albeit positive, shock of the opening up of Eastern Europe, totally unforeseen at that time, and the sudden disappearance of the Soviet sphere of influence which had stopped just 60 km short of Vienna. For Vienna, this meant that the future towards which we wanted to build our bridges had overnight turned into the present. And suddenly Vienna started growing again.

Together with my team, led by Arnold Klotz as Director of Planning, I was fortunate enough to be able to play a part in the period of growth we referred to at that time as the new "Gründerzeit", or "Second Period of Intensive Construction". There were major tasks to be

Stadtentwicklungsplan war neu zu schreiben, die überbordende (Auto-)Mobilität machte ein neues Verkehrskonzept für Wien nötig. Die wachsende Bevölkerung und vor allem die gestiegenen quantitativen wie qualitativen Ansprüche an den Wohnraum und die Wohnumgebung machten ein plötzliches Hinaufschrauben der Widmungen für soziales Wohnen nötig: Von 3.500 Wohnungen pro Jahr kamen wir in kürzester Zeit auf über 10.000 jährliche Widmungen. Völlig neue Stadtteile waren zu entwickeln. Und bei all dem wollten und durften wir keine Qualitätsverluste hinnehmen: Weder sozial, noch ökologisch, noch bei der gestalterischen Qualität.

Die „Neue Gründerzeit" hatte nachträglich betrachtet nicht die erwartete Dynamik erreicht, nicht zuletzt, weil die Öffnung des Ostens schneller als erwartet zur europäischen Selbstverständlichkeit geworden war. Und Mitte der neunziger Jahre schien sich die Größe Wiens auf 1.650.000 Einwohner stabilisiert zu haben. Umso wichtiger war es, die in Wien traditionelle soziale Dimension der Stadtentwicklung zu stärken. Es galt, den Weg zur nachhaltigen Stadt konsequent weiterzugehen.

Derzeit werden nahezu monatlich neue Wohnsiedlungen bezugsfertig, anhand derer wir überprüfen können, ob wir die angestrebte Qualität erreicht haben. Wir haben den Wiener Grüngürtel geschlossen, haben ein umfassendes Grünprogramm beschlossen, Wien liegt als einzige Großstadt der Welt an einem Nationalpark, obwohl – oder weil es mitten in der Stadt ein Donaukraftwerk errichtet hat. Wien hat sein U-Bahn und Straßennetz konsequent weiterentwickelt. Das Verkehrskonzept beginnt zu greifen: Die Parkraumbewirtschaftung wurde auch in Wien zur Selbstverständlichkeit. Die öffentlichen Räume werden zunehmend von den Menschen in Besitz genommen. Wir haben eine grundlegende Reform der Wiener Bauordnung

undertaken. The Urban Development Plan had to be rewritten and the flood of cars into the city made a new traffic concept for Vienna necessary. The growing population and, in particular, its increased quantitative and qualitative demands for improved housing and residential environments have made it necessary to increase the number of social housing units built annually from 3,500 apartments to over 10,000 units within a short time. Entirely new areas would have to be generated in the city and yet we could not – and indeed did not want to – lower our standards regarding social factors, the ecological aspects, and in the field of design.

Viewed in retrospect, this "Second Period of Intensive Construction" did not achieve the desired momentum, not least because the opening up of Eastern Europe became a European reality far more quickly than had been anticipated. And by the middle of the nineties Vienna's population seemed to have stabilized at 1,650,000 inhabitants. Given these figures, it became even more important to strengthen the traditional social aspects of urban development and to consistently pursue our goal of a sustainable city.

At present, nearly every month new housing developments are ready for occupancy and give us the chance to see whether we have attained the desired quality. We have closed the city's green belt and have drawn up a comprehensive ecological program: Vienna is the only city in the world to have a national park at its doorstep, although, or because, it has built a power station on the Danube in the middle of the city. We have consistently expanded Vienna's subway system and road network. The traffic concept has begun to take effect: regulated and time-controlled parking facilities have become a matter of course. Public spaces are increasingly being taken over by the inhabitants of the city. We have implemented a fundamental reform of the

durchgezogen, die der Philosophie einer Reform der Wiener Stadtverwaltung hin zur noch stärkeren Bürgerfreundlichkeit entspricht. Und wir haben uns schließlich bemüht, Wien in der Welt noch besser zu positionieren, da ich 1994 auch die neugeschaffene Aufgabe eines Stadtrates für Stadtaußenbeziehungen übernehmen durfte.

Der Wiener Tourismus, wesentlicher Wirtschaftsfaktor der Stadt, blüht, Wien wird als Wirtschaftsstandort immer attraktiver. Wir unterhalten Büros in Hong Kong, Tokyo und dem 1995 erfolgten Beitritt Österreichs zur Europäischen Union Rechnung tragend in Brüssel. In den USA betreiben wir erfolgreiche wirtschaftliche und kulturelle Promotion.

Stark unterstützt und gefördert ist diese Arbeit von den beiden Bürgermeistern worden, mit denen ich in diesen Jahren zusammenarbeiten durfte. Über zehn Jahre war Helmut Zilk ein Motor dieser Stadt in fast allen Bereichen, der Wiens internationales und kulturelles Selbstbewußtsein gestärkt hat, der geradezu besessen die Stadtverwaltung auf Bürgerfreundlichkeit, auf Service trimmte, der ein besonders herzliches und gutes Verhältnis zu den wichtigen Medien dieses Landes, aber auch über die Grenzen hinweg hatte.

Bürgermeister Michael Häupl ist es, der seine als Umweltstadtrat begonnene Arbeit konsequent weiter betreibt: Er war es, der Wien auf den Weg zur Umweltmusterstadt führte, der damit die Entwicklung hin zur nachhaltigen Stadt ermöglichte. Es ist ihm vor allem auch gelungen, die Wiener Lebensfreude als Qualität weiterzuentwickeln.

Was uns freilich nicht ablenken darf von der Notwendigkeit, große kulturelle Projekte wie das Museumsquartier oder ein Guggenheim-Museum in der künftigen Donau-City konsequent weiterzuverfolgen. Für mich ist nach diesen Jahren der Mitverantwortung für diese Stadt der Zeitpunkt gekommen, eine neue Aufgabe in Europa zu überneh-

Viennese building regulations, which matches our philosophy of a new approach by Vienna's municipal administration towards strengthened proximity to its citizens. And, finally, we have endeavored to further enhance Vienna's image in the world, particularly so since in 1994 I had the honor of taking on the new responsibilities of City Councillor for External Relations. Tourism, which has always been an important economic factor for our city, is flourishing, and Vienna is becoming increasingly attractive as a business location. We maintain offices in Hong Kong, Tokyo and – since Austria's accession to the European Union in 1995 – also in Brussels. In the USA we are running a successful economic and cultural promotion program. All these activities were strongly supported and encouraged by the two mayors with whom I was fortunate enough to work during these past years. For over 10 years Helmut Zilk was the engine of this city in almost every field, and it was he who boosted Vienna's international and cultural self-confidence. He was almost obsessed by the idea of reforming the municipal administration towards a closer contact with and an improved service for its citizens, and he also enjoyed especially good relations both with the leading media of this country and abroad. Our present Mayor, Michael Häupl, is persistently pursuing the goals he set himself as City Councillor for the Environment. It was he who led Vienna towards its image as a modern environmental metropolis and who has enabled its development as a sustainable city. Today, he has become Vienna's very popular mayor and has above all also succeeded in re-promoting a "joie de vivre" atmosphere among the people of this city. But there is still room for improvement and what we have achieved must not deter us from implementing major projects such as the Museum Quarter or the Guggenheim Museum in the future Donau City. After all these years of co-responsibility in this city,

men, bei der ich mein Land Österreich und vor allem meine Stadt Wien und die Interessen meiner Mitbürger zu vertreten habe.

Es ist nicht nur das ein Anlaß, ein wenig Bilanz zu ziehen über dieses Wien im neuen Fin de Siecle. Bilanz nicht im klassischen Sinn mit Zahlen, Daten und Fakten: Es ist keine buchhalterische Bilanz, vielmehr der Versuch, Wiener Atmosphäre der neunziger Jahre einzufangen. Es ist eine erzählerische und bildhaft gestaltete Darstellung einer Stadt, die alle lieben, die an diesem Buch mitgearbeitet haben, und ich möchte hier kurz das Entstehen dieses Buches schildern. Gemeinsam mit Arnold Klotz hatten wir die Idee für diese „Bilanz". In mehreren Gesprächen mit meinen Medienbetreuern Gabriele Philipp und Lothar Fischmann ist dann das vorliegende „Drehbuch für Wien" entstanden, und gemeinsam mit dem PR-Team der Stadtplanung Wien sowie der „Lomographischen Gesellschaft Wien" (die für die eigenwilligen Fotos sorgte) haben wir diesen „Reiseführer" gemacht. Für Besucher, aber auch für die Wiener, die ihre Stadt einmal anders kennenlernen wollen.Nicht alles und jedes, was in diesen letzten Jahren in Wien geplant und umgesetzt wurde, kann hier Platz finden, und niemand von den vielen, vielen Planerinnen und Planern, Architektinnen und Architekten und allen engagierten Menschen dieser Stadt möge uns Gram sein, wenn ihr/sein Name hier nicht aufscheint. Alle werden sich aber hoffentlich im Gesamtbild Wiens wiederfinden, wie es hier in den Worten von Lothar Fischmann dargestellt wird.

Gute Reise also in Wiens Vergangenheit, Gegenwart und Zukunft. Wir haben uns bemüht, ein „Drehbuch" zu schreiben – setzen Sie den „Film" für sich selbst um! Wir haben für Sie „Caroline" durch unser Wien geführt, deren Reise hier beschrieben wird.

Viel Lese- und Reisevergnügen wünscht
Hannes Swoboda

the time has now come for me to take on new tasks in Europe, where I will represent my country and, above all, my city and my fellow citizens. I would therefore like to use this opportunity to take stock of the situation of our City of Vienna at the new fin de siécle. But not in the classical sense of figures, dates and facts, not like a bookkeeper but rather in the form of an attempt to capture the atmosphere of Vienna in the 1990s. It is a narrative and pictorial presentation of a city which is loved by all those who have worked on this book and I would now like to briefly describe how it came into being. We developed the idea of this "stocktaking" together with Arnold Klotz. In the course of several discussions with my media experts, Gabriele Philipp and Lothar Fischmann, this "Film-script for Vienna" was conceived and, with the help of the Municipal Department of Urban Planning and the "Lomographische Gesellschaft Wien" (which supplied the distinctive photos), we have produced this "Guide to the City", which is intended not only for visitors but also for those Viennese who want to get to know their city from a different angle.

Not everything that has been planned and implemented in Vienna during these past few years can be incorporated into this text, and none of the hosts of planners, architects and dedicated people of this city should feel offended if their name is not mentioned. They will, hopefully, recognize themselves in the overall picture of Vienna presented by Lothar Fischmann.

We hope you will enjoy your journey into Vienna's past, present and future. We have endeavored to write a "script" – it is up to you to make the "film"! For you, we have guided Caroline through our City of Vienna and have described her journey in the following book.

We wish you pleasant reading and a good journey
Hannes Swoboda

Prolog
Prologue

7

„We built this city on rock'n' roll", tönte aus den Lautsprechern des Autoradios, als sie den Hollywood Boulevard hinunterrollte. „Jefferson Starship" hießen die Oldies, deren Hit aus vergangenen Jahren der Wiener Peter Wolf produziert hatte. Komisch, daß ihr das gerade jetzt einfiel. Oder doch nicht: Seit einigen Wochen beschäftigte sich Caroline W. mit dieser exotischen Welt im alten Europa. 1.000 Jahre alt war dieses Österreich geworden, in das sie jetzt zum ersten Mal in ihrem Leben fliegen sollte. Die Österreicher sprachen gerne auch vom „Namenstag" ihres Landes.

Als sie auf den Highway einbog, der sie zum internationalen Airport von L. A. bringen würde, hatte sie Zeit, ein wenig darüber nachzudenken, was sie alles gehört hatte über dieses Wien: Der Stau hatte durchschnittliche L. A.-Dimensionen, und sie würde eine gute Stunde bis zum Flughafen brauchen.

Caroline war Mitarbeiterin des neuen „Metropolis TV", eines jener neuen Programmanbieter, die die 500 TV-Stationen beliefern sollten, welche über die neue Digital-Satelliten-Kette weltweit auch „special interests" befriedigen würden. „Metropolis TV" plante gerade eine Serie über die alten Städte in Europa. Und dieses Wien war ihrem Chef als erste Station nicht gerade zufällig untergekommen: Hollywood wimmelte ja vor Leuten in der Film- und Fernsehbranche, die irgendeine Beziehung zum alten Europa, vor allem auch zu jenem sagenhaften alten Österreich hatten.

Billy Wilder zum Beispiel, der gerade mit biblischen neunzig Jahren einen neuen Film plante. Klar, ein paar Junge waren auch dabei. Arnold Schwarzenegger etwa oder dieser Robert Dornhelm.

„We built this city on rock'n' roll" Carolines L.A. war tatsächlich irgendwie auf Musik, auf dem Glitzergeschäft des Kinos, der globalen Unterhaltungsindustrie aufgebaut. Dieser Peter Wolf kam ja auch aus einer Stadt, die auf Musik gebaut war.

"We built this city on rock'n' roll" echoed from the loudspeakers of the car radio as Caroline drove down Hollywood Boulevard. "Jefferson Starship" they were called, those "oldies" whose hit from the past had been produced by the Viennese Peter Wolf. Funny how she happened to think of that just now. Or maybe not so funny. For Caroline W. had been thinking about this exotic world back in old Europe for several weeks now. And Austria, which she was about to visit for the first time, had just become 1,000 years old. And Austrians also liked to refer to this event as the "name-day" of their country.

When she turned onto the highway that would take her to Los Angeles International Airport, Caroline had some time to think about everything she had heard about Vienna. The traffic jam was about average for L. A. so it would take her a good hour to get to the airport.

Caroline was working for "Metropolis TV", a new broadcasting station that would supply 500 TV stations which would also cater to "special interests" all over the world via the new digital satellite chain. Right now, "Metropolis TV" was preparing a series on old European cities. And it was no accident that Vienna had occurred to her boss as the first one. Hollywood and the film and television branch were full of people who had some sort of connection with Europe and particularly with famous old Austria.

Take Billy Wilder, for example, who at the biblical age of 90 was planning a new film. Sure, there were also a couple of young ones like Arnold Schwarzenegger and Robert Dornhelm.

"We built this city on rock'n' rol". Yes, Caroline's L. A. was somehow built up on music, on the glitter of the movies and on universal show-biz. But this guy Peter Wolf also came from a city that was built on music. At her parents' place, their ancestors also came from somewhere back in old Europe, Caroline had watched this really neat concert on TV.

Caroline hatte bei ihren Eltern, deren Vorfahren auch aus irgendeinem Teil dieses alten Europa gekommen waren, dieses witzige Konzert im Fernsehen gesehen. Am Neujahrstag hatte da ein Haufen Musiker in dunklen Anzügen und weißen Hemden ziemlich schwungvolle Musik gemacht. Das Outfit, na ja! Aber die Musik hatte schon ihren Reiz.

Peter Wolf, wußte Caroline von ihrem Freund, der in einem der Musikstudios in L.A. arbeitete, war seinerzeit von Frank Zappa in seine Band geholt worden, obwohl Europäer ja offenbar dauernd nur diese alten Walzer spielten, und in Wien sollte es eine uralte Oper geben. Wolf hatte mit „Wang Chung" gearbeitet, die den Soundtrack zum Film „To Live and Die in L.A." gemacht hatten.

„Walzerstadt Wien", das hatte sich irgendwie eingeprägt, doch Caroline hatte bei ihren ersten Erkundigungen über die Stadt an der blauen Donau, auf die sie ja schon gespannt war, von wegen „blau", mitgekriegt, daß dort nicht alles nur alt war. Irgendwie hatte sie so eine vage Vorstellung gehabt: Ein kaiserlich-königliches Disneyland, eine Museumsstadt, ein Haufen merkwürdiger Menschen wie in diesem alten Film von Roman Polanski: „Tanz der Vampire" hatte der geheißen und irgendwo im Osten von Europa gespielt. Sie mußte lachen, als sie an die Szene im Ballsaal des Dracula-Schlosses dachte: Ob es wohl am Wiener Opernball auch so zuging?

Im Ernst: Sie hatte sich ja mit dem modernen Wien zu beschäftigen. Die UNO hatte dort einen ihrer Hauptsitze, Wien war schon lange die Hauptstadt einer kleinen Republik, die jahrzehntelang am Eisernen Vorhang gelegen war. Und Wien, das wußte sie, war eine kleine Stadt im Vergleich zu den US-Metropolen. Und das mit Disneyland stimmte auch nicht: In einer Architekturausstellung der Stadtplanung Wien hatte sie Bilder vom neuen Wien gesehen, die sie neugierig gemacht hatten. Direkt gegenüber dem hunderte Jahre alten Step-

On New Year's Day a bunch of musicians in dark suits and white shirts had played some pretty swinging music. Their outfit was kind of strange, but the music had its charm.

Caroline knew from her boy-friend, who was working in one of L. A.'s music studios, that Peter Wolf had been invited by Frank Zappa to join his band, although Europeans apparently only played those waltzes, and in Vienna there was supposed to be a really old opera house. Peter Wolf had worked with "Wang Chung", who had made the soundtrack to the film "To Live and Die in L. A.".

"Vienna, City of the Waltzes", had somehow stuck in her mind but the first information Caroline had gathered about the city on the "blue" – you must be kidding! – Danube, about which she was now quite curious revealed that not everything there was old. Somehow she had built up a vague image of a kind of imperial Disneyland, a museum city and a bunch of strange people like in that old film by Roman Polanski "The Dance of the Vampires", which was made somewhere in Eastern Europe. She really couldn't help laughing when she thought of the ballroom scene in Dracula's castle. "I wonder whether that's how it goes at the Vienna Opera Ball?", she thought.

But, seriously now. She had to find out about modern Vienna. She knew that Vienna was one of the headquarters of the UN. And for a long time now Vienna had also been the capital of a small republic, which had for decades been right next to the Iron Curtain. Vienna was also a small city compared with the big cities in the US. And of course it wasn't like Disneyland. In an exhibition on architecture she'd seen pictures of the new Vienna that had made her really eager to see it. Right across the street from St. Stephen's Cathedral, which was hundreds of years old, they'd built a shiny new department store. Apparently there was quite a fuss about it – at least in Vienna.

hansdom hatten sie ein spiegelndes Kaufhaus hingestellt, worüber sich die alten Europäer eine Zeitlang ziemlich gestritten haben sollen. Jedenfalls in Wien. Von COOP Himmelblau hatte sie gehört, den Architekten, die ja auch in L.A. arbeiteten. Das „Schindler House" und das „Mackey House" kannte sie als Dependencen des Wiener MAK (Museum für Angewandte Kunst). Und bei einer Party hatte sie eine ganze Schar junger Architektinnen und Architekten kennengelernt, die gar nicht in ihr persönliches Bild vom alten Europa gepaßt hatten. Silja Tillner zum Beispiel, die mit dem österreichischen Kulturinstitut in New York auch hier in Los Angeles die Ausstellung „Vienna Housing: Trends and Prototypes" gemacht hatte, oder Regina Pizzinini. Und in New York war die Szene begeistert vom Neubau des österreichischen Kulturinstituts, das Raimund Abraham geplant hatte. Keine Spur von architektonischem Disneyland, das diese Österreicher hier zeigten.

Drei Tage sollte sie nun in Wien verbringen. Drei Tage, in denen ihr Experten jenes Wien zeigen sollten, das nicht unbedingt in der Tourismuswerbung gezeigt wird. „Metropolis TV" wollte ein Wien-Feature, das die Entwicklung der alten Stadt in den letzten Jahren zeigen sollte. Konnte ja ganz schön stressig werden. Schließlich sollte sie in diesen drei Tagen auf Spurensuche aus zweitausend Jahren gehen. Angeblich hatten ja schon diese alten Römer in Wien ein Lager gehabt.

She'd heard of COOP Himmelblau, the team of architects that were also working in LA. And she knew about the "Schindler House" and the "Mackey House" in connection with the Vienna MAK. At a party she'd once met a whole bunch of young architects who didn't at all fit into the image she'd built up of old Europe.

Take Silja Tillner, for example. Together with the Austrian Cultural Institute in New York, she had set up an exhibition here in L.A., too – "Vienna Housing: Trends and Prototypes" it was called. Or Regine Pizzinini. And in New York they were all raving about the new building for the Austrian Cultural Institute that Raimund Abraham had designed. No trace of an architectural Disneyland there!

And now she was going to spend three days in Vienna. Three days during which experts would take her round the city and show her things that don't necessarily appear in tourist brochures.

"Metropolis TV" wanted a Vienna feature showing the development of the old city over the past few years. It could prove quite stressful because she was supposed to uncover the traces of 2,000 years of history. Apparently, even the ancient Romans had had a camp in Vienna.

Caroline drove into the airport. She would first fly to New York to take a look at the new CD ROM "Visionaries in Exile", a multi-media presentation about the influence of Austrian architects in the USA. From there she would take a direct flight to Vienna. And tomorrow

Caroline bog zum Airport ein, ihre erste Flugetappe sollte sie nach New York bringen, wo sie sich die erste Präsentation der CD-ROM „Visionäre im Exil" ansehen wollte, jene multimediale Darstellung des Einflusses österreichischer Architekten in den USA.

Von dort gab es dann einen direkten Flug nach Wien. Morgen früh sollte sie dort von einem befreundeten Paar abgeholt werden, das gerade in Baden lebte, einem kleinen Städtchen bei Wien. Und am nächsten Tag sollte sie sich auf den Weg durch die Stadt machen. Mit der U-Bahn. Und zu Fuß! Komisch, diese Wiener, dachte sie noch, gehen zu Fuß durch die Stadt! Aber dann parkte sie bereits ihr Auto ein.

Dieses Buch soll eine Anleitung zu einer Reise durch Wien sein, die man tatsächlich in drei Tagen (mit einem 72-Stunden-Ticket der Wiener Linien) sehr preiswert machen kann. Eine Reise für interessierte Wien-BesucherInnen ebenso wie für alle WienerInnen, die ihre eigene Stadt einmal anders kennenlernen wollen. Begleiten Sie also unsere Caroline auf ihrem Wien-Trip.

Übrigens: „Metropolis TV" gibt es (noch?) nicht wirklich. Und auch Caroline ist eine virtuelle Figur. Aber wer kann das heute noch unterscheiden, in einer zunehmend virtuellen Welt ...

morning she would be met at the airport by a couple of friends who were presently living in Baden, a small town nearby. The next day she would start her tour of Vienna, by subway and on foot. Can you believe it! These funny Viennese, she thought, they still go through the city on foot! By now she had reached the airport and was parking her car.

This book is intended as a self-guided tour of Vienna that can actually be done in three days (with a 72-hour ticket from the Vienna Transport Board) at a very reasonable price. It is a tour not only for interested visitors to Vienna but also for those Viennese who want to see their city from a different angle. And now let's join Caroline on her trip through Vienna. Incidentally, "Metropolis TV" does not (yet?) exist. And Caroline is also a virtual-reality figure. But, today, in our increasingly virtual world, who can tell the difference...?

Twilight Zone
Am Rande der Stadt
On the outskirts of the city

13

74

Der Flug über den Atlantik war angenehm gewesen. Austrian Airlines stimmte Caroline mit einem Wiener Frühstück auf ihre Zielstadt kulinarisch gut ein. Der Bordfilm über Wien zeigte bekannte Wien-Klischees: Die Wiener Sängerknaben, die Sachertorte, die Lipizzaner. Tradition ist ja gut, dachte Caroline, aber das ist ja nun wirklich ein wenig viel monarchistische Folklore. Sie war auf das wirkliche Wien gespannt.

Der Anflug bot ihr schon erste Eindrücke: Über den Wienerwald schwebte der Airbus ein, querte die Donau, die im Morgenlicht wirklich fast blau, wenigstens blaugrau schimmerte. Und sie konnte wie auf einem Modell sehen, wie sich die Stadt rechts der Donau konzentrierte, an die Hänge der Berge schmiegte, wie sie dann geradezu vorsichtig links des Stromes sich hinaustastete in die Ebene. Natürlich: Von den Dimensionen her schien sie viel kleiner als die großen Metropolen in den USA, in Asien und auch in Europa. Ziemlich kompakt eigentlich. Und was Caroline auf den ersten Blick auffiel: Soviel Grün hatte sie in einer großen Stadt noch kaum gesehen.

Der Jet zog noch eine weite Kurve über den Nordosten der Stadt und senkte sich sanft über eine weite Aulandschaft: Hier mußte wohl der Nationalpark sein, von dem sie gehört hatte. Ein Nationalpark am Rande einer Großstadt!

Die Maschine war schon zu tief und zu schnell, als daß sie das neue Donaukraftwerk hätte sehen können. Auch so eine Wiener Geschichte: Ein Kraftwerk mitten in der Stadt und gleich daneben ein Nationalpark.

Als der Riesenvogel ausrollte, war Caroline vollends auf Wien eingestimmt. Wofür schon die Wiener Walzerklänge sorgten, die aus den Lautsprechern perlten. Der Flughafen empfing sie ein wenig abweisend: Viel größer, als sie erwartet hatte. Mußte also doch stimmen, daß Wien eine europäische Drehkreuzfunktion hatte. Und bei der Paß-

Caroline had enjoyed her flight over the Atlantic, and "Austrian Airlines" had given her a taste of her destination with a typically Viennese breakfast. The film about Vienna showed the familiar clichés – the Vienna Boys' Choir, the Sachertorte, the Lippizaner horses. Tradition is all very well, mused Caroline, but that's a bit too much imperial folklore. She was curious to see the real Vienna. The approach to the city gave her the first impressions. The airbus hovered low over the Vienna Woods, crossed the Danube, which really looked almost blue, or at least blue-gray, in the morning light. And like on a model, she could see how the city was concentrated to the right of the Danube, how it hugged the slopes of the hills and then cautiously fingered its way along the left of the river and out into the plains. Of course, it looked much smaller than the big bustling cities of America, Asia or even Europe. Rather compact, in fact. But what Caroline noticed at first glance was the wide expanse of green – she'd never seen so much greenery in a large city before.

The jet made another curve over the north-east of the city and then dropped down over a large stretch of wetlands. This must be where the national park was that she'd heard about. Just imagine, a national park on the edge of a large city!

The airplane was already too low and too fast for Caroline to be able to make out the new Danube power station. This must also be something typically Viennese, she thought – a power station in the middle of the city and right next to it a national park.

By the time the big machine had taxied down Caroline was completely tuned into the Austrian capital, helped by the Viennese waltzes that wafted from the loudspeakers.

The airport she found slightly off-putting. It was much bigger than she had expected. So it must be true that Vienna serves the function of a hub within Eu-

kontrolle fühlte sie sich wie vor abweisenden Burgtoren stehend. Ob das mit der EU-Außengrenze zu tun hatte?

Aber dann wurde Caroline schon von ihren Bekannten in Empfang genommen, die sie in das kleine Städtchen Baden bei Wien brachten. Tat ganz gut nach den beiden langen Flügen, sich in der Kleinstadt zu erholen.

Am nächsten Tag ging es früh los. Caroline sollte den typischen Tagesablauf in Wien miterleben. Und Wien ist zeitig auf den Beinen. Ihre Bekannten nahmen sie mit dem Auto mit zu ihrem Treffpunkt mit ihren Wiener Stadtführern. Merkwürdig: bei einem Park & Ride-Bahnhof sollten sie sich treffen. Aber wie gesagt: Caroline sollte den Wiener Alltag erleben.

Auf der Fahrt über die Autobahn wurde sie ein wenig an die morgendlichen Highways in Los Angeles erinnert. Obwohl es hier noch um einiges zügiger dahinging als daheim, deuteten sich schon die ersten Staus an. Rund 180.000 Menschen, erfuhr sie später, pendelten jeden Tag in die 1,6-Millionen Stadt zur Arbeit ein. Zu viele mit dem Auto. Und ihr fiel auf, daß sich die Stadt schon ganz schön in ihr Umland gefressen hatte. An einem riesigen Einkaufszentrum mit fast US-Dimensionen vorbeifahrend, sah sie erstmals die Silhouette Wiens vom Süden her, fast wie eine Mauerkrone auf den Hügeln des Wienerberges aufgesetzt.

Dann ging es durch eine typische Vorstadtgegend zum Park & Ride an der U6 in Siebenhirten. Und da bekam Caroline ihren ersten Eindruck von neuer Architektur im scheinbar der Tradition verhafteten Wien.

Futuristisch, in der Morgensonne silbern glänzend, stand da inmitten eher gesichtsloser baulicher Umgebung, die südliche Endstation von Wiens längster U-Bahn-Linie. Einen weiten Teil ihrer „Reise" durch Wien konnte sie nun auf Abschnitten der insgesamt 18 Kilometer langen Linie machen, die bis in den Nor-

rope. And at the passport control she felt almost as if she were barred by castle gates. Maybe this had something to do with the borders of the European Union?

But then Caroline was greeted by her friends, who took her to Baden, near Vienna. After two long flights it felt good to relax in this small town.

The next day they set off for Vienna early in the morning. For Caroline was to experience a typical day in the life of the city, and Vienna gets going early. Her friends drove her to the venue with her Viennese guides. Funny, she was to meet them at a park-and-ride station. But, as we said, Caroline was to get to know everyday life in Vienna.

During the drive along the expressway to Vienna she was reminded of the highways in Los Angeles in the mornings. Although the traffic here moved somewhat faster than at home, there were already signs of the first build-ups. Around 180,000 people, as she learned later, commuted every day to the Austrian capital with its 1.6 million inhabitants, too many of them by car. And she noticed that the city had engulfed a lot of the surrounding countryside. Passing a huge shopping center almost the size of an American one, she caught her first glimpse of the silhouette of Vienna from the south, resting like the crest of a wall on the hills of the Wienerberg.

Then they drove through a typical suburban area until they reached the park-and-ride station of the U6 subway line in Siebenhirten. And here Caroline gained her first impression of modern architecture in a Vienna that was supposedly rooted in tradition.

Futuristic and gleaming like silver in the morning sun in its somewhat characterless environment stood the southern terminus of Vienna's longest subway line. Caroline would do a large part of her "journey" through Vienna in stages on this 18 km-long line, which continues to the northern end of the city, trav-

den der Stadt führte und im Süden wie im Norden als Stadtentwicklungsachse fungierte. Weil, wie sie später hören sollte, die Stadt dem Autoverkehr zwar nicht gerade den Kampf angesagt hatte, aber in den letzten Jahren durch gezielte Stadtplanung versucht hatte, unnötigen Autoverkehr zu vermeiden. Wozu eben die Erweiterung und Verdichtung der Stadt an den öffentlichen Verkehrsmitteln gehörte.

Aber der Reihe nach. Ihre Bekannten, die täglich ihr Auto hier in Siebenhirten parkten, um mit der U6 zu ihren Arbeitsplätzen in der Stadt weiterzufahren, stellten sie ihrer Wien-Begleitung vor. Die Stadt unterhält eine eigene Informations-Truppe von geschulten Mitarbeiterinnen und Mitarbeitern, die Wien-Besuchern auch sehr fachspezifische Informationen geben können. Caroline wurde von Susi und Wolf begleitet, die in der Stadtplanung Wien Öffentlichkeitsarbeit machten. Mit ihnen sollte Caroline nun die Stadt „erfahren".

„Twilight Zone" war Caroline eingefallen, als sie in diese Übergangszone zwischen Land und Stadt gekommen war. Ist ja in fast allen Städten ähnlich. An Stadteinfahrten weiß man selten sofort, wo man sich eigentlich befindet. Gerade im Süden Wiens ist das besonders schwer herauszufinden. Denn ein wenig ähnlich wie in Los Angeles erstreckt sich der Ballungsraum schon zig Kilometer hinaus „ins Land".

Wobei sich Wien da in einer besonderen Situation befindet. Noch vor knapp mehr als fünfundsiebzig Jahren war Wien die Hauptstadt Österreich-Ungarns gewesen, eine 2-Millionen-Metropole im Lande Niederösterreich. Als die Monarchie auseinanderfiel und jener kleine Teil, der heute Österreich darstellt, abgetrennt wurde, sollte auch Wien den Status eines Bundeslandes erhalten und wurde von seinem natürlichen Umland getrennt. Ein politischer Gewaltakt, dessen Folgen nicht nur im „Roten Wien" der zwanziger und frühen

ersing the metropolis from north to south as an axis of urban development. Because, as she was later to hear, while the municipal authorities have not exactly declared war on automobiles, in recent years they have tried, through specific urban planning policies, to eradicate unnecessary road traffic. Part of this policy was therefore directed at expanding and intensifying the city's public transport system. But, first things first. Her friends, who every day parked their car here in Siebenhirten and continued on the U6 line to their places of work in the city center, introduced Caroline to the people who would accompany her on her tour of Vienna. The City of Vienna has its own team of trained experts who are able to provide visitors with specialized and technical information about different aspects of the city. Caroline would be taken round by Suzanne and Wolf, who work in public relations in the field of urban planning. With them, Caroline was to "experience" Vienna.

The words "Twilight Zone" had occurred to Caroline when she reached this border area between city and country. It's more or less the same the world over, she thought. When you enter a city you don't quite know where you are. And in the south of Vienna it's particularly confusing because, a bit like in Los Angeles, the conurbations stretch out over several kilometers into the "open country". And Vienna's geographical situation is also unique in this respect.

For just over 75 years ago Vienna was still the capital of the Austro-Hungarian Empire and was at that time a metropolis of 2 million located in the province of Lower Austria. When the monarchy collapsed and the small part of it that today makes up Austria was divided off, Vienna was accorded the status of a federal province and was forcibly separated from its natural environment. This was an act of political violence which left its mark not only on the so-called "Red, or Socialist Vienna" of the twenties and

dreißiger Jahre zu spüren war. Noch heute sind die negativen Auswirkungen spürbar und sichtbar, wie hier im „Niemandsland" zwischen Stadt und Land.

In der dunklen Phase Österreichs, als der Name von den Landkarten verschwand, gab es nicht nur ein Großdeutschland, sondern auch ein Groß-Wien in den Grenzen etwa der heutigen Ballungsregion. 1955 erreichte Österreich wieder seine Unabhängigkeit, und alle „großdeutschen" Spuren sollten getilgt werden. Also bekam auch Wien fast wieder seine engen Grenzen, die sich als problematisches Korsett erweisen sollten.

Heute versucht man, in Zusammenarbeit mit den Bundesländern Niederösterreich und Burgenland wieder eine geordnete Zusammenarbeit in einer „Planungsgemeinschaft" in dieser Wiener Region, aber die ist mühsam. Und so wachsen jenseits des Stadtrandes nach wie vor Einkaufszentren, wachsen, nicht nur im Süden, neue Vorstädte ohne die notwendigen Verkehrsverbindungen

early thirties. The negative effects can still be felt, and seen, as here in this "no man's land" between city and country.

In the dark period of Austrian history when the name "Austria" vanished from the maps, there was not only a "Greater Germany" but also a "Greater Vienna" with the approximate dimensions of today's conurbation. In 1955 Austria regained its independence and all traces of "Greater Germany" were removed. So Vienna, too, reverted almost to its original narrow limits, which were later to prove a problematic corset.

Today, concerted efforts are being made to work together with the provinces of Lower Austria and Burgenland in the interests of mutual cooperation on a "planning community" for this region of Vienna; but this is proving to be a laborious process. And so, beyond the city limits, shopping centers continue to mushroom and new suburbs to spring up, not just in the south of the city, without there being the necessary transport

nach Wien, wo die meisten Menschen der Region ihren Arbeitsplatz haben. Wenn die Zusammenarbeit greift, sollen Siedlungsentwicklung und Verkehrsplanung der Bundesländer und Gemeinden aufeinander abgestimmt sein.

Heute endet auch die U6 am Stadtrand und führt, weil es bisher keine Einigung über gemeinsame Finanzierungen gegeben hat, nicht in die wachsende Region hinaus. Einziges leistungsfähiges öffentliches regionales Verkehrsmittel sind die Schnellbahnen, deren Strecken allerdings in einer Vergangenheit gebaut worden waren, als man diese Siedlungsentwicklungen nicht abschätzen hatte können. Für viele Autofahrer stellt die S-Bahn daher immer noch keine attraktive Alternative dar.

connections to Vienna, where most of the inhabitants of the region work. If this cooperation takes root, then there must be a harmonization between the federal provinces and the local government offices as regards housing development projects and transport planning.

Today the U6 also ends on the outskirts of the city because so far no agreement as to joint financing has been reached and does not continue out into growing peripheral areas. The only efficient form of regional public transport is the rapid suburban train known as the "Schnellbahn", or "S-Bahn", whose tracks, however, were constructed at a time in the past when the development of these housing estates outside the city limits could not have been anticipated. For many drivers, therefore, the S-Bahn still does not offer an attractive alternative to the car.

Fly the tube

„Fly the Tube" hatte vor Jahren ein Werbespruch der Londoner U-Bahn gelautet, um das Verkehrsmittel imagemäßig aufzupolieren. Das ist in Wien nicht nötig: Die U-Bahn ist mit Abstand das attraktivste öffentliche Verkehrsmittel, und sie wird ständig ausgebaut. Attraktiv übrigens nicht nur hinsichtlich der Leistungsfähigkeit. Die in Wien aufgrund der kostenintensiven Wiederaufbautätigkeit nach dem Zweiten Weltkrieg erst relativ spät geplante U-Bahn wurde mit speziellen Charakteristika ausgestattet.

Die einzelnen U-Bahn-Linien sind etwa an ihren Stationsbauwerken erkenn- und identifizierbar. Ein wenig an das Stadtbahnsystem Otto Wagners angelehnt, der um die Jahrhundertwende nicht nur ein Verkehrssystem geplant, sondern auch weithin sichtbare stadtgestalterische Merkmale gesetzt hatte. Und weil auch die spezielle Topographie Wiens (viele Hügel und dazwischen alte Flußtäler, Landschaftsterrassen vom Wienerwald ins Donaubecken) es erfordert, ist die U-Bahn nicht überall eine „Untergrundbahn", sondern verläuft oft an der Oberfläche.

Gerade am Beispiel der U6 hat das zum planerischen Bestreben der letzten Jahre geführt, nicht nur Verkehrsarchitektur zu bauen, sondern gerade im Bereich der Entwicklungsachsen so etwas wie „Identität" zu schaffen.

Waren die Stationsgebäude der U6 im Süden Wiens in ihrer ursprünglichen Planung wenig „charakteristisch" ausgefallen, so wurde durch die Einbeziehung des Architekten Johann Gsteu ein heute in Fachkreisen weltweit beachteter Architekturschwerpunkt gesetzt.

Was Caroline besonders ins Auge sticht: Die geschwungenen Bleche, die nüchternen und doch nicht kalten Formen, die Farbgebung. Nicht gerade, daß es eine „Begegnung der dritten Art" gewesen wäre, aber in der baulichen Um-

Fly the tube

Years ago, "Fly the Tube" was an advertising slogan on the London "tube", or subway system, which was aimed at polishing the image of this form of public transport. This sort of publicity is not necessary here in Vienna, for the subway or "U-Bahn" is by far the most attractive form of public transport, and its network is continually being expanded. But it is not only its efficiency that makes it attractive. In view of the costly reconstruction work following the First World War, the Vienna subway system was built relatively late and was equipped with certain special features.

For example, the individual subway lines can be recognized and identified by their stations, a bit like Otto Wagner's "Stadtbahn", or metropolitan railway. At the end of the 19th century this architect not only designed a comprehensive transport system but also left his imprint on the cityscape in the form of attractive architectural landmarks. And because Vienna's special topography (a lot of hills separated by old river valleys, terraced landscapes from the Vienna Woods to the Danube Basin) so requires, its subway is not only an "underground" system but often also runs above ground.

The U6 is a good example of the urban planning goals of recent years that have endeavored not only to construct a transport system and the corresponding architecture but also, precisely in the area of the development axes, to create a certain type of "identity".

While the station buildings of the U6 in the south of Vienna may not have been very "characteristic" in the original plans, the incorporation of the architect Johann Gsteu has resulted in this project being universally acclaimed in architectural circles. What particularly attracts Caroline's attention is the curved sweep of the metal, its simple but not cold form and the color combinations. Although this wasn't exactly an "encounter of the

gebung wirken diese Stationen wie „UFOs" aus der fernen und doch so nahen Stadt.

Und auch die Züge der U6 wirken eher wie Raumfahrzeuge denn wie herkömmliche öffentliche Verkehrsmittel. Ebenso lautlos gleiten sie aus der Station und bringen Caroline und ihre Begleitung auf die Fahrt durch Wien.

Zu sehen, erläutern ihre Begleiter, ist hier von den bereits vorhandenen wegweisenden Planungen noch nicht viel. Aber es ist erklärtes Ziel der Wiener Stadtpolitik, jene bauliche Verdichtung zu schaffen, die das Städtische ausmacht. Zwar ist schon der eine oder andere interessante Wohnbau zu sehen, aber die nötige Infrastruktur kommt erst mit der geplanten Verdichtung. Auch die Tatsache, daß nur jeder zweite Zug der U6 bis Siebenhirten fährt, zeigt, daß hier noch nicht genug los ist. Los im Sinne von Wohnen und Arbeiten.

Weshalb eben verdichtet werden muß. Vor allem auch, weil man in den engen Grenzen Wiens mit Grund und Boden sparsam umgehen muß. Nicht nur, weil Flächenverbrauch teuer ist, sondern weil sich Wien das Ziel gesetzt hat, seinen hohen Grünanteil zu schützen.

Vor 100 Jahren wurde von weitsichtigen Beamten und Politikern der Wienerwald unter Schutz gestellt, eine Verbauung damit verhindert. Wenn nun die Stadt in die Ebenen wächst, muß dort rechtzeitig auf Natur geachtet werden.

third kind", in their concrete surroundings these stations still appeared like "UFOs" from the distant and yet nearby city, she thought.

The U6 trains, too, seemed more like spaceships than conventional means of public transport. And, just as silently, they glide out of the station to take Caroline and her companions on their tour of Vienna. As her guides tell her, there is still not much to be seen here in the way of architecture, although building plans already exist. But it is a priority aim of Vienna's municipal policies to create the urban density that is characteristic of a city. While one catches sight of the occasional interesting residential building, the necessary infrastructure will only come once the planned population density has been achieved. The fact that only every second U6 train goes all the way to Siebenhirten shows that the area is still somewhat dead and that not very many people are living and working in this part of Vienna.

Which is why there must be a higher population density here. Particularly because, within the narrow city limits, we have to economize on space; not only because land is expensive, but because Vienna has set itself the goal of protecting its large expanse of greenery.

A hundred years ago, far-sighted civil servants and politicians declared the Vienna Woods a protected area, thus preventing the use of its land for building

Und so hat Wien erst vor kurzem beschlossen, seinen Grüngürtel zu sichern. Aber das wird Caroline auf ihrer Fahrt noch im Detail erfahren.

Zwischen der U6-Station Perfektastraße und den Wohntürmen von Alt Erlaa, die links schon zu sehen sind, wurde nicht „auf der grünen Wiese" sondern „In der Wiesen", wie die Gegend trotz sichtbarer Verstädterung immer noch heißt, ein neuer Stadtteil geplant.

Caroline freut sich zu hören, daß eine Frau, Franziska Ullmann, die Planung von rund 700 Wohnungen und 1.000 Arbeitsplätzen übernommen hat. Dabei handelt es sich um den ersten Teilbereich eines Stadtteiles mit insgesamt 4.000 Wohnungen und 5.000 Arbeitsplätzen. 60 Hektar stehen zur Verfügung, der nahe Wohnpark Alt Erlaa bietet bestehende, auch soziale Infrastruktur. Und die U6 eben Anbindung an das öffentliche Verkehrsnetz.

An der U6-Station Perfektastraße entsteht auch ein „multifunktionales Zentrum" mit Schule, Büros und Einkaufsmöglichkeiten.

Linker Hand rücken die Türme des Wohnparks Alt Erlaa immer größer ins Bild. Ein Wohnbauprojekt aus den siebziger Jahren, unter dem Motto „vollwertiges Wohnen" geplant und errichtet. Architekt Harry Glück hat hier versucht, Hochhauswohnen auf damals sozusagen freiem Feld umzusetzen. Herausgekommen ist dabei eine Stadt in der

purposes. But if the city is now expanding out into the plains then the ecological aspects must be taken into account well in advance. This is why the municipal authorities decided just a short while ago to maintain a green belt around the city. But Caroline will hear about that in detail during her trip.

There are plans for redevelopment between the U6 station Perfektastrasse and the high towers of the Alt Erlaa housing complex, which can be seen on the left-hand side. Despite its visible urbanization, this part of the city is still known as "In der Wiesen", or "in the meadows".

Caroline is pleased to learn that a woman, Franziska Ullmann, has taken over the planning of some 700 apartments and 1,000 jobs here. This is the first part of a new development area that will provide a total of 4,000 apartments and 5,000 jobs. 60 hectares are available for this project. The nearby residential block at Alt Erlaa already supplies the necessary infrastructure, also for social needs, and the U6 has now established the link with the public transport network.

Near the U6 station Perfektastrasse a "multifunctional center" is being built, with a school, offices and shopping facilities. To the left, the towers of Alt Erlaa are moving closer. This large housing project was planned and built in the seventies under the motto "high-quality living". What the architect Harry Glück wanted to achieve was the feeling of liv-

Stadt, in der sich die Bewohner laut verschiedenster Umfragen sehr wohl fühlen, die aber auf die sehr kleinteilige Umgebung mit vielen kleinen Siedlungshäusern keine Rücksicht genommen hat. Obwohl für derartigen Wohnbau viel Propaganda gemacht worden war, hat er sich in Wien in dieser Dimension anderswo nicht durchsetzen können. Jahrzehnte nach der Fertigstellung wird jetzt sozusagen die Stadt rundherum „nachgeliefert". Mit der eben beschriebenen Planung „In der Wiesen" und einem lange von Anrainern bekämpften Projekt mit mehr als 500 Wohnungen auf den sogenannten Osramgründen.

Für Carolines Begleiter ein erster Anlaß, auf die gestiegene Bedeutung der Bürgerbeteiligung in Wien hinzuweisen. Bürgerbeteiligung wurde in den letzten Jahren besonders ernst genommen. Um es kurz zu machen: In den meisten Fällen gelang es, wie in diesem Beispiel, gemeinsam mit den Anrainern Lösungen zu finden. Auch wenn dadurch Projekte manchmal umgeplant werden mußten.

Aber es war nicht nur der Druck der Bürgerbewegungen, der eine „sanftere" Stadtplanung bewirkt hat. Harald Sterk, ein leider viel zu früh verstorbener Kultur- und Architekturjournalist, schrieb in einem vom damals scheidenden Planungsstadtrat Fritz Hofmann herausgebenen Buch („Mut zur Stadt") vor fast zehn Jahren: „In Wien ist in der zweiten Gründerzeit, wie man die Phase seit Anfang der sechziger Jahre auch bezeichnen könnte, keineswegs alles, aber doch einiges schiefgelaufen ... mißlungen sind auch so gut wie sämtliche Verbauungen entlang des Donaukanals ... hauptsächlich Werke von Großbüros ... wie sie sich auch in Wien im Verlauf des Baubooms nach amerikanischem Muster herausgebildet haben. Der Trend zu den großen Lösungen forcierte auch die Umbildung der Strukturen. Folgerichtig kam es zur Konzentration von Macht und Einfluß. Die großen Architektur-

ing in a high-rise building, but out in the country, as it were. The result was a city within a city, in which, according to different surveys, the residents are very content, but which, on the other hand, failed to take account of the immediate surroundings characterized by many small houses. Although a lot of publicity was made for this type of housing, it did not take root in such dimensions anywhere else in Vienna. Now, decades after its completion, the city round about is being "delivered" as an afterthought, so to say. Included is "In der Wiesen" project and plans for building more than 500 apartments on the so-called Osramgründen – a project that was for a long time opposed by the residents of the area.

This gave Suzanne and Wolf their first opportunity to talk about the increased participation of Vienna's population in such planning projects. In recent years, more importance has been attached to the contribution made by the citizens. To cut a long story short: in most cases, as the above example shows, solutions could be found in cooperation with the residents of the relevant district, even though this sometimes meant that projects had to be re-planned.

But it was not only the pressure from the citizens that resulted in "softer" urban planning principles. Harald Sterk, a journalist concerned with culture and architecture who, sadly, died prematurely, wrote in the book "Mut zur Stadt" written by Fritz Hofmann, at that time City Councillor for Planning, shortly before he resigned from office almost ten years ago: "In Vienna, in the 'Second Period of Intensive Construction', as we can refer to this building phase beginning in the early sixties, certainly not everything but a number of things have gone wrong ... other failures were virtually all the ugly buildings along the Danube Canal ... mainly large office blocks ... as they sprung up in American style during the building boom in Vienna. This trend towards large-scale projects also necessi-

büros entstanden ... und was vielleicht noch wichtiger war, die Bauträgergesellschaften eroberten ... neues Terrain hinzu. Diese Bauträgergesellschaften ... arbeiteten hauptsächlich mit den großen Architekturbüros zusammen und kauften andererseits Grundstücke auf, die sie zuerst baureif machten und dann den öffentlichen Stellen, aber auch privaten Bauherren anboten. Da es auch sehr bald zu engen Verflechtungen mit der Bauindustrie kam, war das Wiener Baugeschehen bis Mitte der achtziger Jahre in die Kontrolle von wenigen, aber dafür sehr mächtigen Leuten geraten. Seit einiger Zeit versuchen Politiker dieser Entwicklung entgegenzusteuern, was ein sehr schweres und mühevolles Unterfangen ist."

In einem späteren Gespräch wird Caroline von einem Mitarbeiter der Stadt hören, daß es zu dieser Zeit „nur fertig vorgelegte durchgeplante Projekte zur Einreichung" gegeben und die Stadt kaum Mit-Gestaltungsmöglichkeiten gehabt hatte. Erst die Einführung von Gutachterverfahren und Wettbewerbsverfahren führte zu einer Auflockerung dieser starren Situation.

Freilich waren und sind diese Verfahren nicht immer unumstritten, weil sie nicht zuletzt die Kosten in die Höhe treiben. Aber die Qualität der Planungen wurde nachweislich besser – immer sehr kritisch reflektiert von einer starken architekturkritischen Szene in den Medien. Was letztlich dazu geführt hat, daß die Bauträger von sich aus bereits nicht mehr nur an „Hausarchitekten" vergeben, sondern von vornherein die Vielfalt suchen.

Ein wesentlicher Eckpfeiler der qualitätsvollen Wiener Stadtentwicklung gerade im Wohnbau liegt in der neuen Planungskultur: Es gehört zum Planungsverständnis, bereits auf der Ebene städtebaulicher Konzepte bei allen Projekten ab etwa 300 Wohnungen Gestaltungsvorschläge über Wettbewerbe oder wettbewerbsähnliche Verfahren zu

tated structural changes. The result was a concentration of power and influence. Large firms of architects set up offices and, what was perhaps even more important, the building companies gained ground as well. These building companies ... worked chiefly with the large firms of architects and bought up plots of land which they first prepared for development and then offered to public authorities and also to private individuals. Since this soon led to close contacts with the building industry, by the middle of the eighties the Viennese building scene had fallen into the hands of a small group of very influential people. For some time now, politicians have been trying to counteract this development, which is, however, proving to be a difficult and laborious undertaking."

In a later conversation Caroline was to hear that at that time "only tailor-made projects, planned right down to the last detail" were submitted and that the City of Vienna had virtually no say in the design or planning activities. It was only with the introduction of a system of evaluation and competitions that some relaxation of this rigid situation could be achieved.

Naturally, these evaluation and competition processes are not without contention, partly because they involve an increase in costs. But, on the positive side, the quality of the planning has improved considerably, as is always critically reflected in strict reviews of domestic architecture in the media. All this has resulted in building companies now no longer awarding contracts only to "in-house architects" but seeking more variety right from the start.

An important cornerstone of Vienna's high-quality urban development schemes, particularly as regards housing, is embodied in the new approach towards planning. It is a part of the planning principles, starting at the level of urban planning concepts, to collect design proposals and ideas through competi-

ermitteln. Die daraus resultierende Vielfalt kann auch durch die Vergabepraxis bei Grundstücken gewährt werden: heute werden maximal 100 bis 200 Wohnungen pro Bauträger vergeben.

Aber zurück zur Bürgerbeteiligung: Auch sie wurde durch kritisch-sympathisierende Berichterstattung der meisten Medien gefördert und hat letztlich ebenfalls dazu geführt, nicht nur umweltschonend, sondern vor allem menschengerecht zu planen. „Ein Lernprozeß für alle Beteiligten, die Bürger, Planer, Politiker und Beamten", wie Carolines Begleiter anmerken.

Während der U6-Zug die Station Alt Erlaa verläßt, von der man übrigens auch einen schönen Blick zur Silhouette des Wienerberges hat, nochmals ein Blick in die Zukunft: Linker Hand entstehen jetzt rund 520 Wohnungen in sechs- bis neunstöckigen Gebäuden und vierstöckigen Stadtvillen.

„Direkt am Bach – so wohnen Naturfreunde und Sparmeister", titelte eine

tions and similar processes for all projects of around 300 apartments upwards. The resulting diversity can also be ensured through the practice of allocating plots of land. Today, a maximum of 100 to 200 apartments are awarded per building company.

But to return to the participation of the citizens: this was also backed by critical and sympathetic reports in nearly all the media and in the end led to a situation in which present-day planning concepts are not only environmentally-friendly but also take into account the human factor. "This is a learning process for all the participants – the citizens, the planners, the politicians and the civil servants", remarked Caroline's companions.

While the U6 train is leaving Alt Erlaa station, from which, incidentally, there is an attractive view of the Wienerberg, let's take another look at the future. On the left-hand side, some 520 apartments are being built in six to nine-storied buildings and in four-storied city villas.

große österreichische Zeitung über das Projekt, das am Erholungsgebiet des Liesingtales liegt und unter dem Gütesiegel „Betriebskosten-Spar-Haus" auch letzte ökologische Erkenntnisse berücksichtigt.

Nach einem sanften Schwung führt die U6-Strecke an der in den siebziger Jahren errichteten Großwohnanlage „Am Schöpfwerk" vorbei. Obwohl im Vergleich zu Stadtrandsiedlungen anderer Großstädte durchaus differenziert geplant und gebaut, ist hier eine für Wiener Verhältnisse nicht zufriedenstellende Struktur entstanden. Die Bebauung war zu wenig dicht für ausreichende Infrastruktur, die U6 wurde erst vor kurzem fertiggestellt, davor gab es lediglich eine Straßenbahn, und auch die Besiedlungspolitik vergangener Zeiten hat für eine sehr einseitige Zusammensetzung der Wohnbevölkerung gesorgt. Mit verschiedensten Experimenten im sozialen Bereich wird nun versucht, diese Situation zu verbessern.

Hätte Caroline ein wenig mehr Zeit, könnte sie jetzt zu Fuß durch die Stadterweiterungsteile am Wienerberg gehen und dabei durch das auf den traditionsreichen Ziegeleigründen angelegte Naherholungsgebiet spazieren. Caroline sieht dies für einen weiteren Wien-Besuch vor (für Stadtwanderer haben wir die Route im Serviceteil dieses Buches beschrieben). Von der U6 aus kann sie die sich bereits abzeichnende neue Skyline auf dem Wienerberg erkennen (den Businesspark Vienna), die bald ein spektakuläres „Hochhaus" des italienischen Architekten Massimiliano Fuksas bereichern soll.

Fuksas, ein Spezialist für städtische Peripherien, über sein Wiener Projekt: **„Mit dem Gebäude, das ich baue, einem Hochhaus, versuche ich die jetzt existierende Skyline, die noch lückenhaft ist, zu vervollständigen. Das Gebiet dort bildet die Stadtgrenze, ist aber selbst zuwenig definiert."** Das Gebiet ist übrigens Bestandteil einer langjährigen

"Directly overlooking a stream – ideal for nature lovers and economizers" was the way a leading Austrian newspaper described this project that is planned for the recreation area along the Liesingtal and which, with the seal of quality "Maintenance costs-savings-house" also takes account of the latest ecological research.

After a gentle curve, the U6 route leads past the large housing complex "Am Schöpfwerk". Although in Vienna suburban housing developments are planned and built as individually as possible, as compared with other major cities, we are confronted here with what is, by Viennese standards, an unsatisfactory solution. The building density is too small to warrant sufficient infrastructure: the U6 was only recently connected, before this there was only a tram, and the settlement policies of the past made for a very one-sided social set-up of the local population. With different social experiments, attempts are being made to improve this situation.

If Caroline had had a bit more time, she could have gone on foot through the newly-developed areas on the Wienerberg and then have walked along the recreation area located on the grounds of an old brick factory. Caroline has already earmarked this for her next visit to Vienna (for walkers, we have described the route in the service part of this book). From the U6 train she can see the new skyline appearing on the Wienerberg (the Business Park Vienna), which will soon be enhanced by a spectacular "high-rise building" designed by the Italian architect Massimiliano Fuksas.

Fuksas, a specialist in city peripheries, says of his Vienna project: **"With the building that I am creating, a high-rise building, I want to fill in the gaps of the existing skyline. Although this area forms the city boundary, it is still not clearly defined."** This area is, incidentally, part of a long-term urban planning scheme for regeneration plans drawn up by Otto Häuslmayer, in which a number

28

städtebaulichen Entwicklung für ein Stadterweiterungsgebiet nach den Plänen von Otto Häuslmayer, in dem eine Vielzahl von Architekten eine sehr differenzierte neue Wohnlandschaft geschaffen haben.

Die U6 bringt uns jetzt ins „wirkliche" Stadtgebiet. Vorbei an Kleingartenanlagen – einer Wiener (und Berliner) Spezialität. „Schrebergärten" nennen die Wiener liebevoll noch immer die Kleinstgärten, die ihre Blüte in den Nachkriegswirren nach 1918 und 1945 hatten, die aber als „Siedlungen" nie aus dem Stadtbild verschwunden sind. In den letzten Jahren hat die Stadtplanung auf diese „hartnäckige" Existenz reagiert: Unter gewissen baulichen Voraussetzungen ist das ganzjährige Wohnen in Kleingärten erlaubt.

Carolines Begleiter zeigen ihr ein gerade noch von der U6 sichtbares altes Fabriksareal: Auf den sogenannten KDAG-Gründen soll ein „Milleniums-Experiment" stattfinden. Damit, so meinen

of architects have created a highly individual new residential environment. The U6 now brings us into the "real" metropolis. We pass small gardens or allotments – a typical feature of Vienna (and Berlin). These plots of land, which are lovingly referred to by the Viennese as "Schrebergärten", had their heyday in the confusion of the postwar years after 1918 and 1945, but as "settlements" they have still lingered on. In recent years urban planners have reacted to their "stubborn" existence for, subject to certain structural conditions, people are now permitted to live in them all year round.

Suzanne and Wolf point out an old factory site that is just visible from the U6. These so-called KDAG grounds will be used for a "millennium experiment": in order that the 1000-year celebrations not only look backwards in history but also forwards in time a millennium competition will be launched under the motto "1000 Years of Austria". This will give both established and young up-and-

sie, die Tausendjahr-Feiern nicht nur geschichtsorientiert verlaufen, werden in einem „Milleniums-Wettbewerb 1.000 Jahre Österreich" arrivierte, aber auch junge Architekten und interessierte Bürger eingeladen, ihre Vorstellungen vom Wohnen und Arbeiten in der Zukunft unter Einsatz neuester Technologien zu erarbeiten. Bis zu 1.200 Wohnungen mit der Infrastruktur des Jahres 2000, Parks, 150 Arbeitsplätze und ein Kulturzentrum können geplant werden. Wichtig dabei: Die gesellschaftlichen Veränderungen, vor allem die Tendenz zu Single-Haushalten, sollen in neuen Wohnformen ihren Niederschlag finden.

Caroline hinterfragt nochmals die aktuelle Wiener Philosophie der Wettbewerbe. Die Stadt Wien will Monopole im Bereich der Architektur grundsätzlich vermeiden. Wettbewerbe in ihren verschiedensten Spielarten haben sich als bestes Rezept dagegen herausgestellt. Für viele architektonische und städte-

coming Austrian architects, as well as interested members of the population the chance to air their views on living and working in the future, using all the latest technologies.

Up to 1,200 apartments, complete with the infrastructure of the year 2000, parks, 150 jobs and a cultural center can be accommodated here. An important factor to be taken into consideration is changed social environment, the tendency towards single households, for example, and these trends should also be reflected in new forms of housing.

Caroline raises some further questions about the present Viennese competition policies. The answer she receives is that the City of Vienna wants to avoid any kind of monopoly in the field of architecture. And different forms of competition have proved to be the best recipe against this practice. Hence, a process of evaluation and assessment by experts is used in many architectural

bauliche Projekte wurden und werden Gutachter- und Expertenverfahren veranstaltet, mit denen vor allem auch jüngeren Architekten die Möglichkeit gegeben wird, innovative Ideen einzubringen. Wozu auch Direktaufträge der Stadt dienen, wie etwa das Beispiel der jüngeren Schul-Architektur zeigt. Erklärtes Ziel der Stadt ist es, so erfährt Caroline, daß hochwertige Architektur, Wirtschaftlichkeit, Umweltverträglichkeit und gerade bei Wohnbauten der soziale Aspekt im Gleichgewicht sind und ein Ganzes bilden. Beim „Milleniumswettbewerb" wird die Bürgerbeteiligung bereits in der Vorbereitung ganz groß geschrieben: Über ein Directmailing soll ein Maximum an Ideen erfaßt werden, auch direkte Mitwirkung am Planungsprozeß via Internet ist vorgesehen.

and urban planning projects, giving younger architects, in particular, the chance of introducing new, innovative ideas. Which is where direct contracts from the municipal authorities come in, such as, for example, with the recent school architecture. It is one of Vienna's priority goals, Caroline learns, that high-quality architecture, economic efficiency, environmental sustainability and, precisely in the field of housing, the social aspect, are all balanced together to form a harmonious whole. In the "Millennium Competition" great importance will be attached to the participation of the population, even in the preparatory phase. Through Direct Mailing it is hoped that a maximum number of ideas can be generated, while direct cooperation in the planning process via Internet is also envisaged.

Zeitreise
A journey into the Past

35

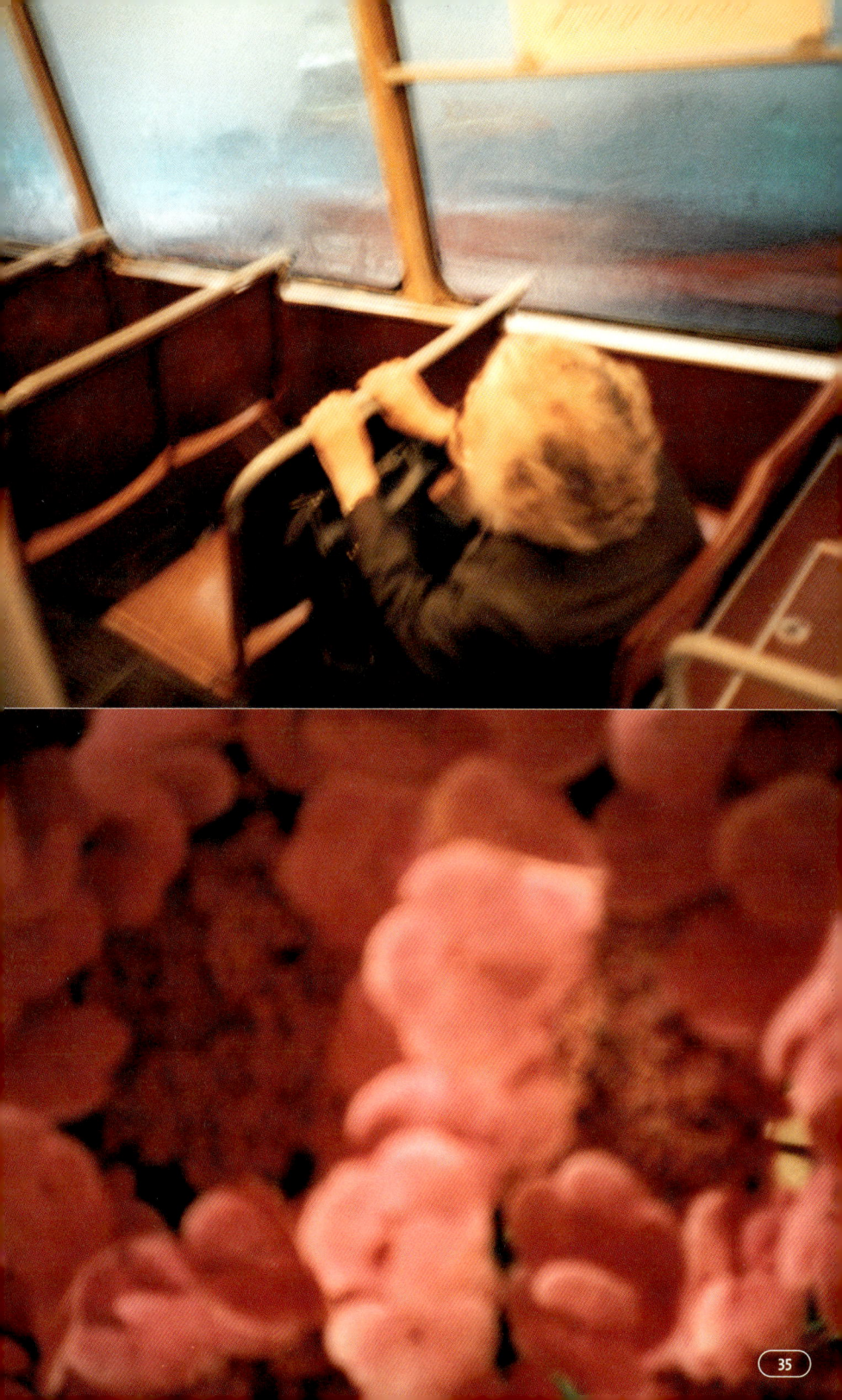

36

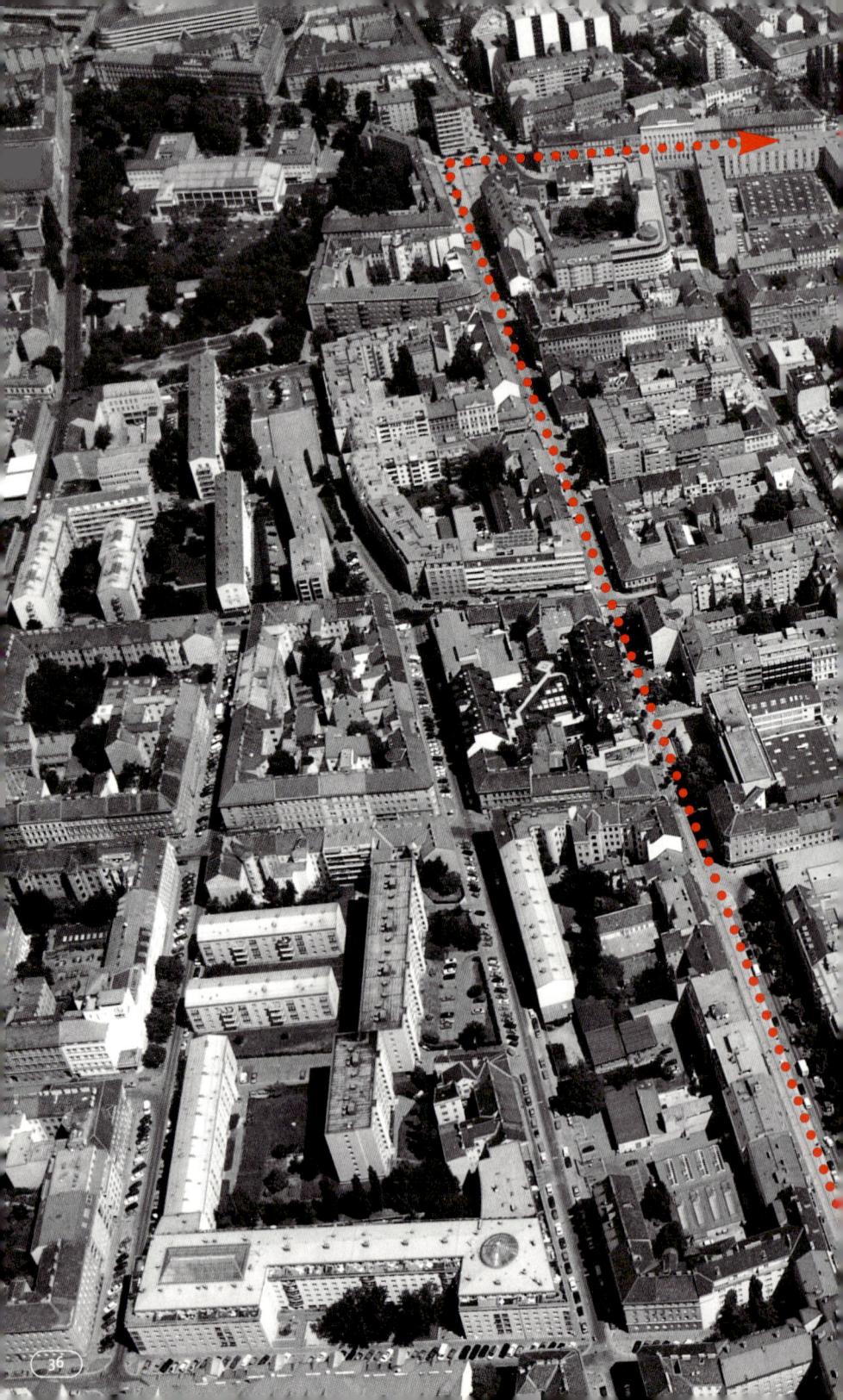

37

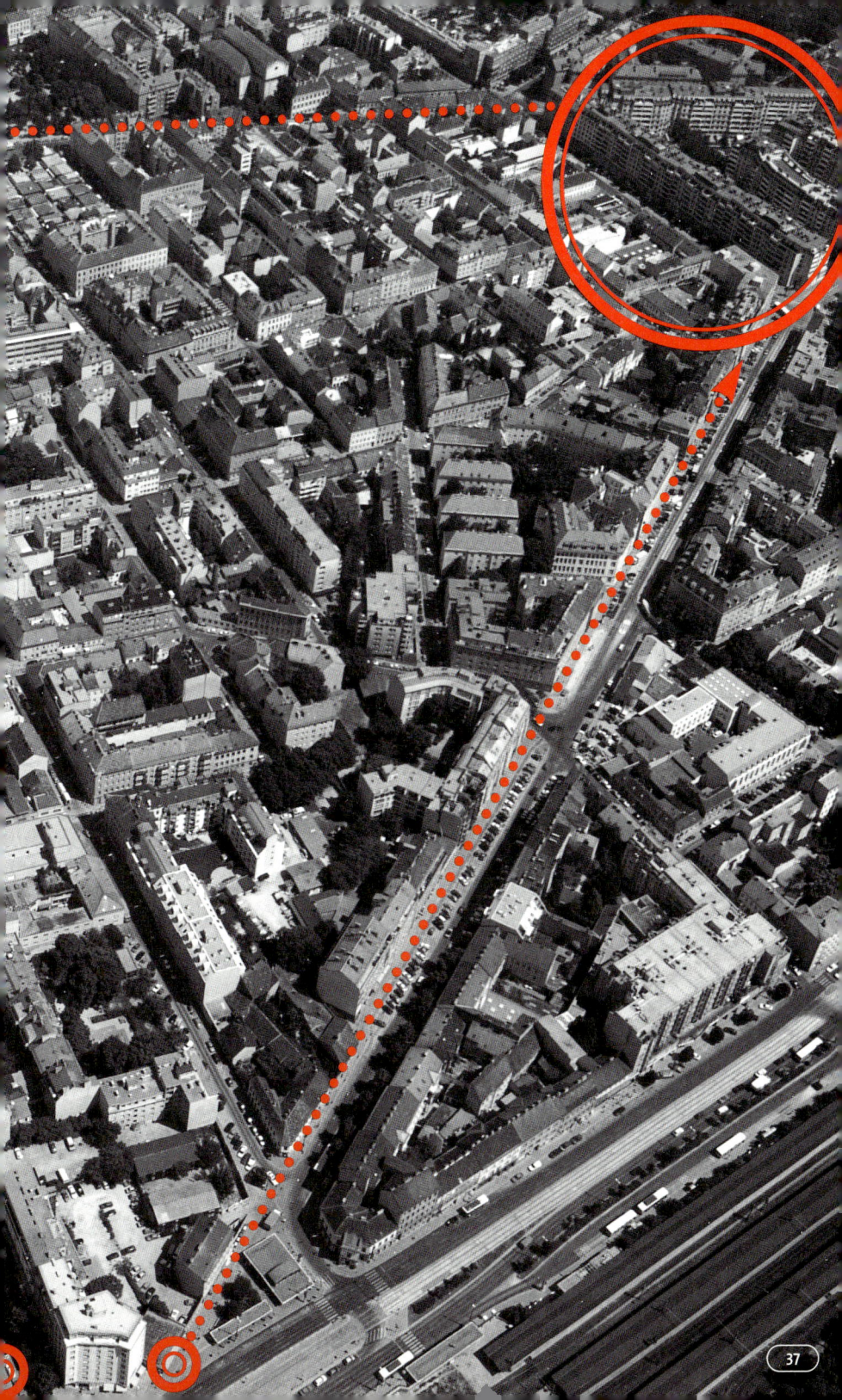

Caroline und Begleitung verlassen die U6 bei der Station Philadelphiabrücke für einen Weg zu Fuß, der sie wie bei einer Zeitreise durch einige Epochen der Wiener Stadtentwicklung führt.

Zuerst überqueren sie die Philadelphiabrücke, nach dem Zweiten Weltkrieg über die hier sehr breiten Gleisanlagen der Südbahn und der Schnellbahn gebaut.

Apropos Bahnanlagen: Während anderswo in Europa in den letzten Jahren innerstädtische Bahnanlagen intensiv überbaut und multifunktional genutzt wurden und werden, erlebte Wien hier eine Phase der „unfreiwilligen künstlerischen Pause".

In der Blütezeit der Eisenbahn im vergangenen Jahrhundert waren die Bahnen, die von der damaligen k. u. k- Residenz- und Reichshauptstadt aus geplant und gebaut wurden, Eigentum verschiedenster privater Bahngesellschaften. Wien erhielt damit mehrere Kopfbahnhöfe, die außerhalb des damals dichtbebauten Stadtgebietes errichtet wurden – so wie man heute Flughäfen in „sicherer" Entfernung der Stadtzentren errichtet.

Und: Wien hatte und hat bis dato keinen Zentralbahnhof, obwohl es für einen „Bahnhof Wien" bereits einen Wettbewerb gegeben hat und ein durchaus attraktives Siegerprojekt vorliegt. Auf den ersten Zug wird der projektierte Bahnhof wohl noch lange warten müssen.

Zurück in die Geschichte: Eine Zwischenlösung, ein Jahrzehnte dauerndes typisches Wiener Provisorium sozusagen, war dann die Errichtung der Stadtbahn, die allerdings vorwiegend unter militärstrategischen Aspekten gebaut worden war.

Wien verfügt daher heute über mehrere mehr oder weniger genutzte Bahnanlagen im heute dichtbebauten Stadtgebiet. Wobei der Begriff „verfügt" an eine Wunde rührt: Die lange Zeit verstaatlichte Bahn, die gerade den mühsa-

Caroline and her companions leave the U6 at the Philadelphia Brücke to continue their journey on foot and to embark upon a route that will take them through several epochs of urban development in Vienna.

First they cross over the Philadelphia Brücke, which was built after the Second World War over the tracks of the southbound railway and the "Schnellbahn", a rapid suburban train, which are very wide at this point.

Apropos railway tracks. Whereas elsewhere in Europe in recent years inner city railway tracks have been, and still are, superimposed with other buildings and then used multifunctionally, Vienna is experiencing an "involuntary pause for reflection" in this respect.

In the heyday of the railroad in the last century the railways that were planned and constructed by Vienna, at that time the residence and capital of the imperial Austro-Hungarian Empire, were owned by several different private railroad companies. This meant that Vienna had a number of railway terminuses which were constructed in regions that in those days lay outside the built-up metropolitan area, just as today airports are built at a "safe" distance from city centers. Vienna did not, and to date still does not have, a central railroad station, although there has already been a competition for a central station, and an attractive winning project already exists. However, the planned railway station will no doubt have to wait a long time for its first train.

But back to history. An interim solution, a typically Viennese provisional measure, as it were, that has already lasted for decades, was set up in the form of the metropolitan railway (we will return to this subject in the course of our tour), which was, however, built largely to fulfill certain military and strategic functions.

Vienna therefore still possesses several stretches of railway tracks (most of which are still used) in its densely built-

men Weg einer sanften Reprivatisierung nimmt, ist Eigentümerin der Bahnanlagen, und über Jahre war es in langwierigen Verhandlungen nicht möglich, diese für die innere Stadtentwicklung dringend benötigten Areale seitens der Stadt zu erwerben oder Grundstücke entsprechend abzutauschen. Gravierendster Fall ist der Nordbahnhof, an dessen Randbebauung die Reise noch vorbeiführen wird. Vielleicht auch abgeschreckt durch die bisher einzige Überbauung, der alte Franz-Josefs-Bahnhof im neunten Bezirk wurde durch ein mehrere Kilometer langes Beton- und Glasgebirge in den siebziger Jahren ersetzt und bildet heute eine unüberwindliche Barriere innerhalb des Bezirkes, wurden keine weiteren Bahnüberbauungen in Angriff genommen.

An dieser Station der Reise, auf der Philadelphia-Brücke, ist rechter Hand ein Areal zu sehen, für das es ein Überbauungsvorhaben gibt, dessen Realisierung aus obengenannten Gründen allerdings irgendwo in der Zukunft liegen dürfte.

Vorstadtboulevard

Vor Caroline liegt nun die „Pforte" zum Beginn unserer kleinen Zeitreise, der Eingang zur Meidlinger Hauptstraße.

Meidling ist einer jener Bezirke Wiens, die vor mehr als hundert Jahren durch die Zusammenlegung mehrerer Vororte entstanden sind. Er ist auch klassisches Beispiel für das Erbe der ersten Gründerzeit: In manchen Vierteln wie zum Beispiel in Wilhelmsdorf, das man besuchen sollte, stammen fast zwei Drittel der Häuser aus der Zeit vor dem Ersten Weltkrieg.

Die Bebauung der Meidlinger Hauptstraße, findet Caroline, zeigt keine historisch wertvollen Beispiele, auch keine architektonischen „Schmankerl" neuerer Herkunft. Unterschiedliche Bauhöhen, unterschiedliche Bau-"Stile" vermitteln noch heute das Bild einer „Vorstadt".

up metropolitan area. The word "possesses", however, opens up old wounds. The railroad company, which was for a long time nationalized and is currently undergoing the laborious process of re-privatization, owns the railway tracks and, despite year-long lengthy negotiations, it has not been possible for the City of Vienna to obtain these urgently needed facilities or to exchange them for pieces of land. The most serious case in point is the North Railway Station (Nordbahnhof), the outer end of which we will pass on our journey. The former Franz Josephs Bahnhof (this is also part of our itinerary) in the 9th district was replaced in the seventies by a several kilometers long cement and glass dome-like construction that today forms an insuperable barrier within the district. Perhaps it was the shock of this superstructure that deterred any further attempts at building over railways in Vienna.

At this point of our journey – the Philadelphia Brücke – we can see a site on the right-hand side for which a superstructure is planned, the implementation of which, however, still lies in the distant future for the reasons mentioned above.

Suburban boulevard

In front of Caroline is now the "gateway" to our short journey into the past, the entrance to Meidlinger Hauptstrasse.

Meidling is one of those Viennese districts that was formed more than a hundred years ago through the amalgamation of several suburbs. It is also a classical example for the heritage of the first "Gründerzeit" or "Period of Intensive Construction". In some parts of Meidling such as, for example, Wilhelmsdorf that we will also be visiting, almost two-thirds of the houses stem from the period before the First World War.

Caroline finds that the buildings in Meidlinger Hauptstrasse are not particularly noteworthy examples and that there are no architectural "delicacies"

41

Dennoch ist die Meidlinger Hauptstraße heute ein Paradebeispiel für die Wiedergewinnung des öffentlichen Raumes, für die Neugestaltung alter Geschäftsstraßen, insbesondere auch, um deren Attraktivität gegenüber den Einkaufszentren jenseits der Stadtgrenzen zu erhöhen. Die Chance für eine umfassende Neugestaltung bot sich, nachdem die U6-Unterquerung der Meidlinger „Altstadt" Anfang der neunziger Jahre fertiggestellt war. In der Straßenmitte war bis dahin eine legendäre Straßenbahn, der „8er", gefahren. Seine Einstellung hatte jahrelange heftige Auseinandersetzungen bis hin zu einer Volksbefragung mit sich gezogen, weil er eine klassische Anbindung an den Gürtelbereich dargestellt hatte.

Die heutige Attraktivität der U-Bahn und das damit zusammenhängende Autobusnetz haben aber die Kritiker verstummen lassen. Und vor allem: Die Fußgänger haben den öffentlichen Raum sozusagen über Nacht in Besitz genommen. Heute präsentiert sich die Meidlinger Hauptstraße als durchgehende Fußgängerzone, die nur zweimal von einer Autostraße gequert wird.

Was Caroline auffällt: Während anderswo Fußgängerzonen mit allerlei nötigem und unnötigem „Mobiliar" wie Blumentrögen aus Beton und ähnlichem vollgestellt werden, ist man bei der Neugestaltung dieses Straßenzuges einen anderen Weg gegangen. Der durch seine Triestiner Herkunft stark mediterran angehauchte Architekt Boris Podrecca hat zusammen mit der Magistratsabteilung für Stadtgestaltung eine zurückhaltende Gestaltung entwickelt: Die neuen Beleuchtungskörper und eigens entwickelten Vitrinen „ersetzen" die alte Achse der Straßenbahngleise und schaffen sozusagen die Orientierung für die Benutzer der Straße. Auf „künstliches" Grün wurde verzichtet, der Straßenraum dafür durch eine „warme" Bodengestaltung und durch einige Ruhezonen „wohnlich" gemacht.

with respect to modern design. With their different heights and styles, the buildings still evoke a typically suburban impression. On the other hand, Meidlinger Hauptstrasse is today a perfect example of how public space can be regained and old shopping streets can be redesigned, particularly with the aim of increasing their attractiveness as against the shopping centers on the outskirts of the city. The chance for an extensive redevelopment scheme was provided by the completion of the U6 subterranean subway passage in the old part of Meidling at the beginning of the nineties. Up to that time, there was a tram line running through the middle of the street, the legendary No. 8. For years its discontinuation provoked heated arguments and even an opinion poll because it represented a traditional transport link with the "Gürtel" ring road.

The attractions offered by today's subway system and its connecting network of buses have, however, now silenced its critics. Even more so because the pedestrians have, as it were overnight, regained and taken possession of the open spaces. Today, Meidlinger Hauptstrasse is an unbroken pedestrian zone, which is only twice intersected by roads for traffic.

What Caroline particularly notices is that, whereas pedestrian zones in other parts of the city are filled with all sorts of "furniture" such as concrete flower troughs and similar decorations, for the redevelopment of this street in Meidling a different approach was used. In conjunction with the Municipal Department for Urban Development, the architect Boris Podrecca, strongly influenced by his birthplace Trieste and by the Mediteranean atmosphere, kept his design simple. The new street-lights and specially designed shop windows "replace" the former "axis" of the tram tracks and provide a kind of orientation for the pedestrians. While there is no "artificial" greenery, the street is highlighted in warm stone and further enhanced by several resting places.

Besonders stark angenommen wird, erfährt Caroline, das Meidlinger Platzl mit einer modernen Brunnenanlage. Insgesamt lädt die Straße zum Flanieren und Bummeln ein und lockt (nicht zuletzt aufgrund der guten Erreichbarkeit mit der U6) Besucher aus anderen Teilen Wiens an.

Freilich – s'wär net Wien! – hat die moderne Architektur auch „aufgeregt": Sie trifft nicht altgewohnte „Geschmäcker", entspricht nicht dem, was viele unter „Gemütlichkeit" verstehen. Aber sie zeigt Mut zu einer ganzheitlichen Gestaltung, verleiht dieser alten Straße eine neue, eigenständige Charakteristik und prägt nicht zuletzt auch das Geschmacksempfinden der Menschen.

Und sie ist ein hervorragendes Beispiel dafür, wie man „alt" und „neu" im Stadtbild zu einer Synthese bringen kann, findet Caroline. Im unteren Teil der Meidlinger Hauptstraße finden sich dann „altgewohnte" Gestaltungselemente wie die Allee und eine Pergola.

A particularly popular spot, as Caroline sees, is the Meidlinger Platzl with its modern fountain. All in all, the street is pre-destined for strolling and sauntering along and, partly on account of its easy accessibility by U6, also attracts visitors from other parts of the city.

Naturally, – otherwise this wouldn't be Vienna ! – this modern architecture has also been a bone of some contention. For it is not in line with traditional tastes and does not correspond to many people's idea of "cosiness". But, on the other hand, it demonstrates the courage of its convictions by lending this old street a new, distinctive character, and has also left its imprint on the tastebuds of its residents.

And Caroline finds it an excellent example of how to blend the "old" and the "new" elements of a city into a successful synthesis. At the lower end of Meidlinger Hauptstrasse we encounter the more "traditional" elements like an avenue and a pergola. The buildings, too, will

Auch bauliche Akzente werden der Meidlinger Hauptstraße noch eine neue Identität im Konzert der großen Wiener Straßen geben: An der Philadelphiabrücke entsteht eine Eckbebauung, die ursprünglich als Hochhaus geplant war, nach langen Diskussionen aber nunmehr zwar einen architektonisch neuen Akzent, allerdings in „gemäßigter" Bauhöhe setzen soll.

Im Wiental wird das „U4" genannte Einkaufszentrum an der gleichnamigen U-Bahn-Linie erweitert und ein markantes Zeichen setzen.

Unsere Reisegruppe setzt die Meidlinger „Zeitreise" fort, indem sie von der U6-Station Niederhofstraße, in deren Umfeld sich markante Büroneubauten befinden, die ebenfalls eine gelungene Synthese mit dem baulichen Altbestand bilden, zurück zur Philadelphiabrücke fährt. Von dort bietet sich ein Weg durch die Wilhelmstraße in das alte Wilhelmsdorf an. Wilhelmsdorf ist einer der ältesten Teile Meidlings und eines

give Meidlinger Hauptstrasse a new identity among the major Viennese streets. On Philadelphia Brücke a corner construction is being erected that was originally planned as a high-rise building but which, after lengthy discussions, will still set new architectural accents but at a "moderate" height.

In the Wiental, the "U4" shopping center, called after the subway line of the same name, is being expanded and will become a prominent feature of this district.

Our tour group continues its journey into the past through Meidling by taking back to Philadelphia Brücke the U6 from the station Niederhof, whose environment is characterized by striking new office blocks which also form a successful synthesis with the existing buildings.

From here, a route leads through Wilhelmstrasse to the old area of Wilhelmsdorf. Wilhelmsdorf is one of Meidling's oldest parts and was one of Vienna's first and largest regeneration areas.

der ersten und größten Stadterneuerungsgebiete Wiens.

Stadterneuerung ist übrigens auch eine typisch wienerische Spezialität, wie unsere Caroline im Vergleich mit anderen europäischen, aber auch amerikanischen Städten feststellt.

Die erste Gründerzeit

Nun hatte Wien das Glück, daß die schweren Bombenangriffe der Amerikaner auf Wien im zweiten Weltkrieg zwar schwere Schäden angerichtet, aber anders als etwa in Dresden und anderen deutschen Städten die Stadt nicht dem Erdboden gleichgemacht haben. So überlebte das historische Bauerbe ebenso wie die Bauten des Roten Wien und eben die Gründerzeitviertel. Stadterneuerung war in den späten siebziger Jahren deshalb notwendig geworden, weil in dem hohen Anteil der Gründerzeitwohnungen die Wohnverhältnisse auf den zeitgemäßen Standard gebracht werden mußten. Die erste Gründerzeit hatte dem Stadtbild zwar durchaus attraktive Fassaden, ganze Viertel und Stadtteile gebracht, die viel von der Identität der Wiener „Vorstadt" ausmachen. Aber die Bauten jener Zeit waren Spekulationsobjekte, die auf jene, für die sie letztlich gebaut worden waren, nämlich die Menschen, keinerlei Rücksicht nahmen.

Die Bauten des „Roten Wien" waren dann die sozialdemokratische Antwort auf diese Ausbeutung von Menschen und städtischer Fläche.

„Licht, Luft und Sonne" hatte die sozialdemokratische Wohnbaupolitik der Zwischenkriegszeit den Menschen versprochen und auch gebracht. So mancher Gemeindebau der Zwischenkriegszeit (weltweit bekanntestes Beispiel: Der Karl-Marx-Hof in Heiligenstadt), wie es sie in großer Zahl auch in Meidling gibt, waren damals auf die „grüne Wiese" gebaut worden. Heute, nach Jahrzehnten, bilden ihre Innenhöfe und

Regeneration is, incidentally, a typically Viennese feature, as Caroline realizes, in comparison with other European and also American cities.

The first "Gründerzeit"

Vienna was lucky in that the heavy bombing of Vienna by the Americans during the Second World War, while inflicting heavy damage did not cause total destruction to the metropolis, as it did in Dresden and other German cities. For this reason, the historical buildings survived, as did the buildings of "Red Vienna" and, with them, the Gründerzeit districts. In the late seventies, regeneration became a necessity because the housing conditions in the majority of the apartments built during the Gründerzeit were substandard.

The first "Period of Intensive Construction" left its mark on Vienna in the form of attractive facades, entire districts and parts of the city which go to make up much of the identity of the typically Viennese "suburb". But the buildings of that period were objects of speculation that did not take into account those for whom it was built, namely the people.

The buildings of "Red" Vienna then provided the Social Democrats' answer to this exploitation of people and municipal terrain.

"Light, air and sun", which the Social Democrat housing policies of the interwar period promised, and also gave, to its people, were also challenges from the point of view of urban planning. Many a municipal housing estate (the best-known example is the Karl-Marx Hof in Heiligenstadt), of which many also appear in Meidling, were at that time built "out in the country". Today, decades later, their inner courtyards and the parks laid out nearby provide green oases and havens of tranquillity away from the noisy bustle of the city.

Regeneration in Vienna had, and still has, the aim of cautious rehabilitation. Cautious because of the building sub-

die Parks, die in ihrem Umfeld errichtet wurden, grüne Oasen, Ruhepunkte im Treiben der Stadt.

Stadterneuerung in Wien hatte und hat vor allem zum Ziel, behutsam zu sanieren. Behutsam, was die Bausubstanz betrifft, also keine Kahlschlagsanierungen. Und behutsam, was die Menschen angeht. Sie sollte leistbar sein und sie sollte die Menschen während der Sanierungen und vor allem danach möglichst in ihrem Viertel belassen.

Stadterneuerung bedeutet vor allem auch das Aufwerten des öffentlichen Raumes. Dazu konnte gerade der U-Bahnbau durch die Folge-Einrichtungen an der Oberfläche beitragen. Dazu haben nicht zuletzt die Gebietsbetreuungen beigetragen: Kommunikationsbüros, die im Auftrag, aber nicht in der Abhängigkeit der Stadtverwaltung vermitteln sollen zwischen den Bewohnern, den Behörden, den Bauträgern.

„Grätzl" nennt man in Wien diese Quartiere oder Viertel oder „neighbourhoods", wie sie anderswo heißen. Die kleinsten Einheiten in der Großstadt sozusagen, den unmittelbaren Lebensraum der Bewohner. Wilhelmsdorf ist dafür ein gutes Beispiel.

„Zentrum" ist der Wohnpark Wilhelmsdorf, eine dichte, aber gut gegliederte neu errichtete Wohnanlage, übrigens auch nach den Ansprüchen des „Vollwertigen Wohnens" errichtet und anders als die Türme von Alt Erlaa sehr

stance, not wholesale redevelopment in other words, and cautious with regard to the inhabitants. It should be affordable and, wherever possible, should permit the residents to remain in their districts, both during the renovation work and afterwards.

But redevelopment also refers to the upgrading of public space. The construction of the subway system made a valuable contribution in this respect through the buildings at street level to its immediate surroundings. And the district offices have also played their part: communication centers, which act on behalf but without dependency on the central municipal administration, provide a means of communication between the residents, the authorities and the building companies.

In Vienna, a special word, "Grätzl", exists for these quarters or neighborhoods: the smallest units in the large city, the direct living environment of its citizens. Wilhelmsdorf is a good example of such a neighborhood. The "center" is the Wilhelmsdorf housing complex, a dense but well-structured development that, incidentally, was also built according to the demands of "high-quality" living and which, unlike the towers of Alt Erlaa, was incorporated into the surrounding area with great sensitivity. It is also flanked by two parks. Wilhelmsdorf Park, Caroline learns, is an excellent example for the new environmental attitude in the city,

rücksichtsvoll in die Umgebung eingefügt. Gelegen zwischen zwei Parks. Der Wilhelmsdorfer Park, erfährt Caroline, ist ein Paradebeispiel für die neue Grüngesinnung in der Stadt, die sich in den letzten Jahren durchgesetzt hat. Hier wurde ein bestehender Park nach der Auflassung eines städtischen Schienenlagers nicht nur erweitert, sondern im Sinne der Aufwertung des öffentlichen Raumes auch durchgestaltet. Hier finden sich Zonen für ruhesuchende ältere Menschen ebenso wie für spielende Kinder. Hier können die aus südlicheren Gefilden zugewanderten Familien ihrem gewohnten Bedürfnis nach dem Leben im Freien nachkommen. Hier wurde erhaltenswertes Grün kombiniert mit moderner (garten)architektonischer Gestaltung. Das geht bis ins Detail: Ein für Wiener Parks ungewöhnliches Blau in der Farbgebung des Mobiliars macht den Park auch in den kaltgrauen Wintermonaten attraktiv.

Eine Besonderheit, die beispielgebend für andere Bezirksteile Wiens wurde: Die Parkbetreuung durch einen Verein namens „Kugel" ist ein neues Wiener Modell für Sozialarbeit im weitesten Sinn. Im kommerziellen Bereich würde man es wohl Animation nennen, was die Parkbetreuer machen. Tatsächlich sorgen sie für den Aufbau von Verständnis zwischen den unterschiedlichen Gruppen der Parkbenützer (jung/alt, Inländer/Ausländer) und versuchen

which has been developing in recent years. After the closing down of a municipal depot, an existing park was not only expanded but also redesigned, with the aim of upgrading public space. Here, there are places for old people seeking repose, as well as for children who want to play. Here, immigrant families from southern climes can fulfill their habitual needs for outdoor life. Here, existing greenery was combined with modern garden architecture. Everything was planned down to the very last detail: blue, unusual for Viennese parks, highlights the garden furniture, making the park attractive also in the cold, gray winter months.

A special feature, that has set a precedent for other districts in Vienna, was the introduction of park supervision by an association called "Kugel", which provides a new Viennese model for social work in its widest sense. In the commercial field, what the park attendants do would probably be termed "animation". And, indeed, their aim is to establish good relations between the different groups of park users (young/old, Austrians/foreigners) and try to resolve conflicts or, ideally, not allow them to arise in the first place.

This park supervision and such neighborhood activities as a whole, was, incidentally, a small but evidently important contributory factor to the fact that the URBAN project for the Gürtel (we will re-

Konfliktlösungen zu erarbeiten, im Idealfall Konflikte gar nicht erst entstehen zu lassen. Diese Parkbetreuung, die Grätzlarbeit insgesamt, war übrigens auch ein kleiner, aber offenbar ausschlaggebender Anlaß dafür, daß das URBAN-Projekt Gürtel Plus von der EU als förderungswürdig bewertet wurde.

Caroline ist etwas verwundert angesichts dessen, was ihr da als „städtische Problemlage" vermittelt wird und was die EU sogar als Fördergebiet bewertet. Erinnerungen an Echo Park, an den öffentlichen Raum amerikanischer Städte, an Städte in Frankreich, die sie besucht hat, werden wach. Slums, meint sie, sehen wohl anders aus. Aber Wien hat eben einen besonders hohen Anspruch an Lebensqualität, wird ihr erklärt.

In der Nähe des Wilhelmsdorfer Zentrums findet sich auch noch ein alter „klassischer" Gemeindebau und ein wenig stadteinwärts der Arndt-Park, ebenfalls ein Paradebeispiel für die neuen Wiener Parks.

turn to this in detail towards the end of our tour) was considered by the EU as being worthy of subsidization.

Caroline is somewhat surprised by what has just been presented to her as "municipal problems" and by what the EU regards as an area worth subsidizing. She recalls Echo Park and the public spaces of American cities, or of cities in France which she has also visited. Slums, she thinks, look somewhat different. But Vienna places particularly high demands on the quality of life, as is explained to her.

Near the center of Wilhelmsdorf there is also another old "classical" municipal housing block and a bit further in towards the city center lies Arndt Park, which can also be considered a model for the new type of Viennese parks.

Die Bäuche von Wien

Die Reiseroute führt jetzt zurück Richtung U6 und am Meidlinger Markt vorbei. Spätestens hier erhält Caroline einen optischen Eindruck von der multikulturellen Zusammensetzung der Wiener Bevölkerung.

Die Wiener Märkte (insgesamt gibt es mehr als 40) waren in den vergangenen Jahrzehnten beinahe zum Aussterben verurteilt. Supermärkte hatten ihnen das Leben schwer gemacht, Inländer hatten das mühsame Geschäft der Marktstandler immer öfter aufgegeben. Erst die Zuwanderung der letzten 10 bis 15 Jahre hat zu einer Wiederbelebung der Märkte geführt, wie man hier in Meidling sehen kann. Sie wurden sozusagen zu den neuen/alten „Bäuchen von Wien". Die Nachfrage der „Ausländer" nach Obst, Gemüse und anderen Lebensmitteln, die Supermärkte in Wien nicht führten, und ihre Geschäftstüchtigkeit haben die Märkte wieder attraktiv gemacht. Und auch die alteingesessenen Wiener haben den Zauber der Märkte wiederentdeckt.

Wiens bekanntester Markt ist wohl der Naschmarkt, der in den Jahren des ersten Weltkrieges auf der damals erfolgten Überplattung des Wientales im Bereich der heutigen U-Bahnstationen Pilgramgasse und Kettenbrückengasse beziehungsweise bis zum Karlsplatz angesiedelt wurde.

Caroline würde dort wohl an den Farmers Market in ihrer Heimatstadt erinnert werden, denn ein Bummel über den Naschmarkt, den sie sich vorgenommen hat, vermittelt einen Eindruck über die Herkunft der altösterreichischen Bevölkerung und über die in jüngerer Zeit Zugezogenen.

The stomachs of Vienna

Our itinerary now takes us back towards the U6, passing Meidling Market on the way. Here, if not before, Caroline gets a graphic impression of the multicultural composition of the Viennese population.

Vienna's markets (there are more than 40 altogether) were often threatened with extinction during the past decades. They suffered from the competition with supermarkets and, more frequently than not, native Austrians gave up the arduous job of running a market stall. It was only with the wave of immigrants over the past 10-15 years that there has been a revival of the markets – as can be seen here in Meidling. They have become, as it were, the new and old "stomachs of Vienna".

The demands of "foreigners" for fruit, vegetables and other foodstuffs that normal supermarkets in Vienna did not stock have made the markets attractive again. And even the traditional Viennese have rediscovered their magic. Vienna's best-known market is undoubtedly the Naschmarkt which, during the First World War extended over the area covering the Wien River between today's subway stations Pilgramgasse and Kettenbrückengasse, stretching down to Karlsplatz.

Here, Caroline would certainly be reminded of the Farmers' Market in her home city and a stroll through the Naschmarkt, of which she has made a mental note, would give her an insight into the provenance, both of the original Austrian population and of the more recent additions in the form of immigrants.

Und noch einen Markt sollte Caroline besuchen, wenn sich Zeit findet: An der U3-Station Johnstraße im 15. Bezirk wurde ein alter Wasserbehälter umgebaut, baulich durch architektonisch anspruchsvolle Zubauten zu einem multifunktionalen Komplex ergänzt und der bestehende Meisel-Markt in die Gewölbe des Wasserbehälters übersiedelt.

Im Zusammenhang mit der Oberflächengestaltung nach dem U-Bahnbau wurde dort auch eine „Wasserwelt" eingerichtet, eine Art Park mit allen möglichen Wasserinstallationen. Lohnt einen Abstecher. Mit der U3 in wenigen Minuten zu erreichen.

Apropos Markt: In der äußeren Mariahilferstraße (an der weiteren Reiseroute gelegen), soll der alte Schwendermarkt ebenfalls in einen multifunktionalen Komplex integriert werden.

If she has time, Caroline should also visit another market. By the U3 subway station Johnstrasse in the 15th district, an old water reservoir has been converted and, with the addition of some architecturally ambitious buildings, expanded into a multifunctional complex, while the existing market has now moved into the dome of the water reservoir.

And as part of the redevelopment plans following the building of the subway, a "water world" theme park was installed with different kinds of water attractions. The detour is worthwhile and can be reached within several minutes on the U3 line.

Apropos markets. In outer Mariahilferstrasse (it is on our itinerary later on) is another market, the old Schwendermarkt, which is scheduled for conversion into a multifunctional complex.

55

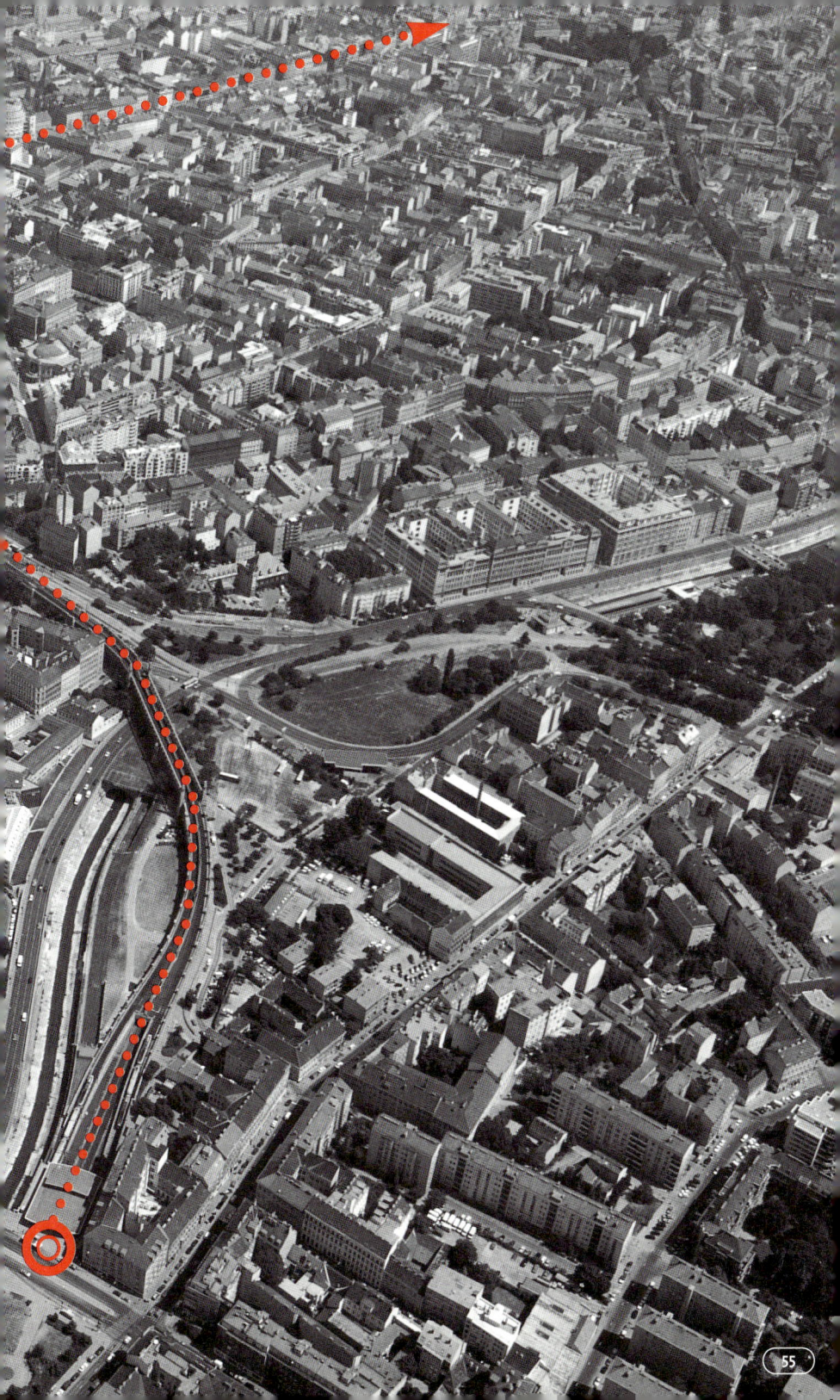

Über das Wiental

Markanter kann man den Wechsel, die Schnittstelle zwischen alt und neu kaum darstellen, als es die Bilder tun, die an den Fenstern des U-Bahn-Zuges vorbeiziehen, wenn er aus dem „Untergrund" der Stadt auftaucht und sich über die Rampe auf die von Otto Wagner konzipierte Brücke über das Wiental schwingt.

Die Videoclip-Generation wird dabei keine Schwierigkeiten haben, für herkömmliche Sehgewohnheiten mag es ein wenig zu schnell gehen. Und leider kann man die Strecke nicht zu Fuß begehen. Caroline läßt sich diesen „Flug" durch und über Höhen- und Zeitschichten der Stadt schildern.

Otto Wagner gilt als der Vater der Stadtbahn, jenes zukunftsweisenden innerstädtischen Schienenverkehrssystems, das vor rund 100 Jahren in Wien in Auftrag gegeben worden war. Wie bereits erwähnt, hatte ein nicht unwesentlicher Teil des Netzes militärisch-logistische Aufgaben zu bewältigen, aber schließlich hat die Menschheit ja auch die Raumfahrt grundlegenden militärischen Überlegungen zu verdanken. Zu weit hergeholt, dieser Vergleich?

„Star Wars" ist Caroline als jenes gigantische Rüstungsprojekt noch in Erinnerung, das kurz vor dem Entspannungsprozeß zwischen den USA und der damaligen UdSSR für Milliardeninvestitionen in die US-Raumfahrt gesorgt hatte. Die Kriegsspielereien sind hoffentlich vorbei. Geblieben ist immerhin die Basis für die Globalisierung der Telekommunikation via Satellit, die immer zuverlässigere Wetterprognose aus dem All und vieles mehr.

Otto Wagner jedenfalls, jener Mann, der Wiens Stadtbild entscheidend mitprägen sollte, war vor der Beauftragung mit den Stadtbahnplanungen ein in der Branche bestenfalls als zweitrangig eingestufter Architekt.

Doch mit der Stadtbahn gelang ihm der große Wurf, der Schritt zum Welt-

Over the Wientāl

The transition from old to new can hardly be more strikingly presented than in the pictures that glide past the windows of the "U-Bahn" as it surfaces from underneath the city and swings up over the ramp onto the bridge over the Wien River designed by Otto Wagner.

While the video generation will have no problems with the speed of the presentation, for more traditional ways of observation it may be a bit too fast. But, unfortunately, one cannot do this stretch of the route on foot. Caroline has this "flight" through different levels of time and space explained to her by her companions.

Otto Wagner is regarded as the father of the metropolitan railway system, which was commissioned around 100 years ago and was at that time considered progressive. As already mentioned, a considerable part of the network fulfilled military and logistic functions. But then mankind also owes space travel to fundamental military considerations. Is this comparison too far-fetched?

Caroline recalls "Star Wars", the gigantic armament project which, shortly before the process of détente between America and the Soviet Union, generated investments totaling billions of dollars into the US aerospace industry. While the war games are, hopefully, a thing of the past, the basis for the globalization of telecommunications via satellite, for better and more reliable weather forecasts from outer space and much more, still remains. Before he was commissioned with the planning and design of the metropolitan railway, Otto Wagner, the man who was to leave such an indelible imprint on the face of this city, was only known within his field as, at best, a second-rate architect. But the construction of the metropolitan railway brought him his lucky break and the step towards world fame. For this Viennese railway was – in its today still unrivaled style – at that time the only

ruhm: Denn diese Wiener Stadtbahn war in ihrem auch heute noch unvergleichlichen Stil zu Wagners Zeit das einzige Massenverkehrsmittel der Welt, das von einem einzigen Gestalter als einheitliches Ganzes entworfen und umgesetzt wurde. Wiens Planer standen daher bei der Vorbereitung der U6 vor der ungeheuer schwierigen Aufgabe, dieses Gesamtkunstwerk in ein zukunftssicheres U-Bahnnetz zu integrieren – oder umgekehrt.

Neben den Schwierigkeiten, in die hundert Jahre alten Stationsbauwerke etwa moderne Aufzugssysteme einzubauen, war wohl die Integration der Wiental-Brücke die herausforderndste Aufgabe. Die nach langer Diskussion über Wert und Unwert dieses Bauwerks bravourös gelöst wurde.

Es lohnt sich, erfährt Caroline, beispielsweise bei der U4-Station Margaretengürtel beginnend, den „Gaudenzdorfer Knoten" zu Fuß zu überqueren, um sich ein Gesamtbild dieser Konstruktion

mass public transportation system in the world which was designed and implemented by a single architect as a unified whole. Which is why the planners of Vienna's subway system were confronted with the immensely difficult task of integrating this "Gesamtkunstwerk" into a sustainable subway network – or vice versa, as the case may be.

Quite apart from the problems of incorporating modern elevator systems into the century-old station buildings, the integration of Otto Wagner's Wiental Bridge was the most challenging task. After lengthy discussions on the pros and cons of this construction, an admirable solution was found.

Caroline learns that it is worth crossing the "Gaudenzdorf junction" on foot, beginning, for example, at the U4 station Margaretengürtel, in order to see this construction in its entirety. The seconds during which the train glides over this bridge also lead through a remarkable cityscape.

zu machen. Die Sekunden, in denen der Zug über dieses Brückenbauwerk hinweggleitet, führen auch über eine bemerkenswerte Stadtlandschaft.

Er überquert die Wien, jenen Fluß, der manchen Geschichtsforschern als Namensquelle für die Stadt dient, wobei heute noch immer keine Einigkeit über die Namensgebung (Vindobona, Wienen, Vienna ...) herrscht.

Was heute von diesem alten Fluß dort, wo er nicht wie hier in Gaudenzdorf überdacht worden war, ist ein schmales, trübes Gerinne, ein städtischer Kanal vielleicht. Und doch kann dieses Gerinne aufbrausen, wenn es stark regnet, wenn die Staubecken im westlichen Wien die Wassermassen nicht mehr halten können. An manchen Tagen brausen gewaltige Fluten durch das Tal. Dann wird den Städtern bewußt, daß es sich nicht um ein urbanes Gewässer handelt, sondern um einen echten Fluß mit natürlichem Ursprung. Jahrhundertelang stellte das Wasser in der Stadt ja eine reale Bedrohung dar: Hochwässer und Seuchen versetzten die Städter in Angst und Schrecken. So waren auch alle Wasserbauten darauf ausgerichtet, die Natur zu bändigen, zu zähmen, sie dem Menschen unterzuordnen. Erst die letzten Jahre haben in Wien die relative Gewißheit gebracht, daß die Menschen die Gewässer der Stadt im Griff haben.

Das in den letzten Jahren gewandelte Verständnis für Natur in der Stadt tut das seine: Für die Renaturalisierung der Wien liegen Pläne vor. Erste Teststrecken im Westen wurden bereits verwirklicht. Im Zuge der Arbeiten an einem neuen Hauptsammelkanal soll diese Gestaltung Schritt für Schritt erfolgen. Heute hindern noch mangelnde Finanzmittel an einer raschen Umsetzung. Für den Bereich des Gaudenzdorfer Knotens existierten übrigens auch Überlegungen, den Wienfluß wieder zu öffnen, ihn tatsächlich erlebbar zu machen.

For the train crosses over the Wien River, which some historians like to regard as the source of our city's name, although there is still no agreement as to the real derivation (Vindobona, Wienen, Vienna...).

What can still be seen of this old river, in places where it is not covered over, unlike here in Gaudenzdorf, is just a narrow, cloudy trickle of water, more like a city canal. And yet this small stream can surge up into a torrent during heavy rain and when the storage reservoirs in the west of Vienna can no longer hold the mass of water. On some days, vast torrents swirl through the valley and then the inhabitants realize that it is not just an urban watercourse but a real river from a natural source.

For centuries, water in the city posed a real threat: floods and plagues terrified the population. For this reason, all river engineering projects were geared towards controlling and taming nature and subordinating it to human needs.

Only recent years have brought Vienna the "relative" security that its inhabitants have at least tamed the Danube. The changed approach towards nature in the city has done its part: plans already exist for restoring the Wien River to a more natural state, and initial tests have already been carried out in the west of the city. During the construction of a main canal to accumulate surplus water, the other redevelopment aspects will be undertaken bit by bit. A lack of funds is currently impeding further implementation of the project. For the area round Gaudenzdorf junction proposals have also been made to open up the Wien River and make it visible again.

This city landscape has seen many potential projects that are still waiting to be implemented. For through this area gushes a second "stream": the "Gürtel", an outer ring road with three lanes of traffic in each direction. This is virtually a city highway which leads through the built-up outer districts. Concentric to the

Wie überhaupt diese Stadtlandschaft schon viele Planungen gesehen hat, auf deren Umsetzung sie noch immer wartet: Durch diese Landschaft rauscht nämlich noch ein zweiter „Strom". Der in jede Richtung aus drei Fahrspuren bestehende „Gürtel". Das ist jene Fast-Stadtautobahn, die als zweiter Ring durch die dichtbebauten Stadtgebiete führt. Konzentrisch zur klassischen Ringstraße und entlang jener Linie, die einst der „Linienwall" markierte. Dabei handelt es sich um eine Art Vorverteidigungslinie, die das alte Wien vor Angriffen schützen sollte, später zu einer Zoll-Linie und erst vor rund hundert Jahren zu einem Boulevard umgebaut wurde, der eigentlich Naherholungsgebiet für die Menschen sein sollte.

Daß genau zu jener Zeit eine Erfindung ihren unaufhaltsamen Weg nehmen sollte, die wir heute als Auto kennen, war damals nicht abzusehen, denkt Caroline. Aus dem Boulevard wurde jedenfalls dank der zunehmenden Motorisierung eine wichtige Hauptverkehrsstraße Wiens und heute donnern in manchen Teilen an die hunderttausend Fahrzeuge täglich durch die Häuserschluchten, erzählt ihre Begleitung.

Noch in den sechziger Jahren, als man sich am Höhe- und Endpunkt der Motorisierungswelle wähnte (welch fataler Trugschluß!), war für Wien ein Stadtautobahnnetz vorgesehen, dessen Rückgrat der Gürtel gebildet hätte.

Caroline versucht, Wien in die Größenverhältnisse von Los Angeles zu transformieren und sieht mehrstöckige Stelzenautobahnen diese Stadtlandschaft gnadenlos zerschneiden.

In den achtziger Jahren, wird sie beruhigt, wurden diese Projektionen unter die Erde verlegt. Ein Tunnelsystem sollte, so die damalige Planungsphilosophie, den Autostrom unter die Erde leiten, so wie den Wien-Fluß.

Abgesehen von den astronomischen Finanzierungskosten scheiterte dieses Vorhaben vor allem auch an einer ge-

---

classical Ringstrasse, it encircles the inner districts, following the line that once marked the site of the old fortification walls or "Linienwall". It was a defense system that, long before "Star Wars", was to protect Vienna from attack and which then became a customs point. Around 100 years ago it was redeveloped as a boulevard, which was originally designed as a recreation area for the inhabitants of the city.

That this took place precisely at the same time that an invention which we know today as the automobile was pursuing its relentless course could not have then been foreseen, mused Caroline. At any rate, thanks to increased road traffic, this boulevard has become an important bypass round the city and today, on some stretches of the Gürtel, around one hundred thousand vehicles per day thunder past the houses, Caroline's companions tell her.

Even in the sixties when it was thought that motorization had reached its peak and would soon come to an end (what a hope!), a city autobahn network was foreseen for Vienna, whose main axis would have been the Gürtel.

Caroline tries to transform Vienna into the dimensions of Los Angeles and visualizes multi-storied expressways mercilessly slicing up the city's landscape.

To her relief, she was informed by Suzanne and Wolf that, in the eighties, this project was planned for underneath the city. Based on the planning philosophy of the time, a system of tunnels was to bring the streams of cars underground, as with the Wien River.

Quite apart from the astronomical financial costs, this project failed mainly because of a changed attitude towards planning. The city, as the creed the new Viennese traffic concept that was developed in the past years dictated, should not allow itself to become subordinated to cars. Attention must focus on people, although, conversely, people must be prepared to change their mobility habits.

wandelten Planungsphilosophie. Die Stadt, so lautet schließlich auch das „Glaubensbekenntnis" des neuen Wiener Verkehrskonzeptes, das in den vergangenen Jahren entwickelt worden war, dürfe sich nicht dem Auto unterordnen. Im Mittelpunkt habe der Mensch zu stehen.

Von dem man freilich auch verlangen müsse, daß er sein Mobilitätsverhalten ändert. Der Anteil der Fahrten in öffentlichen Verkehrsmitteln, per Fahrrad oder das Zurücklegen zumutbarer Strecken zu Fuß sollte stark zunehmen, die Zahl der unbedingt nötigen innerstädtischen Autofahrten drastisch reduziert werden.

Eine wirksame Maßnahme ist eben der Ausbau der U6, in der wir uns noch immer befinden, die nun das Durchqueren der Stadt zwischen dem Süden und dem Norden genau an den „Ufern" der Autoströme am Gürtel in einer Fahrzeit ermöglicht, mit der kein Auto mitkommen kann.

Die Tunnel-Euphorie der achtziger Jahre bescherte Wien ein internationales und interdisziplinäres Planungsverfahren nach dem Wiener Modell der damaligen Donauraumplanungen. Mag sein, daß heute nur wenige der darin entwickelten baulichen Vorstellungen umgesetzt werden können, sicher ist aber, daß dabei wertvolle Erkenntnisse über Sinn und Unsinn von Tunnels in der Stadt, vor allem aber über die Aufwertung des Lebensraumes im Gürtelbereich gewonnen werden konnten, auf die nicht zuletzt in den jetzigen Projekten im URBAN-Verfahren aufgebaut werden kann.

Warum der Bereich Gaudenzdorf so eminent bedeutend, so neuralgisch ist, hat noch einen Grund: Noch ein (Verkehrs)Strom mischt sich hier mit dem Gürtelverkehr. Die Wiener Westeinfahrt verengt sich spätestens hier von der Autobahn über eine Art Schnellstraße zum Flaschenhals alter, gewachsener Straßenzüge.

Deshalb wurde aus dem gesamten Planungsverfahren für den Gürtel ge-

The aim is to increase the number of journeys by public transport, by bicycle and, for reasonable distances, on foot, while at the same time keeping the number of trips by car into the city center to the absolute minimum.

One effective measure is the U6 subway line, in which we are still traveling, and which enables us to cross the city all the way from north to south by following the streams of traffic along the Gürtel in a time that no car can possibly manage.

From the point of view of urban development, the tunnel euphoria of the eighties left urban planners with an international and interdisciplinary planning process based on the Viennese model of the urban planning principles of the time (see also Danube regeneration scheme). While it may be the case that few of the ideas that were generated at that time can be put into effect today, at least valuable knowledge was gained on the advantages and disadvantages of tunnels in a city, as well as upgrading living conditions around the Gürtel, which form the basis for the current projects of the URBAN program.

Another reason why the Gaudenzdorf area is such a critical spot is that a second stream of traffic mingles here with the cars on the Gürtel. The entrance to Vienna from the West autobahn gets narrowed down into a kind of express road, turning into a bottleneck of old streets, overgrown with traffic.

This is why the Gürtel redevelopment project focuses particular attention on the Gaudenzdorf junction. A "Margaretentunnel" is envisaged, which will enable a small park to be laid out above it at street level. Or rather "would" enable, for we are confronted with the negative attitude of the responsible Austrian Federal Ministries to this project. Whereas elsewhere in Austria even the smallest villages have been provided with a generous bypass, here in Vienna around 12,000 directly-affected residents have been left

nau der „Gaudenzdorfer Knoten" projektsreif ausgearbeitet. Hier sollte der „Margaretentunnel" entstehen, der an der Oberfläche eine parkähnliche Landschaft ermöglichen würde, wäre da nicht die bisher stets abweisende Haltung der zuständigen österreichischen Bundesministerien. Während anderswo in Österreich auch kleinste Ortschaften mit großzügigen Ortsumfahrungen versorgt werden, ließ man hier bis heute an die 12.000 unmittelbar betroffene Anrainer im Regen stehen. Für die notwendigen Bundesstraßenbauten ist kein Geld vorhanden. Und angesichts der Budgetsituation auch in den kommenden Jahren nicht zu erwarten.

Verbleiben für eine weitere blitzartige Videoclip-Darstellung noch zwei Bauprojekte auf dem Gaudenzdorfer Knoten: Dort wo der Gürtel sozusagen einmündet in das Wiental, sind auf beiden Seiten markante Hochbauten in Überlegung. Dem U6-Passagier der Zukunft könnte sich also ein kurzer, aber imposanter Blick auf eine neue Stadtpforten-Situation bieten.

Caroline registriert, daß ihr U-Bahnzug schon längst die Station Gumpendorfer Straße erreicht hat und macht einen Blick in ein weiteres Stadterneuerungsgebiet, wobei sie sich mit einer Wiener Besonderheit konfrontiert sieht, den „Künstler-Häusern".

in the lurch. At present, there is no money available to build more highways and, in view of the budgetary deficit, it is unlikely that any further funds can be expected in the near future.

There are just two more building projects for the Gaudenzdorf junction that we can take a quick look at in video tempo: where the Gürtel "flows" into the Wiental, plans are being considered for salient high-rise buildings. Future U6 passengers will then have a short but impressive glimpse of a new situation regarding the entrance to Vienna.

Caroline realizes that her subway train has already reached Gumpendorferstrasse station and here she is greeted, not only with a new redevelopment area but also with another distinctive Viennese feature – houses decorated by artists.

Wiener Künstlerhäuser

Gumpendorf ist ebenso wie das bereits besuchte Wilhelmsdorf eines der ersten Wiener Stadterneuerungsgebiete, das aus heutiger Sicht freilich nicht ganz geglückt ist, wurde doch hier teilweise wenig sanft vorgegangen. Interessant für eine Bestandsaufnahme des neuen Wien ist allerdings eine Entwicklung in unmittelbarer Nähe des alten Raimund-Theaters, das dem Abbruch entging und mittlerweile zum Ruf Wiens als kontinentaleuropäische Musicalstadt beiträgt.

Mehrere weltberühmte Wiener Maler konnten in Wien in den letzten Jahren ihre Kreativität auch in Bauten manifestieren. Caroline und die Mitreisenden machen hier wieder eine kurze Exkursion: Der Name Hundertwasser ist nicht nur in der Kunstszene ein Begriff. Der Maler hat sich im Laufe der Zeit zu einem Hobby-Stadtgestalter entwickelt und Wien eine Reihe von Touristenattraktionen beschert.

Angefangen hat alles mit dem legendären Hundertwasserhaus im dritten Bezirk nahe des Donaukanals. Dort startete er in den späten siebziger Jahren im Kampf gegen „klassische" Architektur und getragen von einem frühen Öko-Bewußtsein sein erstes Projekt. Otto Kapfinger, renommierter Wiener Architekturkritiker und Mitautor des neuen „Wiener Architekturführers", be-

Artist Houses in Vienna

Just like Wilhelmsdorf that we have already visited, Gumpendorf was also one of the first areas in Vienna to be redeveloped. Viewed from today, it was not entirely successful as some parts of the district were not handled with the necessary sensitivity. But for an inventory of the new Vienna there is an interesting development in the vicinity of the old Raimund Theater, which escaped demolition and has, in the meantime, contributed to Vienna's reputation as European capital for Broadway musicals.

In recent years a number of world-famous Viennese artists were given the opportunity of demonstrating their creativity on public buildings. Caroline and her traveling companions again make a short detour. The name Hundertwasser is not only known in the world of art. Over the years, this painter has developed into a hobby urban planner and has presented Vienna with a wide range of tourist attractions. It all began with the legendary "Hundertwasserhaus" near the Danube Canal in the third district. It was here that he took up the gauntlet against "classical" architecture and launched his first project, which was based on an early ecological awareness. The well-known Viennese architecture critic and co-author of the new "Wiener Architekturführer" (Guide to Viennese Architecture) described the phenomenon

schrieb bereits vor Jahren das Phänomen Hundertwasser ausgehend von dessen weltberühmtem Wohnhaus am Donaukanal:

„Indem es den seit den 50er Jahren angewachsenen Innovationsbedarf im Wohnungsbau in einer einzigen spektakulären Geste, in einer rein symbolischen Handlung abfängt, in eine prächtige Kulisse ökologischen Bauens stilisiert, indem es ein Wohnhaus radikal zum Ausstellungsstück und ausschließlich auf seinen Schauwert hin überhöht (in die Löwengasse strömen jährlich mehr ‚Besucher' und Gaffer aus nah und fern als in alle Museumsneubauten am Frankfurter Schaumainkai zusammen) – in all dem verkörpert es (über Wien hinaus) beinahe ein Leitfossil für die Architektur der 80er Jahre schlechthin. Wenn der Grundgedanke der Postmoderne darin liegt, daß das Falsche zum Echten mutiert, weil es nichts Echtes mehr gibt (L. Burckhardt), wenn es heute so ist, daß das Sein sich nur mehr im Design manifestieren und die Kultur nur mehr in der Ironie, in der Allegorie überleben kann, dann ist dies selten (bewußt, unbewußt?) perfekter vorexerziert worden als in der Löwengasse – es sei denn von Hundertwasser selbst durch die äußerliche Verschönerung der Müllverbrennungsanlage Spittelau: Der im Zeitalter der ‚Posthistoire' als veraltet abgetane Widerspruch zwischen Lüge und Wahrheit, Schein und

Hundertwasser years ago, based on his world-famous residential building on the Danube Canal:

"He has created, in a single spectacular gesture and a purely symbolic act, a building that responds to the growing need for innovation in housing which we have seen since the 1950's; his is a building stylized against the splendid backdrop of eco-architecture, an apartment block radically turned into a showpiece and exclusively valued for its visual impact (more 'visitors' and gapers flock to Löwengasse from near and far than to all the museum buildings along the entire Frankfurt Schaumainkai). The building is, quintessentially and beyond the confines of Vienna, a guide to the architecture of the eighties. If the fundamental principle of post-modernism is embodied in the thought that 'unreal mutates to real because nothing real is left' (L. Burckhardt) and if, today, existence is only manifested in design and culture can only survive in irony and allegory, then there could hardly be a more perfect demonstration of this (consciously or unconsciously?) than in Löwengasse – to be outdone only by Hundertwasser himself perhaps in the facade redesign of the Spittelau waste incinerator. The contradiction between lies and truth, reality and unreality, which is viewed as old-fashioned in the age of 'posthistoire', acquires almost baroque dimensions in this huge phantasmagory and appears to

Sein hebt in dieser gigantischen Phantasmagorie in geradezu barocke Dimensionen ab und wird ob solcher Maßlosigkeit offenbar wirklich unsichtbar – virtuell, wie man jetzt sagt."

Zurück nach Gumpendorf: Hier sieht Caroline aus der U-Bahnstation ein Haus, das der von der Stadt Wien dem Maler zur Seite gestellte Architekt in dessen Stil errichtet hat. Und in unmittelbarer Nähe entstand ein Haus nach den Vorstellungen des Malers der Wiener Schule und Liedermachers Arik Brauer, in der nahen Mariahilferstraße entstand eine Hausfassade nach Christian Ludwig Attersee.

Die Reisegruppe setzt die Fahrt fort und sieht kurz ein seltsames Bautenpaar: Kurz vor dem Westbahnhof steht links die Kirche Maria am Siege, ein Gründerzeit-Bau. Und vis á vis hat eine Hotelkette ein etwa gleich hohes Gebäude im Stil international verwechselbarer (oder unverwechselbarer?) Hotelarchitektur errichten lassen. Als danach abschreckendes Beispiel für die Ausnutzung der höchsten Bauklasse in Wien, wie ein hoher Planungsbeamter im Gespräch mit Caroline süffisant anmerkte. In Zukunft soll hier wieder die höchste Bauklasse ausgenützt werden. Allerdings mit jener hohen Qualität, wie sie nunmehr zum Standard geworden ist.

Der U-Bahn-Zug hat mittlerweile die Station Westbahnhof erreicht, und Caroline durchquert ein monumentales

vanish altogether in the light of such boundlessness, becoming, as one would say today, virtual reality."

But back to Gumpendorf. Here is a house, and Caroline can see this from the subway station, that was built by an architect who was put at the disposal of the artist by the municipality of Vienna and constructed it according to his wishes. And, not very far away, another house was built, based on the ideas of the artist of the Vienna School and singer/songwriter Arik Brauer. In nearby Mariahilferstrasse there is a house facade designed by the painter Christian Ludwig Attersee.

The tour party continues on its' way and for a short time sees a an odd couple of buildings. Shortly before the West Railway Station, on the left-hand side, is the Church Maria am Siege, a Gründerzeit building. And across the road from it a hotel chain has erected a building of roughly the same height in internationally recognizable (or unrecognizable?) hotel architecture. To act as a deterrent for the utilization of the highest building category in Vienna, as a high-ranking planning official in a conversation with Caroline remarked self-complacently. In the future the highest building category will again be applied here, however, with the high quality that has now become standard in the Vienna.

Verkehrsbauwerk. Hier schneiden sich unterirdisch unsere Reise-Linie U6 und die als „Kulturlinie" apostrophierte U3.

Das ist eine Durchmesserlinie, die aus dem westlichen Bezirk Ottakring zur Jahrtausendwende bis ins östliche Simmering führen wird. In den bereits fertiggestellten Stationen hat die Stadt Wiener und internationale Künstler mit der Ausgestaltung der Bauten beauftragt. Von Vertretern des Phantastischen Realismus der fünfziger und sechziger Jahre bis zu Videoinstallationen von Nam June Paik reicht die Palette. Und zwischendurch bietet die U3 im City-Bereich Einblicke in die Vergangenheit der Stadt. Ein ausführlicher U-Bahn-Stationsbummel lohnt sich für alle, die Zeit genug dafür haben. An der Oberfläche befindet sich Wiens Kopfbahnhof nach Westeuropa, auch eine stark frequentierte Regionalbahn endet hier. Und mehrere Straßenbahnen sorgen für die Fein-Verteilung der Passagiere. Auch hier hätte übrigens ein Straßentunnel den Autoverkehr unter die Erde bringen sollen, was, wie die anderen Tunnelpläne, verworfen wurde.

Caroline und Begleitung tauchen aus dem Untergrund auf und erreichen den Europaplatz.

The subway train has already reached the West Railway Station and Caroline finds herself walking through a monumental building. At this point, our U6 subway intersects with the U3, commonly known as the "cultural line". This is a diametrical line that starts in the western district of Ottakring and, by the year 2000, will stretch to the furthest eastern point in Simmering. For the station buildings, most of which are now complete, the City of Vienna has commissioned Viennese and international artists with the outer design of the buildings. The selection ranges from exponents of the School of Fantastic Realism of the fifties and sixties to video installations by Nam June Paik. And in the meantime, between the buildings, the U3 gives an insight into the past history of the city. An extensive stroll around the subway stations would be worthwhile for anyone who has the time. At street level is Vienna's railway terminus for Western Europe – a widely used regional train also ends here. And a variety of trams provide for a further distribution of the passengers. Here, too, incidentally, a tunnel was envisaged that would take road traffic underground, but this plan as other plans for tunnels was rejected.

Caroline and her companions come up from the subway onto street level and reach Europaplatz.

Baustelle Europa

So wie sich Wien an einer europäischen „Verwerfungszone" befindet, stellt der Europaplatz eine innerstädtische Verwerfungszone dar.

So wie sich Europa im Um- und Ausbau befindet, fanden die Wiener hier jahrelang eine Baustelle vor, die jetzt langsam Gesicht angenommen hat.

So wie in Europa Ost und West, im weitesten auch Nord und Süd ihre „Mitte" in Wien haben, treffen hier drei Wiener Bezirke aufeinander, schneidet Wiens längste Straße, die in Zeiten der Monarchie die Hofburg mit der Sommerresidenz Schönbrunn verband, den Verkehrsstrom Gürtel, war hier einst eine der wichtigsten Stadtmautstationen für nach Wien Einreisende.

So wie Wien auf der Baustelle Europa mitwirken will beim Aufbau von „Transnationalen Netzen" im Infrastrukturbereich, vor allem beim Ausbau der Hochleistungsbahnen, so stellt dieser Europaplatz innerhalb der Stadt einen der wichtigsten Verkehrsknoten dar.

So wie sich in Europa Völker, Nationen, Regionen einerseits um Erhaltung ihrer Identitäten, andererseits um möglichst viele Gemeinsamkeiten bemühen, waren und sind an diesem städtischen Schnittpunkt Verbindungen und Akzentuierungen in Bau und in Planung.

Building site Europe

Just as, geologically, Vienna lies on a European fault, Europaplatz is on an inner-city fault. Just as Europe is presently in a state of change and expansion, in the same way the Viennese were for years confronted with a building-site that is now gradually taking on shape.

Just as in Europe East and West, in the furthest sense also North and South have their "middle point" in Vienna, here on Europaplatz three Viennese districts meet, Vienna's longest street, which at the time of the Monarchy connected the Hofburg winter palace with the summer residence at Schˆnbrunn, intersects the Gürtel road and what was formerly the most important toll station for people entering Vienna once stood here.

Just as Vienna wants to cooperate on the building-site of Europe in constructing transnational networks in the area of infrastructure and particularly in the expansion of high-speed trains, in the same way this Europaplatz represents one of the most important traffic junctions within the city.

Just as in Europe peoples, nations and regions on the one hand are endeavoring to maintain their identity, and on the other are trying to find as much common ground as possible, in the same way here at this city intersection were, and still are, connections and priorities in building and planning.

67

Planerische Traumbilder

So wie Europa Visionen über seine Erweiterung und seinen Stellenwert in der Welt anstellt, entwickeln hier Visionäre ihre Vorstellungen städtebaulicher Natur.

Nehmen wir den Westbahnhof: Er spielte einst als Kaiserin Elisabeth-Bahnhof in der österreichisch-ungarischen Monarchie eine eher untergeordnete Rolle, weil sich die Hauptinteressen Wiens auf den Norden, Osten und Süden richteten. In den Zeiten des Kalten Krieges wurde er Symbol für die neue West-Orientierung Österreichs und vor der Bedeutungszunahme des Flugverkehrs für viele der hunderttausenden Menschen, die Österreich auf dem Weg vom Osten in die Freiheit durchquerten, ein Symbol wie die Freiheitsstatue in New York.

In den fünfziger Jahren wurde der Westbahnhof nach den Kriegszerstörungen wiedererrichtet und gilt

Planning Visions

Just as Europe is setting up visions as to its expansion and its role in the world, in the same way visionaries in Vienna are developing their ideas on urban planning.

Let us take the West Railway Station as an example. As the former Empress Elisabeth Station at the time of the Austro-Hungarian monarchy it was considered a less important station because Vienna's interests were largely concentrated on the north, east and south. It was only at the time of the Cold War that it became a symbol for the new Austrian orientation towards the West and, before the increased importance of air traffic, for many of the hundreds of thousands of people who passed through Vienna on their way from the East into the freedom of the West it became a symbol like the Statue of Liberty in New York.

In the fifties, the West Railway Station was rebuilt after the destruction of the war years and is today regarded as an ex-

heute als hervorragendes Baubeispiel dieser Epoche. Im Inneren ist, findet Caroline, die Synthese zwischen dem Stil der fünfziger Jahre und der gläsernen Zweckarchitektur zur Verbindung mit dem innerstädtischen Verkehrssystem wirklich gelungen.

Und wieder droht der Westbahnhof zu einem Bahnhof zweiter Garnitur zu werden. Wenn es jemals zu einem „Bahnhof Wien" kommen sollte, für den entsprechende Planungen in den vergangenen Jahren projektreif gemacht wurden und wofür auch die Tunnelverbindung zwischen West- und Südbahn unter dem westlichen Lainzer Tiergarten fix und fertig projektiert ist, dann wird dieser Bahnhof an Bedeutung verlieren. Doch angesichts der Budgetsituation darf man damit rechnen, daß bis dahin noch viele Jahre vergehen werden.

Und so schmieden Visionäre ihre ökologischen Pläne für einen „Stadthügel" auf dem (überbauten) Westbahnhof wohl für eine ferne Zukunft. Der US-amerikanische Wissenschafter und Co-Direktor des Centers for Sustainable Cities, Richard Levine, hat gemeinsam mit einem Wiener Expertenteam den „Stadthügel" als „dreidimensionales urbanes Integrationssystem" entwickelt, das als „Implantat in gesellschaftlich oder funktional unterversorgte Quartiere eingepflanzt wird".

Spannend ist die Idee eines autonomen urbanen Ökosystems allemal, und es bedarf nicht der Schreckensvorstellung eines atomaren Winters oder der Folgen einer weiteren Zerstörung der Erdatmosphäre und des Ozonschildes, um sich einen solchen Stadthügel vorzustellen, bei dem nur die äußerste kompakte Hülle gegen Witterungseinflüsse und Wärme geschützt werden muß. Der „Selbstversorger", in dem sich Energie-Input und Output die Waage halten, ist ein zukunftsträchtiges Konzept. Fraglich ist nur, welche Generation eine Überbauung des Westbahn-

cellent example of the architecture of that era. Caroline finds that the inside of the building is a highly successful synthesis between the style of the fifties and the modern glass functional design as a connection with the metropolitan transport system. And again the West Railway Station threatens to be degraded to a second-rate station. Should there ever be a central railway station in Vienna, relevant plans have been drawn up in the form of projects over the past few years and the tunnel connection between the west and the south highways underneath the Lainzer Tiergarten to the west of the city is also embodied in a project, then this railway station will become terminus for regional trains. But in view of the budgetary situation it can be assumed that this will take several years.

And so visionaries have made their ecological plans for a far-distant future, in the shape of the "city-as-a-hill" project which provides for a superstructure on top of the West Railway Station. In conjunction with a team of Viennese experts, the American scientist and co-director of the Center for Sustainable Cities, Richard Levine, has developed this "city-as-a-hill" concept as a "three-dimensional urban integration system" that will serve as an "implantation to be introduced into socially or functionally underdeveloped districts". The idea of an autonomous urban ecosystem is always an exciting one, and we do not need the terrifying vision of a nuclear winter or the consequences of a further destruction of the earth's atmosphere and the ozone layer before our eyes in order to visualize such a "city-as-a-hill", in which only the outermost compact covering has to be protected against the effects of weather and heat. This self-sufficient system, in which energy input and output are in equilibrium, is a promising concept. The question is only as to which generation will actually see a superstructure built over the West Railway Station. (Models of such railway superstructures

hofes erleben wird, auch wenn ähnliche Überlegungen schon seit Jahren existieren. Bis dato „rechnet sich" eine Überbauung auch nicht.

Traumtürme

Blicken wir also stadteinwärts, Richtung Mariahilfer Straße. Hier, am Mariahilfer Platzl, erinnert sich Caroline, habe doch COOP Himmelblau ein Projekt eines horizontalen und eines senkrechten Turmes entwickelt, das bei einer Werkausstellung im Pariser Centre Pompidou Anfang der neunziger Jahre Aufsehen erregt hatte.

Noch sind es „Traumtürme", noch zögern die Bauträger. Aus stadtgestalterischer Sicht wäre ein solches Signal am Beginn der größten Wiener Einkaufsstraße, des größten urbanen Boulevards nach der Ringstraße, willkommen.

Caroline & Co machen sich zu Fuß auf den Weg „in die Stadt", wie die Wiener sagen, wenn sie den 1. Bezirk, die „Innere Stadt", meinen. Unter ihnen fährt die U3, in die sie alle paar hundert Meter einsteigen könnten, sie haben aber vor, auch ein paar Abstecher in die Seitengassen zu machen.

Sie wandeln also auf Kaisers Spuren, sehen zwar (noch) keine Kutschen, weil die Fiaker vorwiegend innerhalb der Ringstraße verkehren, verfolgen aber seinen Weg Richtung Hofburg.

Noch vor gar nicht allzulanger Zeit litt die Mariahilfer Straße unter den jahrelangen „Wunden", die der U-Bahn-

in Vienna include the North Railway Station.) Relevant plans and considerations have existed for several years now. But, so far, the economics has not been right.

Dream towers

Let's now take a look in towards the city in the direction of Mariahilferstrasse. Here, in Mariahilfer Platz, as Caroline recalls, the COOP Himmelblau team developed a project for a horizontal and vertical tower that caused quite a stir during an exhibition in the Paris Pompidou Center in the early nineties. So these towers are still "dream towers", figments of the imagination, and still the building companies are hesitating. From the point of view of urban planning, such an architectural symbol at the lower end of Vienna's major shopping street, the biggest boulevard after Ringstrasse, would be more than welcome. Caroline & Co make their way on foot "downtown", as the Viennese say when they go into the 1st district, the "inner city". Beneath them is the U3 subway line, which has stations every couple of hundred meters along the way, but they prefer to walk in order to make a couple of detours into some of the side-streets. Now they find themselves following in the tracks of Emperor Francis Joseph, although they do not (yet) see any carriages – the "fiacres" are mainly to be found within Ringstrasse -, and retrace his footsteps down towards

Bau in „Tagbauweise" geschlagen hatte. Die einstige Einkaufs-Prachtstraße drohte abzusacken, geschäftsmäßig. Das verschärfte die ohnehin angespannte Konkurrenz zu den Einkaufszentren am Stadtrand, die Ostöffnung bescherte der Mariahilfer Straße zwar zigtausende kauflustige Gäste aus dem Osten, aber auch eine nicht gerade attraktive Billig-Shop-Szene.

Umso wichtiger war die Aussicht auf eine einmalige, weil unverwechselbar charakteristische Neugestaltung des Straßenbildes.

Benutzten vor dem U-Bahnbau die Autofahrer die Mariahilfer Straße als Zu- und Abfahrt Richtung Innere Stadt, zeigt sich heute ein Fußgängerparadies. Breite Gehsteige laden zum Bummeln ein, das Überqueren der Straße, deren Fahrbahnen reduziert wurden und auf der eine Tempobegrenzung von 30 Stundenkilometern gilt, stellt kein Problem dar. Freilich konnte bei einer derartigen Konzeption keine für alle Verkehrsteilnehmer gleichermaßen zufriedenstellende Verkehrslösung gefunden werden. Anfangs quälte sich der Autoverkehr eher zähflüssig durch, und ein für die Bewohner der angrenzenden Bezirke Neubau und Mariahilf verkehrsberuhigendes Einbahnsystem machte den Lieferverkehr und die Orientierung für Ortsunkundige nicht immer leicht.

Heute zeigt sich bereits, wie anpassungsfähig die Verkehrsteilnehmer sind.

Hofburg Palace. Not too long ago Mariahilferstrasse was still suffering from the year-long "wounds" inflicted by the building of the subway stations, for which a lot of drilling work was done. The former elegant shopping street was threatening to collapse, from the business point of view. The construction of the new subway line sharpened the already strong competition between the shops here and the shopping centers on the outskirts of the city. And while the opening up of Eastern Europe meant that Mariahilferstrasse gained several thousand visitors from the former Eastern Bloc, eager to spend their money, it also meant that it became a cheap shopping area that had lost its specific atmosphere. For this reason, the opportunity to gain a unique and distinctive face-lift for the street was even more important. Whereas, before the construction of the U3 subway line, motorists used Mariahilferstrasse as an approach to the city center, it has now become a paradise for pedestrians. Wide pavements invite the visitor to stroll along them and crossing the road, whose traffic lanes have been reduced and on which there is a speed limit of 30 km/h, is no longer a hazard. In a project of such magnitude, it was naturally difficult to find a solution that satisfied the different types of users. Only in the first months the road traffic crawled through painfully and, while the one-way system brought relief to the residents of the adjoining districts of Neu-

Charakteristische Elemente

Dafür bietet die Umgebung der Mariahilfer Straße eine Fülle von Stellplätzen in Parkgaragen und ein Leitsystem dafür, dessen Anzeigentafeln beweisen, daß die Umstellung vom Auto auf öffentliche Verkehrsmittel zumindest schon teilweise vollzogen ist: Es gibt immer eine große Zahl leerer Garagenplätze. Gestalterisch zeichnet sich die heutige Mariahilfer Straße durch neue Baumpflanzungen und ein dominierendes Beleuchtungssystem aus: In Form und Farbe signalisieren die Masten auch im dichtesten Gewühl, in welcher Straße man sich befindet. Ebenso charakteristisch ist die übrige Stadtmöblierung ausgefallen.

Apropos Stadtmöblierung: Dafür wurde gemeinsam mit einer Meisterklasse an der Hochschule für angewandte Kunst ein Wettbewerb durchgeführt, der einige Musterbeispiele für die Einrichtung im öffentlichen Raum erbrachte.

bau and Mariahilf, it sometimes created problems for those delivering supplies.

Characteristic Elements

On the other hand, the environs of Mariahilferstrasse offer a number of parking spaces in garages, together with an orientation system. The notice signs to this effect show that the changeover from cars to public transport has, at least in part, been fulfilled. There are always plenty of free spaces available in the garages. Today, Mariahilferstrasse's distinctive feature is its lighting system. Even in the largest of crowds, the light masts show by their form and color which street one is in. Another dominant feature is the rest of the decoration. Apropos decoration: in conjunction with a master-class at the College of Applied Art in Vienna a competition was launched which showed some of the best examples of furniture in public spaces.

73

Die grünen Zellen

Wenige Schritte entfernt von der Mariahilfer Straße stoßen wir (in der Kaiserstraße 30, 52 oder in der Seidengasse 31) mitten im dichtestverbauten Bezirk Wiens („Neubau" genannt) auf grüne Zellen. Einer der Schwerpunkte des Wiener Stadtentwicklungsplanes ist es ja, auch im dichtverbauten Gebiet die Umwelt- und Lebensqualität zu verbessern. Angesichts der Notwendigkeit, neue Wohnbauten vorwiegend im dichtbebauten Gebiet zu errichten, wäre also auch hier eher Verdichtung als Abbruch angesagt. Da in diesen Gebieten keine größeren Flächen für neue Grünanlagen zur Verfügung stehen, heißt die Devise „Verdichtung auch beim Grün". Im Rahmen einer Mitteleuropa-Metropolenkonferenz wurde 1994 im Rahmen eines „Pilotprojekts ÖKO 7" zum Thema historische Gärten deren ökologischer und kultureller Funktion größte Bedeutung geschenkt. Anläßlich einer Bestandsaufnahme der Grünoasen in diesem Bezirk wurden damals nicht weniger als 219 Gärten (davon 31 historische), 190 begrünte Innenhöfe und 27 sogenannte Ersatzgärten (zum Beispiel auf Tiefgaragen) registriert.

Im Rahmen einer Novellierung der Wiener Bauordnung und des Wiener Naturschutzgesetzes wurde eine Sicherung dieses wertvollen Grünbestandes vorbereitet. Dazu kamen und kommen

"Green Pockets"

Just a few steps away from Mariahilferstrasse (in Kaiserstrasse Nos. 30 and 52 and in Seidengasse No. 31) and right in the heart of one of Vienna's high-density areas, the district of Neubau, we find pockets of green space. One of the main priorities in the City of Vienna's Urban Development Plan is to improve the environmental and living quality, even in the most built-up zones of the city. In view of the necessity of building residential buildings mainly in the most densely populated areas of the city, it would seem better to increase densities rather than pull down buildings. Since in these areas there are no large expanses which could serve as new green areas, the motto is rather "high-density building but with green areas".

As part of a Central European cities' conference in 1994 within an "ECO 7" pilot project on the subject of historic gardens, attention was focused on their ecological and cultural role in cities. For an inventory of the green oases in this district, at that time no less than 219 gardens (31 of which were historical), 190 green courtyards and 27 so-called substitute gardens (for example on underground garages) were recorded.

As part of an amendment to the Viennese building regulations and the Viennese Nature Conservation Act, provisions to maintain theses valuable

neue Baumpflanzungen im öffentlichen Raum (Ziel: mindestens 1 Baum pro Gasse) sowie, wo immer möglich, die Schaffung neuer Parkflächen. Markantestes Beispiel dafür ist der Andreaspark, der auf knapp 1.700 Quadratmetern auf der Fläche eines Abbruchhauses entstand und in seiner Struktur die „Zimmer" eines Hauses wiedergibt. Auf drei unterschiedlichen Niveaus wurde „Wohngefühl" unter freiem Himmel nachempfunden. Der Minipark ist aus heutiger Sicht ein Idealbeispiel für den Park im dichtverbauten Gebiet, insbesondere für Kinder, deren Begleitpersonen und ältere Menschen.

Ebenfalls ein neues Gesicht zeigt der Siebensternplatz, sozusagen am Eingang zum legendären Spittelbergviertel. Die dortige vorwiegend barocke und über Jahrzehnte devastierte Bausubstanz wurde in den siebziger Jahren als „Luxus-Revitalisierungsprojekt" in ein hoch attraktives Gebiet für Künstler, Kunsthandwerk und Gastronomie verwandelt. Besonders beliebt sind die verschiedenen Märkte, die in den engen Gassen des Spittelberges eine pittoreske Umrahmung finden.

Völlig neu gestaltet wurde in den vergangenen Jahren auch die Neubaugasse, die wichtigste Querung der Mariahilferstraße. Unter Einbeziehung der Anrainer und Geschäftsleute wurde auch hier auf eine möglichst fußgängerfreundliche Gestaltung Wert gelegt.

green areas were prepared. In addition came, and will continue to come, the planting of new trees in public spaces (aim: at least 1 tree per street) as well as, wherever possible, the creation of new parks. The most striking example is that of the Andreaspark, which was laid out on just 1,700 square meters of land on the site of a house that had been pulled down and which, in its structure, reproduces the "rooms" of a house. This means that at three different levels a "feeling of living" in the open air was created.

This mini park is, viewed from today, the ideal example of a park in a high-density area, particularly for children, the adults accompanying them and for old people.

Siebensternplatz, at the entrance to the famous Spittelberg quarter, is also getting a new look. The largely baroque buildings whose building substance, in the course of the past centuries, have suffered from decay, was in the seventies as part of a "luxury revitalization project" transformed into a highly attractive area for artists, craftshops and restaurants. Particularly popular are the different markets which have a picturesque setting against the narrow lanes of the Spittelberg.

Another area that was completely redeveloped in the course of the past years was Neubaugasse, the most important intersection of Mariahilferstrasse. By involving both the residents and the busi-

Zurück in der Mariahilferstraße fühlt sich Caroline plötzlich ins heimatliche L. A. versetzt: Im Gehsteig findet sie ähnlich den Sternen des „Walk of Fame" in Hollywood Fußspuren. „Straße der Sieger" heißt dieser Pfad, der zu einem Einkaufszentrum führt. Österreichs erfolgreichste Sportler verewigen hier ihre Fuß- und Handspuren.

In Mariahilf (6. Bezirk) findet Caroline ebenfalls einige pittoreske Elemente: Zwei Stiegendurchgänge bilden eine Verbindung zur Gumpendorferstraße und lassen die durch die Verbauung nicht mehr sichtbare Geländestufe hinunter ins Wiental erlebbar werden. Die Römer sollen einst hier Wein angebaut haben.

Heute bieten die revitalisierten Durchgänge viele kleine Geschäfte und Restaurants.

Weniger pittoresk als makaber stellt sich ein Erbe des Tausendjährigen Reiches dar: Der Flakturm in der Nähe der Mariahilfer Kirche ist ein unzerstörbares Vermächtnis jenes Adolf Hitler, der Wien zu einer Perle seines Reiches machen hatte wollen und es beinahe in den Abgrund geführt hätte. Für den Flakturm (einige weitere Exemplare zieren andere Bezirke) wurden bereits mehrere Gestaltungskonzepte entwickelt. Unter anderem sollte auch Christo seine Verpackungskünste in Wien demonstrieren. Bisher fand sich allerdings keine Umsetzungsmöglichkeit. Vielleicht gar nicht

ness people, attention was focused here on a design that was particularly pedestrian-friendly.

Back in Mariahilferstrasse, Caroline suddenly has the feeling of being at home in L. A. For on the pavement she finds footsteps, similar to those of the stars in the "Walk of Fame" in Hollywood. This street, which leads to a shopping center, is called the "Street of the Victors" and records the hand and foot imprints of Austria's most successful sportsmen and women.

In Mariahilf (6th district) Caroline also sees picturesque parts. Two small passageways form a connection to Gumpendorferstrasse and permit a view down into the Wiental. Apparently the

Romans once grew wine here. Today, these revitalized passageways house various small shops and restaurants.

Rather less picturesque, macabre in fact, is a legacy of the German Reich. The antiaircraft tower near the Mariahilfer Church is an indestructible memory of Adolf Hitler, who wanted to make Vienna the pearl of his Reich and in doing so almost destroyed it. Several design concepts have already been developed for redesigning and using this antiaircraft tower (there are some more examples in other districts as well), among them by the packaging artist Christo. To date, however, there was no possibility to realize any of the projects. Maybe it's not such a bad idea to keep them as they

so schlecht, denkt Caroline, immerhin gehören auch derartige Bauten zum historischen – wenn auch ungeliebten – Erbe einer Stadt.

Europäisches Interface

Gleich daneben findet Caroline eines der ältesten Kinos Wiens, das Apollo-Kino, das vor kurzem auf den neuesten technischen Standard gebracht wurde und Hauptspielstätte der Wiener Filmfestspiele „Viennale" ist.

Die Mariahilfer Straße selbst wird in der warmen Jahreszeit immer mehr auch für die in Wien sogenannten Schanigärten (die Tische auf dem Gehsteig vor Lokalen) genützt.

Wenn Wien auch kein mediterranes Klima aufzuweisen hat, haben die Wiener die Rückgewinnung des öffentlichen Raumes sehr genossen. Sosehr sie als Autofahrer über scheinbar verlorenen Straßenraum jammern, so sehr haben sie als Fußgänger genau diesen öffentlichen Raum der breiten Gehsteige, der autofreien Gassen und Plätze in Besitz genommen.

Im untersten Teil verbreitert sich die Mariahilfer Straße und Caroline hat einen ersten Blick auf die historische Innenstadt. Knapp vor dem querenden Getreidemarkt, steigt Caroline die Stiegen auf der rechten Seite hinunter und kommt in die Rahlgasse, in der das vor kurzem eingerichtete „Europaforum

are, mused Caroline. After all, such buildings are part of the historical, if unpopular, heritage of a city.

European Interface

Just nearby, Caroline finds one of the oldest cinemas in Vienna, the Apollo Cinema, that was recently adapted to modern technical standards and is now the main location for the Viennale – the Vienna Film Festival.

Mariahilferstrasse itself is a favorite haunt in the summer months on account of its so-called "Schanigärten", small areas in front of restaurants where one can sit outside at tables. Even if Vienna is by no means Mediterranean in

climate, the Viennese much enjoy the regaining of the public space. As much as they, as drivers, complain about the lost road space, the more they, as pedestrians, have taken possession of this public space of wide pavements, car-free streets and squares.

Towards its lower end, Mariahilferstrasse becomes wider and permits Caroline a first view of the historic inner city. At the end of the street, shortly before the intersecting Getreidemarkt, Caroline climbs down the steps on the right-hand side and enters Rahlgasse, in which the recently established Europaforum Wien has its headquarters. At the instigation of the City of Vienna, this institution provides for a kind of "European interface",

Wien" seinen Sitz hat. Diese Einrichtung sorgt im Auftrag der Stadt sozusagen als „europäisches Interface" für Verbindungen zwischen Wien und Europa, dem europäischen Westen wie dem Osten. Veranstaltungen, Diskussionsrunden, Einladungen vor allem von Vertretern der Städte aus Ost und West haben einen Diskussions- und Gedankenaustausch auf europäischer Ebene angeregt, der den Wienern selbst ein wenig Gusto auf „Europäisches" machen soll.

Im selben Haus wird auch über die Zukunft nachgedacht: „Club of Rome"-Guru Dennis Meadows hatte vor Jahren die Idee zu einer Wiener Internationalen Zukunftskonferenz entwickelt und mit Unterstützung der Stadt umgesetzt. Jetzt arbeitet eine „Zukunfts.Station Wien" an der Aufarbeitung von Fragen und Lösungen der nachhaltigen Entwicklung im regen internationalen Gedankenaustausch.

supplying connections and maintaining contacts between Vienna and Europe, both the European West and East. A range of events, discussions, invitations, above all from representatives of the cities from East and West, have incited a round of discussions and exchange of views that should give the Viennese a bit of a taste for "things European".

And in the same house on the same location there are thoughts as to the future. "Club of Rome" guru Dennis Meadows years ago had the idea of setting up an international Vienna Conference on the Future and with the support of the city was able to put his ideas into practice. Now a "Future.Base Vienna" is working out all the questions and solutions of sustainable development within the framework of an animated and international exchange of views.

Kultur ohne Zukunft – Zukunft ohne Kultur?

Der Gebäudekomplex am unteren Ende der Mariahilferstraße bildet schließlich den kulturpolitischen Streitgegenstand Wiens seit Jahren schlechthin: Das „Museumsquartier" im ehemaligen Messepalast, davor als kaiserliche Hofstallungen bekannt.

Es ist die „unendliche Geschichte" von der Wiener Kulturseele, die sich hier erzählen ließe. Wir wollen es kurz versuchen. Die zweite österreichische Republik, die es in den fünfzig Jahren ihres Bestehens geschafft hat, dieses kleine Land, dem noch vor 70 Jahren kaum ein Mensch in Europa Überlebenschancen gegeben hat, zu einem der „reichsten" Länder Europas, der Welt zu machen, hat kein einziges repräsentatives Kulturgebäude zustande gebracht.

Während Wien in historischem Kulturerbe manchmal geradezu zu versinken scheint, während es aus dem Roten Wien ein auch baulich hervorragendes Erbe zu verwalten hat, sind die neuen Kultureinrichtungen spärlichst. Einzig der nach der Weltausstellung 1958 aus Brüssel nach Wien verbrachte österreichische Pavillon beherbergt, versteckt hinter dem Südbahnhof, das Museum des zwanzigsten Jahrhunderts.

Als typisch wienerisches Provisorium steht immer noch am Karlsplatz jener Container, der einst für eine Ausstellung im Messepalast gebaut wurde und aufgrund seiner hervorragenden Nutzungsqualität als Übergangslösung für eine Kunsthalle verwendet wird. Sehr zum Mißfallen vieler Kulturkritiker und nörgelnder Wiener übrigens, die in diesem bunten Bau in der städtebaulichen Wüstenei des Karlsplatzes eine Verschandelung sehen.

Hier, in den Gefilden der ehemaligen Hofstallungen, deren Fassade nach Entwürfen von Fischer von Erlach gebaut worden war und die nach Jahren minderwertiger Nutzungen und als Messe-

Culture without a Future – A Future without Culture?

The complex of buildings at the lower end of Mariahilferstrasse has been the source of a cultural and political bone of contention for several years now: the "Museum Quarter" in the Messepalast and, in front of it, the former imperial stables.

This is the "eternal story" of the Viennese cultural soul that could be unfolded at length here. We will try to make it brief. The Second Austrian Republic, which, in the 50 years of its existence, has succeeded in making this small country that, just 70 years ago, hardly anyone in Europe gave a chance of survival, one of the "richest" in Europe or even in the world, has still not managed to produce a single representative cultural building .

Whereas Vienna seems almost to be buried in historical treasures and while Socialist Vienna produced some splendid examples of architecture for future generations to maintain, the new cultural institutions are few and far between. The only building of note is the former Austrian Pavilion from the World Exhibition in Brussels in 1958 that was brought to Vienna and re-assembled, Concealed behind the South Railway Station it now houses the Museum of the 20th Century.

As a typically Viennese provisional measure, on Karlsplatz there is still the container that was originally built for an exhibition in the Messepalast and which, because of its excellent functionality, now serves as a temporary solution for art exhibitions. Much to the chagrin of many culture critics and complaining Viennese, incidentally, who view the colorful building in the urban wilderness of Karlsplatz as a disgrace.

Here, in the area of the former stables for the imperial court, whose facade was built according to plans by Fischer von Erlach and which, after years of use for second-rate events and a trade fair, are now in danger of falling into decay, the

standort zu verfallen drohen, soll nun das österreichische Kulturdenkmal des zwanzigsten Jahrhunderts, der Republikbau schlechthin entstehen.

Umgeben von den großen Museen der Monarchie, am Rande der Innenstadt, erreichbar mit zwei U-Bahn-Linien und der Straßenbahn, aufgeschlossen durch die Mariahilfer Straße, ist eine Vielfalt kultureller Einrichtungen geplant. Seit rund 15 Jahren laufen die Planungen, zwei Wettbewerbsstufen haben ein Projekt gebracht, das durch einen signifikanten „Leseturm" ins Auge stach, und vielen ein Dorn im Auge war und ist. Eine seltsame Allianz aus Lodenmantelträgern, Kultur-Beschützern und Veränderungsverhinderern bildete eine Bürgerinitiative, die in manchen österreichischen Meinungsbildnern gar heftige Unterstützung fand.

Gefragte und ungefragte Kulturexperten aus aller Welt mischten sich in die Wiener Diskussion ein und selbst I. M. Pei, jener Mann, der den Pariser Louvre mit der weltberühmten Glaspyramide aufgewertet und der in Cleveland, USA, das erste Museum des Rock'n'Roll geplant hatte, sprach sich gegen diesen Leseturm aus.

In aufwendigen Simulationen wurde versucht, die Wirkung auf die Stadtsilhouette darzustellen, die sich übrigens gerade in diesem Gebiet im Laufe der Jahrhunderte äußerst uneinheitlich entwickelt hatte.

Irgendwann im Laufe der Diskussion wurde dann auf den Turm verzichtet, um wenigstens die anderen Einrichtungen realisieren zu können, doch die Auseinandersetzungen wurden und werden weitergeschürt. Zudem kommt, daß sich die Kassen in Bund und Land Wien bedrohlich leerten und Finanzierungen zwar zugesagt wurden, aufgrund der heutigen finanziellen Situation aber wieder zu wackeln drohen. Wobei die Geldknappheit allzuoft als Ausrede für mangelndes kulturelles Bewußtsein gebraucht wird.

Austrian cultural monument of the 20th century and the incarnation of 'the' building of the Republic is to be created.

Surrounded by the great museums of the monarchy, on the edge of the inner city, easily accessible through two subway lines and the tram and adjacent to Mariahilferstrasse, a variety of cultural institutions are being planned here. For the past 15 years or so the plans have existed; two competitions have produced a project that, on account of an eye-catching tower – the so-called "Reading Tower", attracted great attention and for many was, and still is, a thorn in the side. A strange alliance of Lodenmantel wearers, culture protectors and innovation opponents formed a citizens' initiative, which found solid backing from some of Austria's opinion-makers.

Cultural experts, both invited and uninvited, from all over the world intervened in the Vienna discussions on this subject and even I. M. Pei, the man who crowned the Paris Louvre with the renowned glass pyramid and who in Cleveland, Ohio, planned the first Museum of Rock-'n-Roll, opposed the construction of this reading tower. In complicated simulations, attempts were made at representing the effects on the city skyline which has, incidentally, over the years developed in this area into a highly inharmonious whole.

At some point during the discussions the idea of the tower was dropped in order to at least be able to implement the other installations, but the arguments were, and still are, underway. In addition, there is the fact that both federal funds and those of the province of Vienna are rapidly diminishing, and although financing was promised, in view of the current financial situation it has again become uncertain. Although it must be said at this point that lack of funds is all too often used as an excuse for a dearth of cultural awareness. It may well be that the functions for which the Museum quarter was proposed are too little future-orien-

Mag sein, daß die Nutzungsvorschläge für das Museumsquartier zu wenig zukunftsorientiert waren, mag sein, daß die Diskussion von den Intellektuellen zu abgehoben geführt worden ist.

Mag sein, daß ein „Leseturm" in der Zeit der Informationsrevolution nicht gerade als Leuchtturm in der unruhigen See des Cyber-Meeres geeignet ist. Mag vor allem auch sein, daß, wie der Berliner Kulturwissenschafter Thomas Macho meint, Zukunft derzeit ohne Kultur geplant wird.

Macho in einem Beitrag für die deutsche „Zeit" im April 1996: „**Das Schweigen der Futurologie über Kunst und Kultur scheint sich demnach zu spiegeln im Schweigen der Künstler, Kritiker und Intellektuellen über die Zukunft. Zukunft ohne Kultur – Kultur ohne Zukunft: praktiziert wird eine antifuturistische Allianz, eine Art von kulturellem ‚Selbstschutz vor der Zukunft' ... Die im futurologischen Angstmanagement praktizierte Ignoranz des Kulturellen spiegelt sich in einer kulturellen Zukunftsabstinenz, die nicht selten zu Melancholie und Verzweiflung disponiert."**

Mag sein, daß manche Teile der lokalen Kulturszene zu rückwärtsorientiert sind, daß die Erinnerungen an den Namenstag Österreich vor tausend Jahren, die Erinnerungen an die vergangene Jahrhundertwende schöner und angenehmer sind als die kulturelle Auseinandersetzung mit dem und die Bewältigung des zwanzigsten Jahrhunderts, das Österreich nicht immer gut aussehen ließ. Viele Jahre dauert dieses Jahrhundert, dieses Jahrtausend nicht mehr – und es wird ein Prüfstein für die Wiener Kultur sein, ob sie sich selbst noch zu dieser Zeitenwende auch baulich einprägsam dokumentiert.

Indessen hat sich im weitläufigen und verwinkelten Areal des Museumsquartiers ein kulturelles Biotop entwickelt, das auch seinen eigenen Reiz hat: Das Wiener Architekturzentrum, wo seit einigen Jahren subtile Ausein-

---

tated and it may well be that the discussions were conducted at too high a level by the intellectuals. It may also be the case that a "reading tower" in the age of an information revolution is not exactly a lighthouse in the troubled waters of the Cyber sea. It could also be the case that, as the Berlin cultural expert Thomas Macho says, at the moment the future is currently being planned without any culture. In a contribution for the German newspaper "Zeit" in April 1996 Macho said: **"The silence of futurology in the spheres of art and culture seems to be logically followed by and reflected in a silence on the part of artists, critics and intellectuals as to the future in general. A future without culture – culture without a future: what is being practiced is an anti-futuristic alliance, a kind of cultural 'self-protection against the future' ... The practiced ignorance of cultural matters embodied in futurological angst management is reflected in a cultural abstinence of the future, which all too often leads to melancholy and desperation."**

It may be that some sectors of the local cultural scene are too oriented towards the past and that the memories of the birth of Austria 1,000 years ago and of the last turn of the century are more attractive and pleasant than the cultural discussions about them and the coming to terms with the events of the 20th century, which did not always show Austria in a good light. This century has lasted many years; the millennium will soon come to an end and it will be a touchstone for the Vienna cultural scene as to whether it leaves an imprint at this turning point in time, also in the field of architecture. In the meantime, in the extensive and labyrinth-like area of the Museum Quarter, a cultural biotope has developed that also has its own charms: The Viennese architectural center is where for several years now subtle discussions with contemporary architects have been conducted under the direction of the internationally renowned architec-

andersetzung mit zeitgenössischem Planen und Bauen unter der Leitung des international renommierten Architekturexperten Dietmar Steiner stattfindet. Es ist auch integraler Bestandteil des geplanten künftigen Nutzungsmixes, mit der Zielsetzung, ein österreichisches Architekturmuseum zu schaffen.

Dieses Architekturzentrum veranstaltete zusammen mit der Stadtplanung Wien auch 1995 erstmals die international beachtete Ausstellungs- und Veranstaltungsserie „80 Tage Wien", die es sich zur Aufgabe gemacht hatte, die vor allem bauliche Weiterentwicklung Wiens an zentralen Punkten, aber auch sozusagen „vor Ort" zu dokumentieren und die Wiener und Wien-Besucher zum Nachdenken darüber zu animieren.

„Durch ihre überbordende Fülle erzeugt die Ausstellung ein beinahe euphorisches Gefühl, nämlich das, in einer unglaublich prosperierenden Metropole zu leben, ja an einer neuen Gründerzeit teilzuhaben ... Als informativ und erfolgreich in der Vermittlung städteplanerischer Vorhaben haben sich die parallel zur Ausstellung angebotenen Busrundfahrten erwiesen, in deren Rahmen ausgewählte Projekte vorgestellt werden ... Ansonsten kann man nur hoffen, daß einiges von der Aufbruchstimmung dieser Architekturfestwochen erhalten bleibt und daß architektonische Projekte nicht durch Unentschlossenheit und Verzögerungstaktiken zu Bildern einer Ausstellung degradiert werden. Sonst wäre Wien eines Tages, in Abwandlung eines

ture expert Dietmar Steiner. The center, incidentally, is also an integral component of the planned future mix of uses, with the aim of creating a Viennese museum of architecture. This architecture center also organized, in conjunction with the Vienna Urban Planning Department, for the first time in 1995 the internationally acclaimed exhibition and events series "80 Days in Vienna", which had the goal of documenting particularly the development of building in Vienna at central points but also, as it were, "on the spot" and of animating both the inhabitants of Vienna and the visitors to the city to further thoughts on this subject.

"Through the enormous wealth of exhibits the exhibition evokes an almost euphoric feeling, namely that of living in an incredibly prosperous metropolis and of being part of a new Gründerzeit or "Period of Intensive Construction"... The bus tours organized in parallel to the exhibition offered a selection of projects to be visited and proved to be informative and successful in conveying the ideas of the urban planners... Apart from this, it can only be hoped that something will remain of the mood and spirit of innovation of this architectural festival and that architectural projects do not become degraded to being just pictures of an exhibition through indecision and delaying tactics. If this is the case, then Vienna one day, in the approximate words of Italo Calvino will become 'the city which tells

Wortes von Italo Calvino, ‚die Stadt, die sich selbst erzählt', aber nichts Neues zu sagen hat", schrieb dazu Andrea Hurton im Oktober 1995 in der „Neuen Zürcher Zeitung".

Der „Kunstraum Wien" und das „Depot" bieten Präsentationen zeitgenössischer Kunst, verstehen sich aber auch als Diskussionsforen und kulturstrategische Schaltstellen. Das „Kindermuseum", das „Tabakmuseum" und der Hauptsitz jenes Vereines, der dieses Buch mit den Illustrationen versorgt hat, der „Lomographischen Gesellschaft", haben hier Platz gefunden. Vorübergehend hatte auch die Rockmusik einen Spielort. Musical und Tanz fanden Aufführungs- und Probeorte. Auch für Caroline hat dieses Kulturbiotop seinen Reiz, doch stellt sich die Kardinalfrage für Österreich, für seine Bundeshauptstadt, welchen Stellenwert es seiner Kultur des zwanzigsten Jahrhunderts gibt, wie sehr es zu dieser Epoche auch steht. Nicht zuletzt darum geht es bei der Diskussion um das Museumsquartier. Vielleicht aber ist auch die österreichische Seele noch nicht so gefestigt, sich selbst im Spiegel zu betrachten.

Während Carolines Wien-Reise findet gerade im Wiener Gemeinderat eine heftige Diskussion zum Thema statt und Wiens Bürgermeister Dr. Michael Häupl gibt ein klares Bekenntnis zum Wiener Beitrag für das Museumsquartier ab: Eine Kultur- und Tourismusmetropole wie Wien kann auf eine derartige Kulturstätte nicht verzichten.

its own story' but which has nothing new to add" wrote Andrea Hurton on the subject in October 1995 in the "Neue Zürcher Zeitung". The "Kunstraum Wien" and the "Depot" present exhibitions of contemporary art but also regard themselves as forums of discussion and contact points for culture strategies. The Children's Museum, the Tobacco Museum and the main headquarters of the society that has provided the illustrations for this book, the Lomographische Gesellschaft, are also to be found here. It also offered rock musicians a temporary place to play its music, while musicals and dance events had and still have a place to rehearse and perform. For Caroline, too, this biotope has its charms, but the cardinal question for Austria and for its capital city is that of which role it wishes to give its 20th century culture and to what extent it stands behind the culture of this epoch. This is what, in effect, all the discussions concerning the museum quarter are about. It could, however, also be that the Austrian soul is not yet ready to take a look at itself in the mirror. While Caroline is busy doing her trip round Vienna, in Vienna's City Council Offices heated discussions are taking place on this subject and Vienna's Mayor Michael Häupl has openly given his views on the part Vienna has to play in the whole discussion on the museum quarter: a cultural and tourist metropolis like Vienna cannot do without such a cultural center.

Im Wohnzimmer Wiens
In the Salon of Vienna

85

86

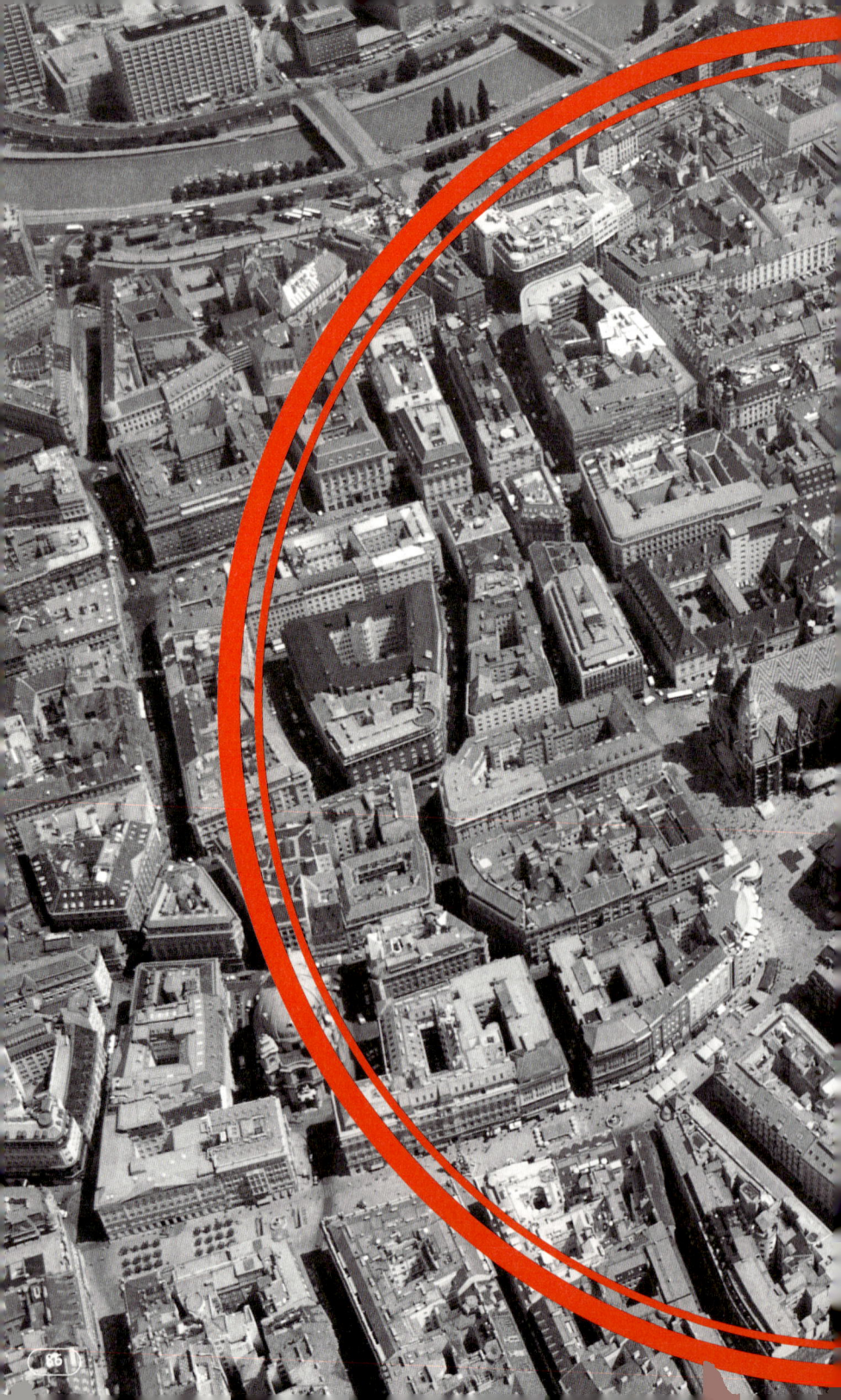

87

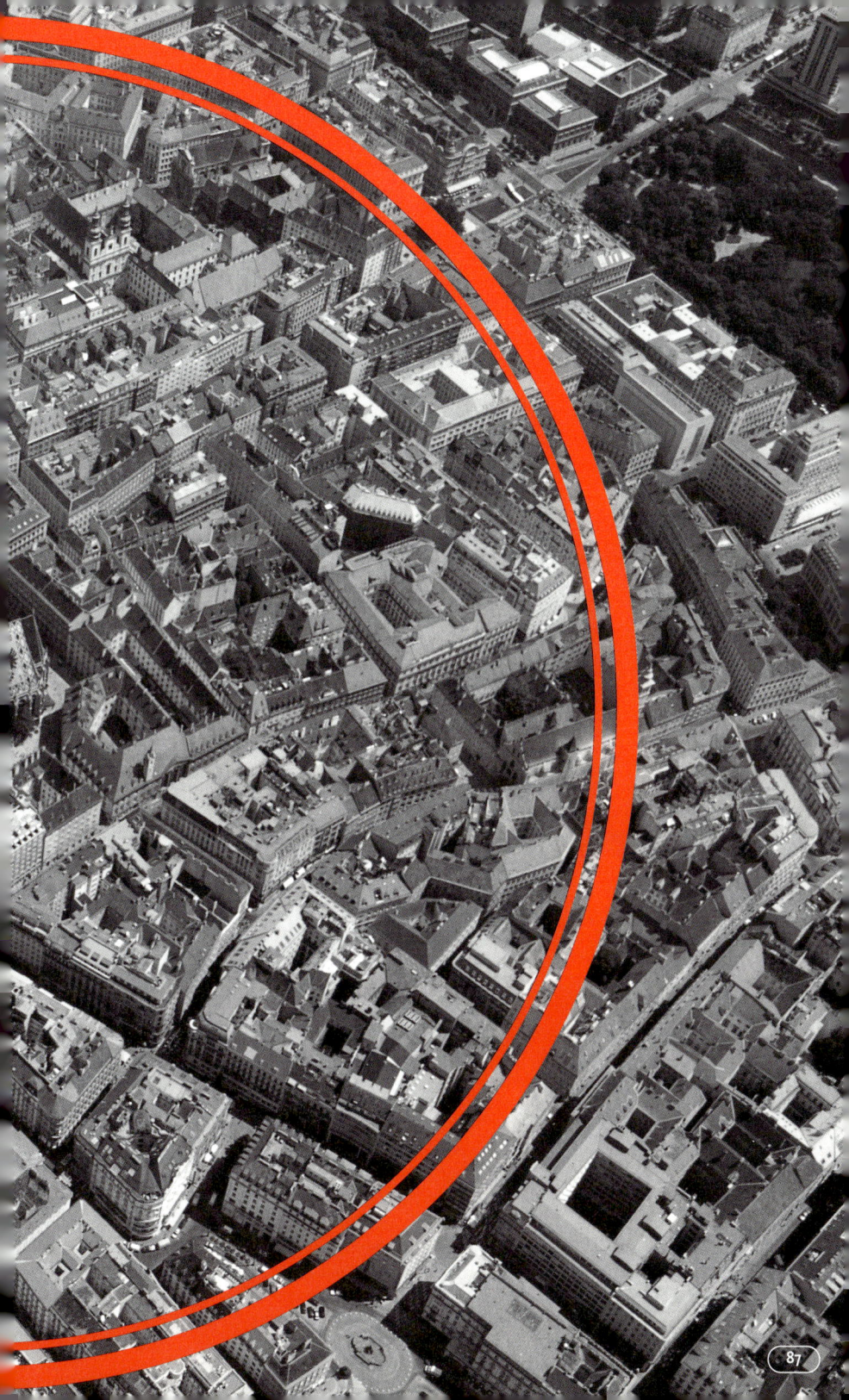

„Warum gehen wir eigentlich so viel zu Fuß bei unserer Wiener Reise?" fragt sich Caroline, die sich eine ähnliche Stadtwanderung im heimatlichen Los Angeles kaum vorstellen kann. Hier, in der Wiener City, „der Stadt", wie alle Wiener sagen, wenn sie ins Zentrum fahren oder gehen, beginnt sie zu verstehen, warum man eine Stadt sozusagen im Gehen erfahren muß. Jedenfalls eine europäische Stadt. Und jedenfalls Wien.

Caroline läßt sich treiben beim Flanieren durch die City, ohne festgeschriebene Wanderroute, will einfach schauen und nachdenken, ein wenig philosophieren und reflektieren. Kein anderer Ort, die alten italienischen Städte oder einige spanische vielleicht ausgenommen, lädt dazu so sehr ein wie die „Innere Stadt", wie dieser Bezirk, die historische Kernstadt, auch heißt.

Flanieren? Woher kommt eigentlich dieser Begriff? Walter Benjamin, der große Kulturphilosoph, hat ihn verwendet, als er schrieb: „**Die Straße wird zur Wohnung für den Flaneur, der zwischen Häuserfronten so wie der Bürger in seinen vier Wänden zuhause ist. Ihm sind die glänzenden emaillierten Firmenschilder so gut und besser ein Wandschmuck wie im Salon dem Bürger ein Ölgemälde; Mauern sind das Schreibpult, gegen das er seinen Notizblock stemmt; Zeitungskioske sind seine Bibliotheken und die Caféterrassen Erker,**

"Why are we doing so much of our tour on foot?", Caroline asks herself, and can't imagine walking such a lot in her home town Los Angeles. But here in the center of Vienna, the first district, or "the city", as all the Viennese say when they go – or rather walk – downtown, she begins to understand why one should walk to get to know a city. At least a European city. And certainly Vienna.

Caroline just wants to stroll through the city, without any fixed goal, wants to look around and think, philosophize and reflect a little. There can hardly be any other places – with the exception, perhaps, of the old Italian cities or maybe some Spanish ones – that are so ideal for strolling in as this "inner city", as the historic core of Vienna is also called. To stroll, or "flanieren". What is the origin of the term? Walter Benjamin, the great cultural philosopher, used it when he wrote: **"For the 'flâneur' the street becomes an apartment; he feels just as much at home between the rows of houses as other citizens do in their own four walls. For him the shiny, enamel firms' nameplates are a better wall-decoration than an oil-painting at home; walls are the desk on which he rests his note-pad; news-stands are his libraries and the bay-windows of the coffee houses from which, when his work is done, he looks out over his household."**

The enamel nameplates don't really fit in today, Caroline thinks, he should

von denen aus er nach getaner Arbeit auf sein Hauswesen heruntersieht."

Das mit den Emailschildern paßt vielleicht nicht mehr heutzutage, denkt sich Caroline, da müßte man eher von den Neonlichtern sprechen, aber sonst ist vieles stimmig von diesem Bild, hier in Wien.

Und Cees Nooteboom, der holländische Parade-Literat unserer Zeit, gedenkt des Flaneurs besonders oft. Kein Wunder, begegnet er doch in seiner Heimatstadt Den Haag dem Ur-Flaneur in Gestalt eines Denkmales für Eduard Elias (jüdischer Schriftsteller und Journalist, Aristokrat und Kosmopolit und eben auch unter dem Pseudonym „Flaneur" bekannt).

Nooteboom setzte ihm in einem Beitrag für das deutsche Wochenmagazin „Die Zeit" unter dem Titel „Die Sohlen der Erinnerung" ein journalistisches Denkmal: „Die Geschichte der Architektur ist auch die Geschichte der schlechten Architektur, denn, das wird jeder Flaneur Ihnen bestätigen können: Eines haben alle Architekten, die guten wie die schlechten, gemein: Um das, was sie bauen, wenn sie bauen, kommt man im wahrsten Sinne des Wortes nicht herum, es steht da. Es steht immer und überall herum. Wir sehen es sogar, wenn wir nicht hinschauen. Wer mit dem menschlichen Maß seiner Schritte durch eine Stadt geht, ist Perspektiven, Artikulationen des Raums, Panoramen, über ihm steil

rather speak of neon lights, but otherwise much of all that is still true, here in Vienna.

And Cees Nooteboom, the Dutch prototype of the modern writer, often refers to the "flâneur". Small wonder, actually, as in his home town of The Hague he meets the original stroller per se in the guise of a statue of Eduard Elias, a Jewish writer and journalist, aristocrat and cosmopolitan, also known under the pseudonym "flâneur".

In a contribution for the German weekly newspaper "Die Zeit" entitled "Die Sohlen der Erinnerung" (The Soles of Memory), Nooteboom pays him journalistic tribute: **"The history of architecture is also the history of bad architecture –**

this, every flâneur can confirm. There is one thing that all architects, both the good and the bad, have in common: whatever they build, we can't get round it, in the literal sense of the word. For it is there, standing around, everywhere and for ever. We can even see it when we are not looking. Anyone who goes through a city on foot is exposed to perspectives, articulations of space, panoramas, steep walls climbing upright above him, empty and full rooms, which not he but someone else has thought up and created."

One of those Viennese flâneurs, who has been sauntering through this city professionally, as it were, is Armin Thurnher, chief editor of the critical Viennese newspaper "Falter". In a travel article

aufragenden steilen Wänden, leeren und gefüllten Räumen ausgesetzt, die nicht er, sondern ein anderer erdacht und gestaltet hat."

Einer jener Wiener Flaneure, der diese Stadt seit nunmehr fast zwei Jahrzehnten sozusagen beruflich durchstreift, Armin Thurnher, Chefredakteur der kritischen Wiener Stadtzeitung „Falter", hat diesen ersten Bezirk Wiens in einem Reisebericht für deutschsprachige Touristen einmal einen „Salon aus Fleisch und Blut" genannt.

„Eine Weile sah es so aus, als würde der Erste Bezirk in Schönheit sterben. Dann füllten sich die Paläste mit Beisln, Theater machten wieder Theater, und siehe da, heute ist ‚der Erste' Wiens Wohnzimmer", erinnert er sich. Und Thurnher resümiert aus persönlicher Erfahrung: „So lange ist es auch wieder nicht her, da krönte der Erste Bezirk die These, Wien sei nichts als eine Ansammlung von langweiligen Dörfern. Wer etwa vor 20 Jahren an einem heißen Sommernachmittag das Unternehmen gewagt hätte, der damals auch in ihrem innersten Zentrum von Autos befahrenen Innenstadt einen Besuch abzustatten, dem konnte es geschehen, daß er weder Mensch noch Tier erblickte. Von jenen Fiakern, die im Schatten des Stephansdomes und in der prallen Hitze des Heldenplatzes heute stundenlang auf ihre internationalen Fuhren warten, war ebensowenig zu sehen, wie von einem

written for German-speaking tourists, he described Vienna's 1st district as a "salon of flesh and blood".

"For a while it looked as if this city's 1st district would die in solitary splendor. But then the palaces began to fill with small restaurants, the theaters began to produce plays and today 'the 1st district' has become Vienna's living room", he recalls. And Thurnher sums up from his own personal experience: "Not so long ago the 1st district reflected the theory that Vienna was little more than an accumulation of boring villages. Twenty years ago, anyone who was brave enough to risk a visit to the center of the city, at that time still open to cars, on a hot summer afternoon could find himself in deserted streets with not a person or animal in sight. There was not a trace of the 'fiacre', the Viennese carriages that today wait for hours in the shadow of St. Stephen's Cathedral and in the blazing heat of the Heldenplatz for their custom, nor even of a street café. In those days the visitor might have had difficulties in finding any restaurant open at all and would have probably retired, bored and disheartened, to the Prater or to an eatery on the outskirts of the city. Since then, a lot, but not everything, has changed. The inevitable pedestrian zones were created and have filled up with international street musicians, In many 'Grätzl' (the Viennese word for the immediate neighborhood) the road traffic has decreased, while the colorful mix of bars

Straßencafé. Ja, der Besucher hätte wohl Schwierigkeiten gehabt, überhaupt ein offenes Lokal zu finden, und hätte sich gelangweilt oder entmutigt in den Prater oder in eine an der Peripherie gelegene Ausflugsgaststätte zurückgezogen. Seither hat sich vieles, aber nicht alles geändert. Die üblichen Fußgängerzonen wurden eingezogen und bevölkerten sich mit internationalen Straßenmusikanten, der motorisierte Verkehr wurde in einigen „Grätzln" (so nennt man hier die nächste Nachbarschaft) einigermaßen beruhigt, ein buntes Nebeneinander der verschiedensten Lokalitäten ließ stellenweise geradezu systematische Nachtschwärmerviertel entstehen. Die U-Bahn karrt das Volk aus den entlegensten Bezirken heran ... Und selbstverständlich hat sich das Bild auf den Gassen verändert. Einen unbelebten Winkel wird man heutzutage selbst am Sonntag kaum zu irgendeiner Tages-, Nacht- oder Jahreszeit finden. Ist Wien modern geworden? Das Zentrum der meisten modernen Großstädte ist längst in der einen oder anderen Weise zur Fiktion erstarrt. Entweder handelt es sich um ein Vergnügungsviertel, das erst nachts erwacht, oder um eine Verwaltungsstadt, die nachts erstirbt. Und wenn beides zutrifft, so fehlt es doch an Bewohnern."

Und an noch einen Wiener Flaneur soll hier erinnert werden, an den be-

and restaurants has in some parts of the city even led to the systematic creation of districts for night-birds. The subway transports the population from the remotest corners of the city into the center ... The street scene has, of course, changed: Even on a Sunday, whatever the time of day, night or year, it is barely possible to find a quiet, secluded corner. Could it be that Vienna has become modern ? The centers of most present-day cities have long since become fiction, in one way or another. They have either become nightlife districts that only wake up at night, or central business districts that go to sleep in the evening. And when both are the case, then there are no inhabitants."

And we should recall yet another Viennese flâneur, Harald Sterk, who in his inimitably precise and pithy way describes like no other the dichotomy of old and new in Vienna: "Despite all the destruction that the Second World War wrought on the city, both the bombings and the fighting in April 1945, until the early sixties Vienna largely remained a 19th century city. After the decision to expand the city in 1857, which was late as compared with other European capitals, first of all Ringstrasse with all its monumental buildings was constructed and then, in the wake of industrialization, because the masses that streamed into the city in search of work were in need of housing, the districts with small rented apart-

reits erwähnten Harald Sterk, der kurz und prägnant wie kaum ein anderer zusammengefaßt hat, was das Spannungsfeld zwischen alt und neu in Wien ausmacht: „Hauptsächlich war ... Wien bis zu Beginn der sechziger Jahre, bei allen Zerstörungen, die der Zweite Weltkrieg verursacht hatte, sowohl der Bombenkrieg als auch die Kämpfe im April 1945, eine Stadt des 19. Jahrhunderts.

Nach dem – im Vergleich zu anderen europäischen Hauptstädten – späten Beschluß zur Stadterweiterung im Jahre 1857 wurde zunächst die Ringstraße mit ihren Monumentalbauten errichtet und in der Folge, weil die im Verlauf des Industrialisierungsprozesses zuströmenden Massen immer mehr Wohnraum benötigten, die Zinskasernenviertel in den Vorstädten. Wie immer man die Ringstraße beurteilt – als pompöses Museum der historischen Baustile, wie das lange Zeit geschah, oder als Ausdruck eines Zeitalters, das schöpferisch mit der Vergangenheit umging -, ihre Erbauer haben wesentlich zur Identität Wiens beigetragen, ja das großstädtische Wien erst geschaffen", charakterisierte Sterk etwa die Wiener Ringstraße.

Nicht ahnen konnten die Planer der Ringstraße wohl, daß hier gegen Ende des vergangenen Jahrhunderts die ersten sichtbaren Demonstrationen der aufstrebenden Arbeiterklasse stattfinden würden: Weil offizielle Demonstrationen in Wien verboten waren, gingen

ments out in the suburbs. However one views Ringstrasse – as a pompous museum of buildings in neo-historical style, which was for a long time the case, or as an expression of an age that creatively came to terms with the past – its architects made a considerable contribution to this city's identity and, indeed, actually shaped the metropolis of Vienna", said Sterk of Ringstrasse.

The planners of Ringstrasse could not foresee that, at the end of the last century, it would form the backdrop for the first visible demonstrations by the rising working classes. Since official demonstrations in Vienna were forbidden, on the 1st of May every year the workers "went for a walk" along Ringstrasse. Today, we still uphold the tradition of the May Day parades in Vienna, mainly to commemorate the great era of "Red Vienna" and the hard, but successful years of reconstruction after the war.

Away from the Automobile

Vienna was also late in its decision to construct a subway system. Whereas in Budapest, Vienna's imperial sister city and greatest historical rival, the first subway line was put into operation one hundred years ago, in Vienna it took until the sixties of this century for a decision as to the planning and financing of this costly means of transportation to be made.

die Arbeiter Wiens jeweils am 1. Mai auf der Ringstraße „spazieren". Noch heute hat sich die Tradition der Maiaufmärsche in Wien gehalten. Heute wohl als Erinnerung an die große Zeit des Roten Wien, an die harten, aber erfolgreichen Jahre des Wiederaufbaus.

Weg vom Auto

Spät ist in Wien auch die Entscheidung für den U-Bahnbau gefallen. Während in der k. u. k.-Schwesterstadt Budapest, die immer in harter Konkurrenz zu Wien gestanden ist, bereits vor hundert Jahren die erste U-Bahn in Betrieb genommen wurde, dauerte es in Wien bis in die sechziger Jahre dieses Jahrhunderts, bis man sich zur Planung und Finanzierung dieses aufwendigen Verkehrsmittels entschloß.

Den heute sichtbaren Erfolg hat Armin Thurnher beschrieben. Erst die U-Bahn (heute kreuzen sich zwei Radiallinien am Stephansplatz, zwei Tangentiallinien umschließen den ersten Bezirk) ermöglichte es, die Innenstadt autoarm zu gestalten und ließ das wohl weltweit einmalige Ambiente des „Wohnzimmers der Stadt" entstehen.

Stichwort autoarm: Im ersten Bezirk mußte die neue Wiener Verkehrspolitik, die sich zum Ziel gesetzt hat, den öffentlichen Verkehr zuungunsten des Autoverkehrs zu stärken, um eine nachhaltige Stadtentwicklung zu ermöglichen,

The visible success of this venture is described by Armin Thurnher in the following way: it was only the construction of the subway (today two radial lines intersect at Stephansplatz and two tangential lines encircle the 1st district) that succeeded in keeping road traffic in the city center to a minimum, thus creating the universally unique atmosphere of a "city living room" in Vienna.

Apropos traffic reduction: in the 1st district the new Viennese traffic policy, which had set itself the goal of improving public transport to the disadvantage of road traffic in order to enable sustainable urban development, was put to a severe test. The "fight" for the introduction of limited parking zones everywhere in the city lasted for years and it was also a hard struggle to keep historical squares free from cars. Caroline, who has just visited Josefsplatz and the Franziskanerplatz, can hardly imagine the city full of cars, as it was in the past. But still the fight persists.

The City Hall employees were the pioneers, in the positive sense of the word. The inner courtyards of the City Hall, once chockablock with vehicles, have been car-free for years. In the courtyards of the Hofburg and the University of Vienna such measures have not yet been taken.

But to return to Ringstrasse: it is still flooded with cars and the recovery of public space by the pedestrians has not

ihre wichtigsten Bewährungsproben bestehen. Jahre dauerte der „Kampf" etwa um die Einführung einer flächendeckenden Kurzparkzone, mühsam war der „Kampf" darum, historische Plätze autofrei zu machen. Caroline, die den Josefsplatz und den Franziskanerplatz besucht, kann sich die Autowüste vergangener Zeiten gar nicht vorstellen. Und dennoch ist der „Kampf" noch nicht beendet.

Pioniere im positiven Sinn waren da die „Rathausmänner": Die Höfe des Rathauses, einst vollgestopft mit Autos, wurden bereits vor Jahren sang- und klanglos geräumt.

In den Höfen um die Hofburg etwa ist dies nur teilweise gelungen, auch im Bereich der Alten Universität.

Zurück zur Ringstraße: Sie ist heute noch immer autoüberflutet, die Rückgewinnung des öffentlichen Raumes durch die Fußgänger ist hier noch nicht von Erfolg gekrönt. Sehr wohl haben aber die Radfahrer Besitz genommen von den Alleen entlang des Ringes. Der Ring-rund-Radweg ist Bestandteil eines heute bereits mehrere hundert Kilometer umfassenden und ständig wachsenden Radwegenetzes, das in den letzten Jahren stark ausgebaut wurde.

Architektonisch bietet die Ringstraße die nur durch wenige „Ausreißer" unterbrochene einheitliche Gestaltung ihrer Gründerzeit. Lediglich einige Hotels und leider auch Bundesverwaltungsgebäude, die mehr oder weniger eigene Planungshoheit haben, ließen teilweise heftige Diskussionen über Gestaltungs- und Geschmacksfragen aufkommen.

Tu felix Austria

Ein baulich interessantes Projekt der letzten Jahre ist der „Ringstraßengalerien" genannte Gebäudekomplex nahe der Oper, von den Architekten Holzbauer und Lippert und dem Team Neumann, Hlaweniczka und Lintl geplant. Passagen haben sich in Wien ja nie wirklich durch-

been entirely successful as yet. However, the bikers have taken possession of the avenues along Ringstrasse reserved for cyclists. This is just one part of a network of cycle tracks that extend for several hundred kilometers through the city and that have been greatly expanded in recent years.

From the architectural point of view, on the whole Ringstrasse presents that unity of design which was characteristic of the Gründerzeit period during which it was built. Just a few hotels and, unfortunately, also Federal Administration buildings, which more or less have their own planning sovereignty, provided for some heated discussions on the subject of design and questions of taste.

Tu felix Austria

One of the most interesting building projects of recent years is the "Ringstrassengalerien", a complex of buildings near the State Opera House that was designed by the architects Holzbauer and Lippert and the team Neumann, Hlaweniczka and Lintl. Shopping arcades have never really taken root in Vienna, although one would have thought that the weather here, particularly in the winter months, would provide a challenge for such architecture. All over the world there seems to be a shopping arcade boom; in the USA shopping malls are big hits, also from the point of view of urban planning. Caroline thought of the "Mall of America" in Minneapolis with its 420,000 kilometers and also of the world's largest shopping center, the West-Edmonton Mall in Canada.

If one views the boom in arcade-building as a reaction to the "inhospitableness of cities", as the philosopher

setzen können, obwohl das Wiener Wetter eigentlich in der kalten Jahreszeit geradezu eine Herausforderung zum Passagenbau darstellen müßte.

Weltweit herrscht ja geradezu ein Passagenboom, in den USA sind die „Malls" die großen städtebaulichen Renner, Caroline denkt etwa an die „Mall of America" in Minneapolis mit ihren 420.000 Quadratmetern oder an das weltgrößte Shopping-Center, die West-Edmonton-Mall in Kanada.

Wenn man den Passagenboom auch als Reaktion auf die „Unwirtlichkeit der Städte", wie sie der Philosoph Alexander Mitscherlich vor mehr als dreißig Jahren definiert hat, sieht, mag dies erklären, warum sich „Mall"-ähnliche Einrichtungen nur an der Wiener Peripherie durchgesetzt haben. Die Ringstraßengalerien jedenfalls, eingebettet in einen Komplex, der auch Hotels umfaßt, „schotten sich vom Innenstadttreiben eher ab, als daß sie sich diesem öffnen", wie der Wiener Architekturkritiker Horst Chris-

Alexander Mitscherlich defined this phenomenon more than 30 years ago, this may well serve as an explanation as to why mall-type developments have only taken root on the outskirts of Vienna. "The 'Ringstrassengalerien', at any rate, embedded in a complex that also comprises hotels, seem to insulate themselves against the bustle of the inner city, rather than opening up to it", says the Viennese architect Horst Christoph.

Christoph, provocative, on the new type of arcades: **"They have little in common with the classical historic arcade. Their vertical structure is more of a variation of the traditional architecture of the department store. And, unlike arcades, they don't provide any connection between streets; instead of sauntering through the city the shopper floats up the city's moving staircases and then, from an elevated viewpoint, looks down over urban life."**

Which, as Caroline discovers, can best be done from Vienna's most prominent

toph meint. Christoph provokant über den neuen Typ der Passagen: „Mit der historischen Galerie haben sie aber wenig zu tun. Ihre vertikale Gliederung variiert eher die traditionelle Kaufhausarchitektur. Anders als die Passagen stellen sie keine Verbindung zwischen Straßen her, statt durch die Stadt zu flanieren, entschwebt der Benutzer der Rolltreppen der Stadt und wird, von erhöhtem Aussichtspunkt aus, zum Voyeur des urbanen Lebens."

Was sich, wie Caroline feststellt, am besten von Wiens wohl prominentestem und provokantestem „Neubau" in der alten Stadt tun läßt. Vom sogenannten „Haas-Haus" am Stephansplatz.

Als 1995 im deutschen Architekturmuseum in Frankfurt am Main unter der Ägide des neuen Leiters Wilfried Wang, eines profunden Wien-Kenners, die Ausstellung „Österreichs Architektur im zwanzigsten Jahrhundert" zu sehen war, geriet der Architekturspezialist der „Frankfurter Allgemeinen Zeitung" ins

and provocative modern building in the city center, the "Haas Haus" opposite St. Stephen's Cathedral.

1995, when the exhibition "Austria's Architecture in the 20th Century" was held at the German Museum of Architecture in Frankfurt am Main under the aegis of its new director, Wilfried Wang, himself, incidentally, highly knowledgeable of Vienna, the architecture expert of the "Frankfurter Allgemeine Zeitung" broke out enthusiastically.

"You, fortunate neighbour, build" Dieter Bartetzko captioned this article and found the following words for Vienna: "Tu felix Austria: the overwhelming scope of the built heritage and the splendid backdrop of the scenery managed to keep the brutal cement blocks of the sixties and seventies at bay. We who have personally experienced the 'inhospitableness of cities' and still feel it, despite all the repairs undertaken to different cities, look with envy at our neighbor. Ernst Hiesmayr's Viennese 'Juridicum', part of

Schwärmen. „Du aber, glücklicher Nachbar, baue", titelte Dieter Bartetzko und fand für Wien folgende Worte:
„Tu felix Austria: Die Übermacht der historischen Bausubstanz, auch die grandiosen Naturkulissen, hielten in Österreich den Betonbrutalismus der sechziger und siebziger Jahre im Zaum. Neidisch schaut unsereins, der die beton-diktierte ‚Unwirtlichkeit der Städte' am eigenen Leib erfahren hat und, trotz aller Stadtreparaturen, noch immer erfährt, auf den Nachbarn. Ernst Hiesmayrs Wiener Juridicum aus den Jahren 1968 bis 1984 ragt wie ein vertäutes Raumschiff aus dem Häusermeer; ein Unikat, das der Historismus ringsum zum reizvollen Exotikum steigert. Daß Hans Holleins Wiener Kerzengeschäft Retti, bekannt als Keimzelle der Postmoderne, bereits 1965 entsand, hat man fast vergessen. Nun tritt seine Affinität zur Technik-Euphorie jener Jahre hervor, die Ähnlichkeit mit den Raumstationen und Schaltzentralen zwischen Cape Canaveral und ‚Raumschiff Orion'. Zugleich möchte man Wiener Verbindlichkeit erkennen, die zur klirrenden Weltraumchiffre einen Hauch Fiaker-Romantik beisteuerte. Doch wenn solche Wien-Klischees sich überhaupt als architektonischer Niederschlag ausmachen lassen, dann in ihrer scharfen, wahrheitsnahen Form. Diese schließt sonderbarerweise den Kreis zwischen Fin de siecle und Gegenwart. Beim Anblick der neueren Bauten assoziiert man Otto Wagners zwischen Mausoleum und Moderne changierendes Postamt oder Adolf Loos' ägyptisierendes Tempelpathos, das im Erdgeschoß des Michaelerhauses die moderne Askese des Aufbaues gegenzeichnet. Schnitzlers Untergangslüste und Altenbergs Ironie, auflebend im schneidenden Widerspruch Thomas Bernhards oder Elfriede Jelineks: Holleins 1990 vollendetes Haas-Haus am Wiener Stephansdom destruiert und erneuert in einem Atemzug die Bauharmonie ringsum. Die provokativ vorgeschobene

the University of Vienna, built between 1968 and 1984, soars like a spaceship from the sea of houses; a unique piece of architecture that makes the buildings around, built in neo-historical style, seem fascinatingly exotic. One tends to forget that Hans Hollein's candle shop Retti, generally regarded as the origin of post-Modernism, was built as early as 1965. Now its affinity with the technological euphoria of those years comes to the fore, its similarity with the space stations and switching stations between Cape Canaveral and 'Spaceship Orion'. At the same time, tribute must be paid to Viennese courtesy, which has added a touch of 'fiacre romanticism' to the cool tones of outer space. But if such Viennese clichés can be decoded at all as architecture, then as a sharp truism. Strangely enough, this closes the gap between the fin de siécle and the present. A glance at the more recent buildings evokes associations with Otto Wagner's Postal Savings Bank, midway between mausoleum and Modernism, and Adolf Loos's Egyptian temple pathos that, nestling on the ground floor of the Michaelerhaus, seems to strive against the modern asceticism of the building. Schnitzler's predictions of decay and Altenberg's irony, revived in the cutting contradictions of Thomas Bernhard and Elfriede Jelinek: Hollein's Haas Haus opposite St. Stephen's Cathedral, completed in 1990, in a single breath both destroys and revives the harmony of the buildings in its immediate environment. The provocatively protruding glass capsule floats as a reminder in design form of the rounded corners of the Roman fort buried beneath and functionally structures and takes possession of public space. Today we see that this was a prelude to the 'Second Period of Intensive Construction', as it was christened at the end of the eighties. And again, the local citizen, mesmerized by Berlin's urban planning stunts, is amazed: even if Potsdam Platz is at present 'Europe's

gläserne Rundkapsel schwebt als gestaltete Erinnerung an die Eckrundung des dort ergrabenen römischen Kastells und gliedert sinnvoll besitzergreifend den öffentlichen Raum. Heute zeigt sich, daß dies ein Auftakt der Ende der achtziger Jahre proklamierten ‚neuen Wiener Gründerzeit' gewesen ist. Wieder staunt der hiesige, von Berlins städtebaulichen Kraftakten gebannte Besucher: mag augenblicklich der Potsdamer Platz ‚Europas größte Baustelle' sein, die Wiener Projekte ‚Museumsquartier' und ‚Donau-City' stehen dem deutschen Unternehmen weder an Größe noch säkulärem Anspruch nach."

Caroline ist fasziniert von dieser Analyse, fasziniert vor allem vom Blick aus dem Café des Haas-Hauses auf den gegenüberliegenden Dom, fasziniert von der Geschichte der Auseinandersetzung um diesen provokanten Bau: jahrelang hatten sich die Wiener gestritten, ob denn ein solches Gebäude nun gerade an einem solchen Platz erbaut werden dürfe, jahrelang war diese Auseinandersetzung auch ein Beweis dafür, daß in kaum einer anderen Stadt der Welt Architektur und Stadtgestaltung so zum Thema öffentlicher Auseinandersetzungen geworden sind wie in Wien. Jahrelang hatte geradezu ein Kulturkampf darum getobt, ob gegenüber dem Dom ein „Tempel des Konsums" errichtet

largest building-site', the Viennese projects for a 'Museum Quarter' and a 'Donau City' are in no way inferior to the German undertakings, neither in size, nor in their secular demands."

Caroline is fascinated by this analysis and, above all, fascinated by the view from the Haas Haus CafÈ onto the Cathedral opposite, fascinated by the history of the arguments engendered by this provocative building: for years the Viennese had been arguing as to whether such a modern building should be erected in such a place and for years these quarrels were proof of the fact that in hardly any other city in the world are the themes of architecture and design so controversial as here in Vienna.

For years a virtual cultural war had broken out as to whether a "mecca of consumerism" could be put up opposite a cathedral. And now a new cultural war is being waged about the Museum Quarter.

Vienna's mayor at the time, Helmut Zilk, who was particularly interested in the upkeep of the historical city center, then put his foot down: yes, Hollein could put up his building. And today the Haas Haus has been accepted by the Viennese, is in fact hardly noticed by them, unlike the millions of gaping tourists who every year crane their necks before it in order to take photos.

werden dürfe. Ein Kulturkampf, wie ihn Wien nun wieder um das Museumsquartier erlebt.

Wiens damaliger Bürgermeister Zilk, dem die Erhaltung der historischen Innenstadt besonders am Herzen lag, hatte dann ein Machtwort gesprochen: Hollein durfte bauen. Und heute ist das Haas-Haus von den Wienern akzeptiert, fast nicht mehr wahrgenommen – im Gegensatz zu den Millionen staunender Touristen, die sich jährlich davor die Hälse verrenken und Kameras schwingen.

Planet Hollywood im Steffl

Was Caroline wundert: Von dieser Innenstadt haben die Multis der Gastronomie- und Unterhaltungsszene noch kaum Besitz ergriffen. Keine Hamburger am Dom, kein „Hard Rock-Cafe" am Graben – wo doch jede Stadt stolz ist, auf diese Errungenschaften amerikanischer Kultur. Sogar in Peking sind diese Pioniere der US-Kultur bereits heimisch geworden. Wien hat sich, erfährt sie, bisher erfolgreich gewehrt gegen diese Form neuer globaler Kultur. Wiens Innenstadt sollte nicht zum Touristenghetto verkommen – gerade angesichts der Tatsache, daß die Stadt Touristenmagnet mit weiter aufsteigender Tendenz ist.

Planet Hollywood in Vienna

What surprises Caroline is that the multinational corporations of the gastronomic and entertainment branch have hardly penetrated the 1st district. There are no hamburgers near the Cathedral, no hard rock cafēs on Graben – usually every city is only too proud to show off such achievements of American culture. Even in Communist Beijing these pioneers of US culture have taken root. She learns that Vienna has so far managed to stave off this type of new, universal culture. The city center should not be degraded as a tourist ghetto, particularly since the Austrian capital has become a tourist magnet and this trend is steadily continuing.

The city center, the "living-room of the city" should conserve its identity, but without forbidding each new development. For Vienna also does not want to dictate certain tastes.

Perhaps it can best be explained by the policy of protected areas, which has been successfully applied in the city. The secret of success lies in the cautious handling of new and old. What is old and worthy of preservation is preserved, and in places where the city needs new stimuli, innovations are admitted and encouraged.

In other words, the urban planners have taken on the task of designing the set but not the costumes, of writing the script, but not giving the final stage directions.

Die Innenstadt, das „Wohnzimmer der Stadt", sollte seine Identität behalten, ohne freilich jede neue Entwicklung zu untersagen. Denn man will in Wien auch keine Geschmacks-Diktatur ausüben. Vielleicht läßt sichs am besten mit dem Schutzzonengedanken erklären, der in Wien erfolgreich angewendet wird: Es ist der behutsame Umgang mit alt und neu, der das Erfolgsgeheimnis ausmacht. Altes wird bewahrt, wo es bewahrenswert ist, neues zugelassen und animiert, wo die Stadt neue Impulse braucht.

Die Stadtplanung übernimmt es, wenn man so will, das Bühnenbild zu gestalten, nicht aber die Kostümausstattung, das Drehbuch zu schreiben, nicht aber die letzten Regieanweisungen bis ins Detail.

Mag sein, daß dies auch Österreichs Hollywood-Größe Arnold Schwarzenegger beeindruckt hat, der mit seinen Partnern Bruce Willis und Sylvester Stallone eines seiner „Planet Hollywood"-Lokale unbedingt am Stephansplatz etablieren wollte. Mag sein, daß es eines Neins der Stadtplanung gar nicht bedurft hatte, weil alle Beteiligten so viel Sensibilität aufgebracht haben. Wie auch immer: „Planet Hollywood" wird auch in Wien heimisch – wäre ja auch anachronistisch, wenn jene Stadt, die einst soviel zum Werden Hollywoods beigetragen hat, der Kulturform des 20. Jahrhunderts neben der Rockmusik eine Absage erteilt

Maybe this was what impressed Austria's Hollywood star Arnold Schwarzenegger when, together with his partners Bruce Willis and Sylvester Stallone, he wanted to open one of his "Planet Hollywood" eateries precisely in Stephansplatz.

Maybe the "no" from the urban planners was not necessary because all those involved showed such sensitivity. Be that as it may: "Planet Hollywood" will also find a home here in Vienna. For it would be anachronistic if this city, which once contributed so much to the making of Hollywood, were to reject a form of 20th century culture that has taken its place alongside rock music: "Planet Hollywood" will take up residence just a few hundred meters down the road from St. Stephen's Cathedral, in the department store called, ironically enough, "Steffl", the pet name the Viennese give to their cathedral ...

Apropos living room: Caroline is impressed by the modern "street furniture" that not only blends in with the historic atmosphere of the city but also attracts attention along newly-designed streets and open places.

"Time and again the question arises of an appropriate redevelopment of streets and public places and, in this connection, of the appropriate design of furniture for them. Particularly in a city like Vienna with a wealth of historic buildings the decision between contemporary and old-style furniture is not an

hätte. „Planet Hollywood" wird wenige hundert Meter vom Stephansdom Einzug halten, pikanterweise im Kaufhaus „Steffl".

Stichwort Wohnzimmer: Caroline fallen die modernen „Stadtmöbel" auf, die sich zurückhaltend und dennoch markant in das historische Ambiente der Stadt ebenso einfügen, wie sie in den neugestalteten Straßenzügen Akzente setzen. „Immer wieder stellt sich die Frage nach einem zeitgemäßen Design der öffentlichen Straßen und Plätze und nach der Auswahl geeigneter Stadtmöbel. Besonders in einer Stadt mit wertvoller historischer Substanz fällt die Entscheidung zwischen zeitgemäßer und historisierender Möblierung oft schwer und sollte von kompetenten, international bewährten Fachleuten getroffen werden. Aus diesem Grund wurde in Wien der Arbeitskreis Stadtmöblierung ins Leben gerufen mit dem Ziel, das Wiener Stadtmöbel teils mit bestehenden, teils mit neuen Elementen auf die funktionellen und ästhetischen Ansprüche unserer Zeit abzustimmen: Das heißt, nicht alles über einen Kamm scheren, sondern individuelle und identitätsstiftende Gestaltungsarbeit zu leisten", heißt es dazu im Vorwort zur von der Stadtplanung Wien herausgegebenen Broschüre „Wien, Stadtmöbel". Darin sind Entwürfe und Ausführungen international bekannter Architekten und junger Wiener Studenten von Tele-

easy one and should be made by a competent team of international experts. For this reason a Working Group on street furniture was set up with the aim of bringing the external furniture of this city into line with the functional and aesthetic requirements of our times, both by incorporating the existing pieces and by creating new ones. This means not making them all the same, but designing individual pieces with their own identity", written in a foreword on this subject in a brochure entitled "Vienna, Urban Furniture" by the Vienna Department of Urban Planning.

This contains designs and models by internationally acclaimed architects and young Viennese students for telephone booths, trash cans, benches, mailboxes and other "pieces of furniture" for public places that are gradually becoming a feature of the cityscape.

Apropos public spaces: during her walkabout Caroline has noticed with what attention to detail the Viennese decorate even the smallest corner of their city. And here, in the downtown pedestrian area, she admires the different types of designs for pavements. At the end of her stay her companions will present her with a brochure entitled "Urban Space Experience", which contains an extract of some 250 of the most interesting designs for streets and squares over the past years.

fonzellen, Mistkübeln, Sitzbänken, sogenannten Postzwischenlagern und anderen „Möbeln" im öffentlichen Raum dokumentiert, die nach und nach Einzug ins Stadtbild halten.

Apropos öffentlicher Raum: Caroline hat bei ihrem Spaziergang auch bemerkt, mit welcher Detailliebe in Wien auch kleinste Flecken öffentlichen Raumes gestaltet sind. Hier, in der Wiener Fußgängerzone, bewundert sie die unterschiedlichsten Bodengestaltungen. Ihre Begleitung wird ihr dazu am Ende der Reise eine Broschüre mit dem Titel „Stadt-Raum erleben" geben, die einen Auszug aus den rund 250 interessantesten Gestaltungen dieser öffentlichen Räume aus den letzten Jahren darstellt.

Holocaustmonument

Caroline steigt wieder hinunter, in die Geschichte Wiens. Den Michaelerplatz hat sie bereits gesehen: Dort wurde ebenfalls nach einem Entwurf von Hans Hollein der Einblick in die Geschichte Wiens architektonisch umrahmt. Bis in die Römerzeit lassen sich hier die Spuren der Bautätigkeit verfolgen. Und das im Schatten jenes Hauses, das vor siebzig Jahren für mindestens ebensoviel Aufregung gesorgt hatte, wie Holleins Haas-Haus. Wien hatte damals die erste Auflage des Kulturkampfes um ein Bauwerk erlebt, als Adolf Loos sein „Haus ohne Augenbrauen" hinstellen wollte. Noch dazu im Angesicht der kaiserli-

Holocaust Memorial

Caroline returns to Vienna s past. She has already visited Michaelerplatz: there she caught a glimpse of the very early beginnings of the city – Roman Vienna, framed in a modern architectural presentation by Hans Hollein. And this just a stone's throw from the house that, 70 years ago, created just as much of a stir as Hollein's Haas Haus. When Adolf Loos wanted to build his "house without eyebrows" just round the corner from the Hofburg and its baroque environment, the first cultural war with the authorities broke out.

To quote Armin Thurnher: **"The fuss made about buildings in Vienna's 1st district is understandable. For everything**

chen Hofburg und barocker Umgebung. Armin Thurnher sei hier nochmals zitiert: „Die Aufregung um Bauwerke im Ersten Bezirk scheint verständlich: Alles geschieht hier quasi in der Auslage Wiens, daher ist jedes Bauwerk dazu verurteilt, ein potentielles Wahrzeichen zu sein ... alles, was in diesem Ersten Bezirk an kultureller Manifestation geschieht, gerät in eine Atmosphäre des Kulturkampfes."

Was etwa bei der Errichtung von Alfred Hrdlickas „Mahnmal gegen Krieg und Faschismus" bei der Albertina zu spüren war, das heute ebenfalls in die städtische Selbstverständlichkeit eingegangen ist. Und was sich beim „Holocaust"-Mahnmal wieder abspielt, wenn auch vergleichsweise abgeschwächt: Als Wiens Stadtarchäologe Ortolf Harl am Judenplatz die Überreste der vermutlich ersten und bei einem Pogrom 1421 zerstörten Synagoge aus dem mittelalterlichen Wien entdeckte, wurde die Idee geboren, dort den Holocaust-Opfern ein Denkmal zu setzen. Im Andenken an die Kristallnacht sollte 1996 das in einem Wettbewerb siegreich hervorgegangene Mahnmal von Rachel Whiteread eröffnet werden. Rachel Whiteread hat dazu einen Stahlbetonkubus mit nach außen gekehrten Bibliothekswänden geschaffen. Nach Meinung der international besetzten Jury unter Vorsitz von Hans Hollein, der neben vielen anderen Simon Wiesenthal

that goes on here happens, as it were, in the shop window of the city, so that every building is fated to become a potential landmark ... any new cultural activity that is undertaken in the 1st district is done in an atmosphere of cultural war."

This was also the case when Alfred Hrdlicka's anti-war and anti-Fascist monument "Mahnmal gegen Krieg und Faschismus" was unveiled across the road from the Albertina, although today it is hardly noticed by the residents. And it is the same story with the "Holocaust Monument", albeit in somewhat diluted form. When Vienna's archaeologist Ortolf Harl discovered on Judenplatz the remains of what was probably the first synagogue in medieval Vienna – it was destroyed in a pogrom in 1421 – the idea was conceived of erecting a monument on this site to the victims of the holocaust. As a remembrance of the "Crystal Night" in 1938 when Jewish shops were plundered and destroyed, the winning model by competition winner Rachel Whiteread is planned to be erected here in 1996.

Rachel Whiteread's model consists of a steel and concrete cube with library walls facing outwards. In the opinion of the international jury led by Hans Hollein, to which Simon Wiesenthal and the Mayor of Vienna among many others also belonged, this monument best symbolizes the survival of the Jewish culture in words, writing and books. The City of Vienna has paid its Jewish popula-

und der Wiener Bürgermeister angehörten, symbolisiert dieses Mahnmal am besten das Fortleben des Judentums im Wort, in der Schrift, im Buch.

Ein besonderes Denkmal hat die Stadt Wien ihrer jüdischen Bevölkerung durch die Renovierung und den architektonisch gelungenen Ausbau des Jüdischen Museums der Stadt Wien in der Dorotheergasse durch das Team „Eichinger oder Knechtl" gesetzt.

Küche und Kultur

Caroline, die nach dem Besuch des alten jüdischen Viertels um die Judengasse auch mit einigem Entzücken die Lokallandschaft des sogenannten Bermudadreiecks erforscht, spaziert dann durch die ebenfalls ungeheuer lebendige Lokalszene der Bäckerstraße und der anschließenden Gassen ins älteste Viertel und erste Sanierungsviertel Wiens: Gleich hinter dem Stephansdom wurden in der Blutgasse uralte Häuser luxussaniert, ein wenig weiter findet sie in der Ballgasse die engsten Gassen des mittelalterlichen Wien.

Stichwort Lokale: Die Wiener Küche ist weltberühmt. Sie spiegelt die Vielfalt

tion a special tribute through the renovation and architecturally successful expansion of the "Jewish Museum of the City of Vienna" in Dorotheergasse by the team "Eichinger oder Knechtl".

Kitchen and Culture

After visiting the old Jewish quarter around Judengasse Caroline is delighted to discover the "Bermuda Triangle" with its bars and restaurants, and then walks through Bäckerstrasse, which is also full of eateries and wine-bars, and its adjoining small streets into the oldest part of the city and the site of its first redevelopment. Directly behind St. Stephen's Cathedral some extremely old houses in Blutgasse have been converted into luxury apartments, and a bit further along in Ballgasse are the narrowest streets of medieval Vienna.

Apropos restaurants: the Viennese cuisine is world-renowned and reflects the variety of the nations and cultures that have established themselves in Vienna. For there is actually no such thing as "Viennese" cuisine! It is a blend of Bohemian, Hungarian, Balkan and Italian dishes, which have found their way to the Austrian capital. This mixture makes for a typically Viennese mèlange and is as varied as the origin of the Viennese themselves. Multiculture? On the menus of Viennese restaurants this is a matter of course. And the growing selection of

der Nationen und Kulturen wieder, die sich in Wien gefunden haben. Denn: „Wiener" Küche gibt es eigentlich nicht wirklich! Es sind die böhmischen, ungarischen, balkanischen und italienischen Gerichte, die hier Eingang gefunden haben. Ihre Mischung bildet eine typisch wienerische „Melange", vielfältig wie die Herkunft der „Wiener". Multikultur? Auf den Wiener Speisekarten ist sie selbstverständlich. Daß daneben das „Ethno"-Küchenangebot in Wien den Vergleich mit London oder New York nicht scheuen muß, spricht für Wiens gelebte Internationalität, denkt sich Caroline.

Durch die Wollzeile schlendert sie Richtung Ring, wo sie am Luegerplatz wieder auf die Reste des mittelalterlichen Stadt stößt: Beim Bau der U-Bahn wurden dort die Spuren eines Stadttores sichtbar gemacht. Nach einem Besuch des MAK, dessen Ableger sie ja aus Los Angeles kennt, und das hier in Wien zu einem der vitalsten Zentren moderner Kunst geworden ist (Caroline stöbert im ausgezeichneten book shop nach Wien-Literatur), wandert sie über das Wiental, das hier offen liegt und in den kommenden Jahren im Zuge der Neugestaltung von Wiental und Donaukanal zu einer innerstädtischen Erholungslandschaft neu gestaltet werden soll, Richtung Landstraße.

Neben der Betonwüste der Bundesamtsgebäude zwischen Ring und Wien-

"ethnic" specialties in restaurants means that Vienna now compares very favorably with London or New York, a sign of the city's increasingly international atmosphere, thinks Caroline.

She now strolls down Wollzeile towards Ringstrasse and on the way encounters further traces of the medieval city on Luegerplatz: during the construction of the subway system parts of a city gate were uncovered. After a visit to the Museum of Applied Art, whose offshoot she knows from Los Angeles and which here in Vienna has become one of the most lively centers of modern art (Caroline browses in the excellent bookstore, looking for books on Vienna), she walks down to the Wiental, which here – unlike the point at which she crossed over it for the first time in Gumpendorf, is exposed. There are plans to redevelop the Wiental and Danube Canal in the coming years and to create a new recreation area in the heart of the city, stretching towards Landstrasser Hauptstrasse.

Next to the conglomeration of federal office buildings between Ringstrasse and the Wien River, the signal blue colour of the modern headquarters of "Bank Austria" attracts her attention. Following a fire a few years ago both the interior and exterior were re-designed by Günther Domenig, who several years ago caused quite a stir with his concept for a subsidiary of this bank in Favoritenstrasse. The transparent glass and metal design with

fluß sticht als moderner Bau das Hauptgebäude der „Bank Austria" in sattem Blau ins Auge. Nach einem Brand wurde es von Günther Domenig, der bereits vor mehreren Jahren durch ein Filialgebäude dieser Bank in der Favoritenstraße für Aufsehen gesorgt hatte, innen und außen neu adaptiert. Die transparente Glas- und Metallgestaltung mit viel Grün und viel Wasser im Inneren erinnert Caroline ein wenig an die Atrien in amerikanischen Hochhäusern.

Unmittelbar neben diesem Gebäude liegt eines der letzten innerstädtischen Hoffnungsgebiete für die Stadtentwicklung: Über den Bahnanlagen des Verkehrsknotens Wien Mitte soll ein Gebäudekomplex mit mehreren Hochhäusern entstehen. Die fertigen Pläne dafür liegen angesichts der europaweiten Immobilienflaute noch in der Schublade.

Alles Walzer

Caroline erholt sich schließlich im schattigen Stadtpark, nicht ohne das Denkmal für Johann Strauß besichtigt zu haben, jenes ersten weltweit gefeierten „Popstars" aus Österreich, der mit seinen Walzerklängen das Image Wiens als Musikstadt geprägt hat, wie die Beatles die britische Vormacht in der Popmusik unseres Jahrhunderts gefestigt haben. „We built this city on rock'n' roll?" – Das alte, neue Wien scheint Caroline eher auf den Walzerklängen der Strauß-Dynastie zu schweben. Wenn auch die Töne der Gegenwart immer stärker einfließen. „Fusion" auf wienerisch sozusagen. Der US-Hit des Wieners Falco fällt ihr ein: „Rock me, Amadeus".

Caroline bleibt noch ein Besuch am abendlichen Rathausplatz.

Anders als in anderen Großstädten der Welt ist das Wiener Rathaus keine Tintenburg, es ist vor allem unter Bürgermeister Zilk geöffnet worden als

its displays of greenery and water inside reminds Caroline a little of the atriums in American high-rise buildings.
Directly adjoining this building is another potential area for urban development in Vienna. Above the railway tracks of the Wien Mitte junction, a complex of buildings with several high-rise buildings is planned. However, in view of the Europe-wide stagnation in the field of real-estate, the plans for this are still tucked away in a drawer.

"Alles Walzer" – It's Time to Waltz

Caroline takes time to rest for a while in the shade of the Stadtpark. On her way she takes a look at the statue of Johann Strauss, Austria's first "pop star" who, with his waltz melodies, shaped Vienna's image as a city of music, just as the Beatles have dominated the present-day pop scene of our century.
"We built this city on rock`n`roll?" The old, new Vienna still seems to float to the strains of the Strauss waltzes, she thought. Even if the tones of the present are to be heard ever more distinctly – a "Vienna-style" fusion, as it were. The American hit by the Viennese singer Falco suddenly occurs to her: "Rock me, Amadeus"...
Caroline still has time for a visit to the Rathausplatz that evening. Unlike in other major international cities the Vienna City Hall is not a bureaucratic fortress: particularly under Mayor Helmut Zilk it was opened up as a center of

Kommunikationszentrum, als Veranstaltungszentrum von den „Wiener Vorlesungen" bis zum „Life Ball", dessen Ruf bis ins weitaus AIDS-bewußtere Hollywood vorgedrungen ist.

Der Platz vor dem Rathaus ist auch so etwas wie der große Festplatz für Wiener und Besucher aus aller Welt geworden. Der Bogen der Veranstaltungen rund ums Jahr spannt sich vom Eislaufplatz nach dem Vorbild des New Yorker Rockefeller Centres über Zirkus, Festwochen, das mittlerweile legendäre Freiluftkino in den Sommermonaten, Rockkonzerten bis zum Christkindlmarkt.

Diesen Christkindlmarkt nahm zusammen mit ähnlichen Veranstaltungen in anderen Städten Neal R. Peirce von der Washington Post Writers Group zum Anlaß, sich mit einem Vergleich amerikanischer und europäischer Städte zu beschäftigen. Unter dem Titel „Unlike America, Europe hasn't Mugged its Cities" schrieb er:

„Vienna has reinvented its Advent market, a tradition traceable to 1298 (wobei er nicht weiß, daß der Christkindlmarkt in Wien auch in den schlechtesten Zeiten immer existiert hat, Anm. d. Verf).

Yet even if city-loving Europeans begun to emulate American's search for automobility and a yard to call one's own, they haven't committed the almost unpardonable sin of American metropolises – letting big chunks of the center cities and older neighborhoods sink into decay. Instead, virtually every European city has preserved, rebuilt and continued to invest, invest, invest. The Europeans seem intent on preserving and rebuilding a public order of shared transportation and shared streets and plazas. Americans, with their private cars, socially stratified malls and gated communities, seem to be racing in the other direction toward faceless exurbia."

Wobei Caroline feststellen muß, daß Wien auf dem europäischen Weg am weitesten fortgeschritten ist: Die größte zusammenhängende Fußgängerzone

communication and events, ranging from the "Vienna Lectures" series to the "Life Ball", a charity event whose fame has spread all the way to AIDS-conscious Hollywood. The square in front of the City Hall has also become a kind of large festival ground, both for the Viennese and for visitors from all over the world. The variety of events throughout the year ranges from an ice-rink like that of the New York Rockefeller Center, to circuses, the Vienna Festival, the now legendary open-air cinema during the summer months, rock concerts and, last but not least, the Advent market.

Neal R. Peirce from the Washington Post Writers Group used this Advent market, together with similar events elsewhere, as a basis for his comparison between American and European cities.

Under the title "Unlike America, Europe hasn't Mugged its Cities", he wrote the following:

"Vienna has reinvented its Advent market, a tradition traceable to 1298 (he appears not to know that the Vienna Advent market has always existed, even in the hardest of times, comment by the author). Yet even if city-loving Europeans have begun to emulate Americans' search for automobility and a yard to call one's own, they haven't committed the almost unpardonable sin of American metropolises – letting big chunks of the city centers and older neighborhoods sink into decay. Instead, virtually every European city has preserved, rebuilt and continued to invest, invest, invest. The Europeans seem intent on preserving and rebuilding a public order of shared transportation and shared streets and plazas. Americans, with their private cars, socially stratified malls and gated communities, seem to be racing in the other direction towards faceless exurbia."

And here Caroline concedes that Vienna is by far the most progressive in Europe in this respect: it has the largest single pedestrian zone and, as her companions told her, there is nowhere, at least

hat es, und, wie sie sich erklären läßt, ist jedenfalls in der Innenstadt kein Punkt weiter als 300 Meter von einem öffentlichen Verkehrsmittel entfernt.

Cybervienna

Caroline steht also vor der neugotischen Konstruktion des Wiener Rathauses. Was ihr besonders bemerkenswert erscheint: Diese alte bauliche Manifestation des Bürgerwillens – die Wiener Bürgerschaft der Gründerzeit hat das Rathaus als bewußte Demonstration gegen die Allmacht des Kaiserhauses gesetzt. Aber das Rathaus ist auch der Nukleus für das Digitale Wien geworden.

Cybervienna in Neugotik? Ein Neuschwanstein des virtuellen Raumes? Nein, hier, im Rathaus, wo viele der Verwaltungseinheiten angesiedelt sind, hat man sich seit langem Gedanken gemacht, wie man der von US-Vizepräsident Al Gore angesagten Herausforderung des „Information Highways" auf

not in the 1st district, that is more than 300 meters away from a public transportation system.

Cybervienna

Caroline stands in front of the Neo-Gothic building of Vienna's City Hall. What she finds particularly remarkable is that this old architectural manifest of the citizens' will – the citizens of the Gründerzeit period used the City Hall as a deliberate demonstration against the omnipotence of the House of Hapsburg – has become the nucleus for digital Vienna.

A Neo-Gothic Cybervienna? A Neuschwanstein Palace in virtual space? No, here in the City Hall, which houses several administrative bodies, thought has for a long time been given to the question as to how we in Vienna are to meet what American Vice-President Al Gore has termed the "challenges of the Information Highway". Vienna's Urban Planning Department has taken up with en-

wienerische Art am besten entsprechen kann. Die Stadtplanung Wien hat geradezu begeistert die Idee einer „Global Village"- Veranstaltungsreihe aufgenommen und die riesige Volkshalle des Wiener Rathauses dafür zur Verfügung gestellt. Jährlich treffen sich hier Theoretiker mit Praktikern aus Verwaltung und Wirtschaft, um den Wiener Zugang zum Cyberspace zu beraten und vorzubereiten.

Mittlerweile ist das alterwürdige Gebäude glasfiberverkabelt und Homebase einer Digitalen Stadt.

Caroline fühlt sich an das sonnige Kalifornien erinnert, wo der Cyberspace eine ähnliche reale Heimat hat wie die Filmindustrie, die Unterhaltungsmusik und die Computerindustrie, vor allem deren Softwarespezialisten.

Vom Cyberspace schwärmte „Grateful Dead"-Songtexter und Mitbegründer der einflußreichen „Electronic Frontier Foundation", John Perry Barlow, dieser sei „die größte funktionierende Anarchie, die je auf dem Planeten Erde erfunden wurde".

Und Gundolf S. Freyermuth, in White Mountains (USA) lebender Autor des Buches „Cyberland. Eine Führung durch den High-Tech-Underground", meinte über das Potential des Computers als „Traummaschine ..., die das beste und radikalste Talent einer Generation anzog, wie es einst die Künste oder die Politik und zuletzt die Rockmusik getan hatten. Ihre Rolle spielt heute die Computerkultur. Das Woodstock der Gegenwart liegt im Cyberspace, die Cyberutopie sieht den Menschen im Medium der Technik, befreit von seinen sozialen wie biologischen Zwängen. Daß die neuen Utopien des technischen Fortschrittes ausgerechnet im ehemals Wilden Westen entstehen, ist mehr als ein historischer Zufall. Unzweifelhaft lebt hier die Sehnsucht nach Veränderung und Abenteuer noch stärker als der ängstliche Wunsch nach Erhalt des Erreichten."

thusiasm the idea of a series of events entitled "Global Village", and held here in the City Hall. Every year theoreticians meet with practians in administrative and economic fields in order to discuss how to link up and prepare Vienna's entry into cyberspace. In the meantime, this old historical building has been fitted with glass fiber cables and has become the home base of a digital city.

Caroline is reminded of sunny California where cyberspace is just as real as the film industry, entertainment music and the computer industry, but particularly its software experts.

John Perry Barlow, song writer of "Grateful Dead" and co-founder of the influential "Electronic Frontier Foundation", raved about cyberspace as "the largest functioning anarchy that has ever been founded on the planet earth".

And Gundolf S. Freyermuth, from White Mountains (USA), author of the book "Cyberland. A Tour through the Hi-Tech Underground", described the potential of the computer as a "Dream machine ... that has attracted the best and most radical talents of a generation, as did formerly the arts and politics and, latterly, rock music. Their role has today been taken over by computer culture. Today's Woodstock lies in Cyberspace, cyber utopia visualizes man in the medium of technology, freed from his social and biological constraints. That the new utopias of technological progress are located in the former Wild West of all places is more than a mere historical coincidence. Without doubt the yearning for change and adventure is even stronger here than the timorous desire to maintain the attained and familiar."

John Perry Barlow, a declared follower of the French theologian Teilhard de Chardin, who is regarded as the prophet of cyberspace, sees the aim of cyber utopia as "the Great Work". According to Teilhard de Chardin the "omega point" of human development has now been targeted.

John Perry Barlow, deklarierter Anhänger des alten französischen Theologen Teilhard de Chardin, den viele als Propheten des Cyberspace betrachten, sieht als Ziel der Cyber-Utopie gar „das Große Werk". Frei nach Teilhard de Chardin werde damit der „Omegapunkt" der menschlichen Entwicklung angesteuert.

Es wäre nicht Wien, wenn man hier nicht auch seine europäischen Zweifel an diesen grenzenlosen Utopien hätte. Und ein wenig wird hier auch der osteuropäische Denkeinfluß spürbar: Stanislaw Lem, der große europäische Utopist und Zukunftsphilosoph, etwa sieht die Entwicklung etwas differenzierter. In einem Interview mit der Wiener Tageszeitung „Der Standard" meinte er auf die Frage, ob er „weniger Naivität im Umgang mit Internet" befürworte: „Ja. Alle kriegen ganz glänzende Augen, wenn von Bill Gates die Rede ist. Schön für ihn, daß er ein Privatvermögen von 14 Milliarden Dollar angehäuft hat. Nichts dagegen. Aber entweder reden wir hier von Leuten, die sehr schnell extremen Reichtum erlangen, oder wir reden von einer ganz neuen technologischen Entwicklung. Die enormen Summen, die da bewegt werden, markieren noch keinen Quantensprung in der menschlichen Entwicklung: Es ist noch nicht der Eintritt ins angebliche Paradies des 21. Jahrhunderts."

Hier will Wien als Stätte der Begegnung, der Kommunikation mit jahrhundertelanger Erfahrung des Vermittelns auch zwischen unterschiedlichsten Systemen und Kulturen ansetzen. Ohne in die eine oder andere angesprochene Richtung sich extrem entwickeln zu wollen, setzt man hier auf den pragmatischen Umgang mit den neuen Technologien: Wien ist als Digitale Stadt im World Wide Web vertreten, und es fördert vor allem Einrichtungen der Telearbeit. Nicht als Ersatz für die traditionellen Arbeitsstätten, sondern als Experiment dafür, wie das Auslagern von Tätigkeiten in die Nähe der Wohnorte

This would not be Vienna if no doubts were expressed about these boundless utopias. The influence of the Eastern European mentality has also doubtless left its mark: the great European utopian and futurologist Stanislav Lem, for example, sees the development somewhat differently. In an interview with the Austrian newspaper "Der Standard", when asked whether he advocated "a less naive approach towards Internet", he answered: "Yes, indeed. Everyone goes starry-eyed when the name Bill Gates is mentioned. It's great for him that he has amassed a personal fortune of 14 billion dollars. No problem. But either we're talking about people who have become extremely rich extremely fast or we're talking about a completely new development in technology. The enormous sums of money that are at stake do not yet mark an enormous stride in the development of humankind. We have not yet reached the entry to the apparent paradise of the 21st century."

This is where Vienna wants to interact as a meeting place, as a center of communication, with hundreds of years of experience in mediation, also between greatly varying systems and cultures. Without wishing to tie ourselves down to going in one or the other direction, we aim at taking a pragmatic approach to the new technologies, Vienna is, as already mentioned, represented in World Wide Web and it supports particularly installations for teleworking. Not as a substitute for traditional work places but rather as an experiment as to how the shifting of activities to somewhere near one's home affects people's transportation habits, for example.

Can unnecessary journeys be avoided if one sets up teleworking offices on the outskirts of the city? Teleworking offices, which through the teamwork of several people in an office would help to reduce the danger of isolation of simply working from home. For, as was explained to Caroline, in cyberspace Vienna is also re-

sich beispielsweise auf das Verkehrsverhalten der Menschen auswirkt. Können nicht notwendige Fahrten vermieden werden, wenn man Telearbeitsbüros an der Peripherie unterbringt? Telearbeitsbüros, die nicht zuletzt durch das Zusammenarbeiten mehrerer Menschen in einem Büro auch die Gefahr der Isolation des reinen Heimarbeitsplatzes verringern sollen. Denn Wien, läßt sich Caroline sagen, setzt auch im Cyberspace auf seine soziale Kompetenz. Wenn es gelungen ist, in den vergangenen sieben Jahrzehnten die soziale Grundhaltung in allen Lebensbereichen „durchzuziehen", müßte dies doch auch in den Welten des virtuellen Raumes möglich sein, ist man jedenfalls in der Stadtplanung Wien zuversichtlich. Besonders wichtig: Wien will die Chancengleichheit im Zugang zu den neuen Medien fördern, und es will den Umgang mit der neuen Technologie zum Bildungsprinzip machen.

Hans Christian Heintschel, einer der jungen Wiener Stadt-Flaneure, hat ein solches Telecenter besucht: „Erste Blicke in die Zukunft werden hier schon gewährt. Nahe der Grenze. An der Peripherie. So ein Ort ist etwa in der Autokaderstraße, nahe der Brünner Straße, zu finden. Ein schlichtes, unauffälliges Gebäude von außen. Von innen ist es die Welt, die ganz runde Welt, die einem gegenübersitzt. Der Blick auf die Welt hat einen bezifferbaren Durchmesser: achtundzwanzig Zentimeter mißt die Länge, zweiundzwanzig Zentimeter die Höhe. Ähnlich wie die kleinen Fenster von Raumschiffen, durch die Astronauten sehnsüchtig ihre Erde vom dunklen, kalten Weltall aus grüßen, stehen hier die Computer herum. In der Autokaderstraße sitzen keine Astronauten, sondern Menschen dieser Stadt, die sich, freiwillig oder von der alltäglichen Arbeitswelt karenziert, auf etwas vorbereiten, das Zukunft genannt werden kann."

lying on its social competence. If we have succeeded during the past seven decades in pushing through our basic social attitude in all spheres of life, then this must also be possible in the world of virtual space. Of this, Vienna's urban planners are quite confident. And what is particularly important is that the City of Vienna wants to support equal opportunities as concerns the access to the new media and aims to include the management of new technologies in its educational programs.

Hans Christian Heintschel, one of Vienna's young city flâneurs visited such a telecenter: "So this is where we gain our first glimpse of the future. Here, on the outskirts of Vienna, near the city boundary. Here, in Autokaderstrasse, near Brünnerstrasse. From the outside, a plain, inconspicuous building. From the inside, one gets a view of the world, the wide, round world. This view of the world that one sits opposite has a measurable diameter: 280 mm in length, 220 mm in height. Like small windows of spaceships through which the astronauts gaze with longing at their planet earth from the dark, cold universe, the computers stand and stare. In Autokaderstrasse there are no astronauts but people, people of this city who, either voluntarily or because they have been made unemployed, are preparing themselves for something called the future."

In the near future such "offices" will be set up in cooperation with large companies and even if the step into the paradise of teleworking cannot be mastered overnight, there are high hopes for success. Just as now the new communication media for a better participation by the population is currently being tried out. As far as the designation of building land is concerned, this can be commented on from the outside and the millennium competition for a new redevelopment project in Meidling mentioned towards the beginning of this book will be strongly aided by Internet.

In der nächsten Zeit werden in Wien weitere derartige „Büros" in Zusammenarbeit mit großen Firmen entstehen, und wenn man sich auch nicht erwartet, von heute auf morgen den Schritt ins Telearbeits-Paradies zu machen, sind die Erwartungen hoch angesetzt. Ebenso wie der Einsatz der neuen Kommunikationsmittel für die Bürgerbeteiligung gerade erprobt wird. Zu Flächenwidmungsplänen kann man in Wien heute schon dezentral Stellung nehmen, und der „Milleniums-Wettbewerb" für ein neues Stadtteilprojekt in Meidling ist bereits stark internet-gestützt. Wien will auch in der „philosophischen" Entwicklung des Cyberspace mitmischen, will sein kommunikatives Potential einbringen und wird dafür die „Global Village"-Veranstaltungen nützen. Es will aber auch seine Rolle als „Frontstadt" der Europäischen Union nützen: Hier in Wien sollen virtuell auch die Know-how-Transfers zwischen Ost und West moderiert werden, hier soll etwa ein europäisches „hub" eines UNO-Netzwerkes für HABITAT entstehen, und hier soll auch „Green Cross" mitarbeiten, jene globale Organisation, der ein Michael Gorbatschow ebenso angehört wie eine Yoko Ono, und die sich ebenfalls die Nutzung des Cyberspace für den globalen Erfahrungsaustausch zum Ziel gesetzt hat.

Wenn es gelingt, die Wiener Kaffeehauskultur in den Cyberspace zu transferieren, denkt sich Caroline, könnte es dort etwas weniger kühl zugehen ...

The City of Vienna also wants to contribute to the "philosophical" aspects of this development, wants to incorporate its communications potential and will use the events of the "Global Village" program to this end. Moreover, Vienna also wants to make use of its role as a "frontier city" within the European Union: here in Vienna we can effect the transfer of know-how between East and West through virtual technology, here in this city we will create the European "hub" of a UN network for HABITAT and here we will also cooperate with "Green Cross", the global organization to which Mikhail Gorbachev belongs, and Yoko Ono, and which has also set itself the goal of using cyberspace for an international exchange of views.

If they succeed in transferring coffeehouses to cyberspace, thinks Caroline, then it might be a bit less cool there ...

Lightning Vienna

After all this philosophizing and strolling or surfing through real and virtual worlds, Caroline decides to see some of the city's night-life and experience "Vienna by light". And even during her preparations for Vienna she read that this city has had quite a history of lighting and that it still plays an important role today. Although she wouldn't see the City Hall in festive illumination tonight she had read that there was a strong tradition for floodlighting in Vienna. In his book "Stadtlichter" (City Lights) Harald Sterk also described the political dimensions of light: **"Anyone**

Wien leuchtet

Nach soviel Philosophie, nach dem Flanieren durch reale und virtuelle Welten beschließt Caroline, sich noch die nächtliche Lichterstadt Wien zu geben. „Wien leuchtet" hatte sie gelesen, „Vienna by light" könne sie erfahren. Und schon in der Vorbereitung auf ihren Wien-Besuch war ihr aufgefallen: Der Umgang mit dem Licht in dieser Stadt hat Geschichte und wird auch heute sehr bewußt gepflegt. Das Rathaus sieht sie zwar heute nicht in der Festbeleuchtung, aber sie hat nachgelesen, welche Tradition Beleuchtung in dieser Stadt hat. Harald Sterk hat in seinem Buch „Stadtlichter" auch die politische Dimension des Lichtes beschrieben: **„Wer sich nicht darum kümmert, daß er die Verbreitung des Lichtes kontrolliert, dem entgleitet auch die Macht und der ist schließlich zum Untergang verurteilt."**

Heute ist Licht keine Frage der Macht, es ist Teil unseres Lebens geworden. Es hat aber über die ästhetische Funktion hinaus eine wichtige Aufgabe gerade in Städten: Es vermittelt Sicherheit.

who neglects to control the dispersion of light soon loses sight of power and is then doomed to destruction." Today, light is not a question of power, it is a part of everyday life. But, in addition to its aesthetic function, it also serves another important purpose, especially in cities: it gives security.

Die „kleine Donau"
The "small" Danube

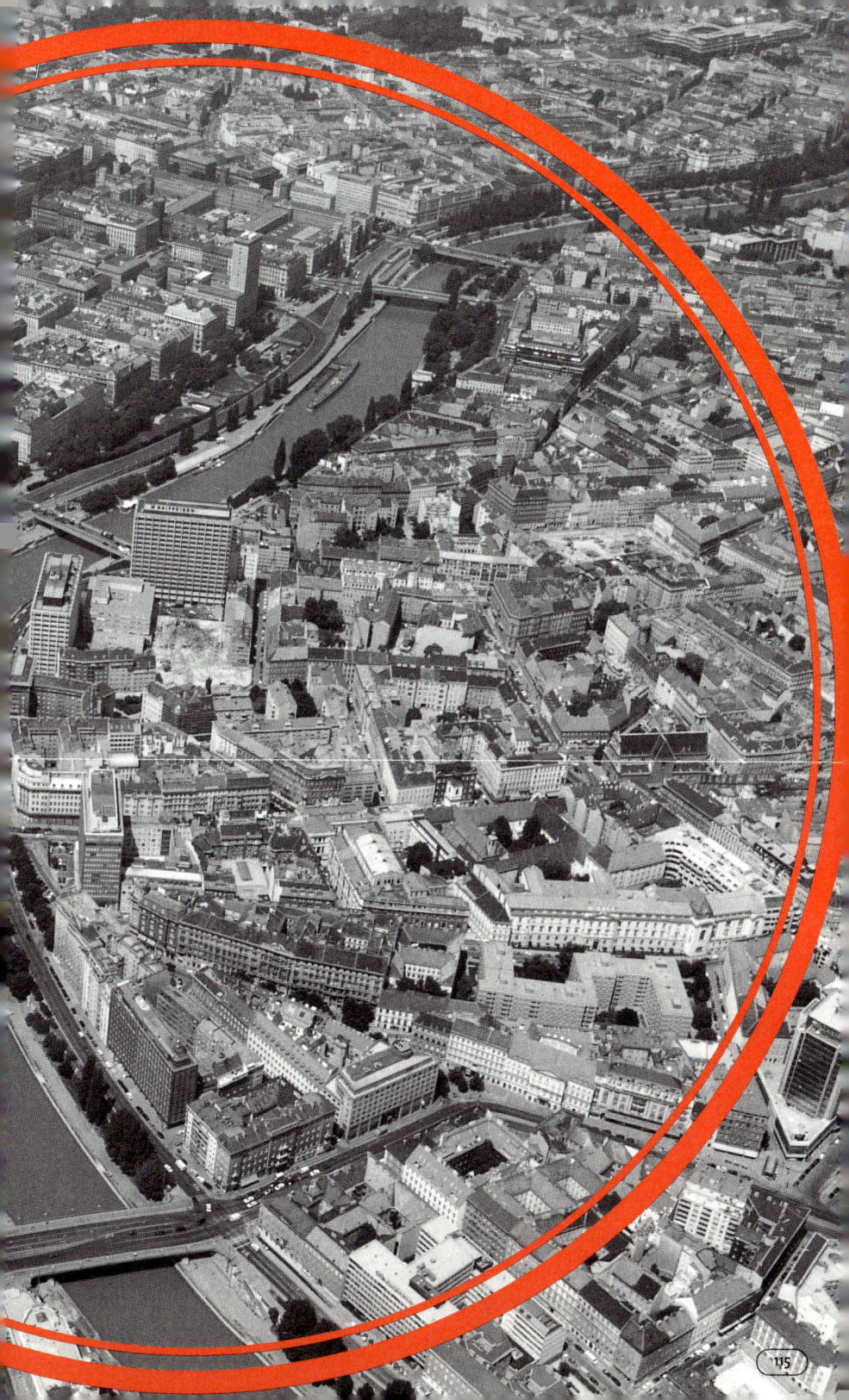

Unvorstellbar, daß hier einst die Donauwellen an die Gestade des alten Wien schlugen. Was wir heute als „Donaukanal" kennen, der Versuch, diesen Wiener Canale Grande in „Kleine Donau" umzubenennen, ist bisher erfolglos geblieben, war tatsächlich einst der wichtigste schiffbare Arm des Donaulabyrinths im Wiener Raum.

Die Kanal-Gestalt bekam dieses Gewässer dann anläßlich der Gesamtregulierung der Donau in den Jahren 1870-1875. Die Schiffe wurden weitestgehend auf die „Große" Donau umgeleitet, heute dümpeln am Donaukanal gerade noch einige Ausflugsboote, fest verankert liegt die alte „Johann Strauß" der selig entschlafenen „Ersten Donaudampfschiffahrts-Gesellschaft". Touristen wird hier Wiener Walzerseligkeit samt zugehöriger Verköstigung geboten.

Doch der Kanal zeigt wieder mehr Leben als noch vor wenigen Jahren. An Wochenenden finden sich hier diverse Märkte, die Radler haben auch die Donaukanalufer in Beschlag genommen, und es gab sogar die Überlegung, das einst hier heimische Donaukanalbad wieder in Betrieb zu nehmen.

Einen wesentlichen Impuls zur Aufwertung des Donaukanals setzt der Bau eines Hauptsammelkanals: Im Zuge dieser Bauarbeiten werden die Ufer neu gestaltet. In den letzten Jahren wurden hier die planerischen Vorarbeiten geleistet. Der Landschaftsplaner Oberhofer hat bereits Teststrecken für eine naturnahe Gestaltung des Kanals im Unterlauf im dritten Bezirk eingerichtet, die später auch im Oberlauf dieses wohl zentralste Wiener Erholungsgebiet prägen wird. Für den städtischen Mittelteil hat Architekt Podrecca Entwürfe geliefert. Wann die endgültige Gestaltung erfolgen kann, ist derzeit nicht konkret absehbar, denn die Mittel für den Bau des Hauptsammlers tröpfeln nur langsam.

It's difficult to imagine that the waves of the Danube once broke against the banks of old Vienna here. What we know today as the Danube Canal – the attempt to rename this Viennese Canale Grande the "small Danube" has so far been unsuccessful – was actually once the most important navigable arm of Vienna's Danube labyrinth. This waterway got its appearance as a canal at the time of the Danube regulation between 1870 and 1875. Most of the ships were diverted onto the "big" Danube and today just a handful of excursion boats drift down the Danube Canal; the "Johann Strauss", an old ship from the "Erste Donaudampfschiffahrts-Gesellschaft, the Danube Steamer Company, which now no longer exists, is moored here permanently and is today a floating café offering not only food and drink but also Viennese waltzes.

But the Danube Canal shows more signs of life than just a few years ago. At weekends it plays host to a variety of markets, cyclists ride along its banks and proposals have even been considered for reopening the former Danube Canal baths on their original site.

A priority feature of the regeneration scheme for the Danube Canal is the construction of a new main canal to collect surplus water. While this is under construction, the banks of the canal are redeveloped. During the past few years the preparatory planning work for this project has already been carried out. The landscape planner Oberhofer has also experimented with a "natural" design concept for the canal on test areas along its lower reaches in the 3rd district, which will later on also be applied to the upper reaches and characterize what will become Vienna's most central recreation area. The concept for the urban middle part of the Canal was drawn up by the architect Boris Podrecca. But just when the final project will be initiated cannot be predicted with certainty, for the money needed for the construction of the new canal is only trickling in slowly.

Kulturkanal

Bis dahin bleibt daher das neue Beleuchtungsprogramm für die Donaukanalbrücken die nächtliche Hauptattraktion. Die Lichtgestaltung setzt aber nicht nur optische Highlights, sie dient auch einem höheren subjektiven Sicherheitsgefühl im Bereich der Brücken.

Entlang des Donaukanals hat sich auch die neue Wiener Festkultur angesiedelt, in der warmen Jahreszeit gibt es immer mehr Veranstaltungen an den Ufern. Langsam, aber sicher wird der Donaukanal zu einer innerstädtischen Architektur- und Kulturmeile: Hatten die Bauten der Wiederaufbauzeit nach dem Zweiten Weltkrieg wenig städtisches „Gesicht", blitzen zwischen den grauen Fassaden immer mehr neue Schmuckstücke oder sind gerade in Planung oder im Entstehen.

Im zentralen Bereich des Kanals, dort wo Caroline ihre Stadtwanderung durch den zweiten Bezirk (Leopoldstadt) beginnt, entsteht nach den Plänen von Hans Hollein ein 70 Meter hohes Haus einer Versicherung, das ein städtebauliches Signal erster Ordnung wird. Es markiert den Beginn der Taborstraße, einer jener Wiener Einkaufsstraßen, die sich trotz Konkurrenz der Märkte am Stadtrand im Aufwind befinden.

Der Hollein-Entwurf setzt durch seine Vielfältigkeit und Eigenständigkeit außerdem einen positiven Kontrapunkt zu dem gegenüberliegenden Verwaltungsgebäude. Und hat schon dafür gesorgt, daß auch die dort ansässige Versicherung Adaptierungspläne wälzt. Die weiteren architektonischen Akzente am Donaukanal sind das Versicherungs-Gebäude von Boris Podrecca oberhalb der Friedensbrücke und das fast vis-á-vis entstehende Wohnprojekt von Zaha Hadid.

Seine nachhaltigen Spuren hinterlassen hat am Donaukanal auch der Gaudi-Interpret von Wien: Das von Hundertwasser gestaltete Donaukanalschiff führt unersättliche Bewunderer seiner

Culture Canal

Until such time, the new floodlighting program for the bridges along the Danube Canal will no doubt remain the main nocturnal attraction.

The lighting not only sets optical highlights but also provides for an increased feeling of subjective security in the environs of the bridges.

The banks of the Danube Canal also serve as a new backdrop for the new Vienna Festivals and during the summer months they offer a increasing number of open-air events.

Slowly but surely, the Danube Canal is becoming part of the inner city architectural and a cultural mile: even if the buildings of the reconstruction period following the Second World War barely had an urban look about them, today an increasing number of new and attractive buildings enliven the gray facades roundabout. Others are planned or currently being built.

Along the central area of the Canal, where Caroline will begin her walk through Leopoldstadt, the 2nd district, a new block, 70 meters high and designed by Hans Hollein, is being built for an insurance company; the building is expected to become the pièce de rèsistance of urban planning. It will stand at the beginning of Taborstrasse, one of those Viennese shopping-streets that, despite competition from the supermarkets on the outskirts of the city, is on the upswing.

The diversity and individuality of Hollein's design marks a positive counterpoint to the administration offices vis-à-vis. So much so that the insurance company located in the latter block is already considering adaptation plans to its own building. Other points of architectural interest along the Danube Canal are a building near Friedensbrücke, also belonging to an insurance company, designed by Boris Podrecca, and a housing project almost opposite by Zaha Hadid.

phantastischen Kulissen vom Kunsthaus im dritten Bezirk (nahe dem „Original" der Wiener Hundertwasser-Häuser) bis zum Fernwärmewerk Spittelau und den noch von ihm zu überarbeitenden Bürogebäuden unmittelbar daneben. Die U6 führt in weiterer Folge daran vorbei.

Nicht zu vergessen an Wiens Canale Grande: Das erste Hochhaus der Nachkriegszeit, der Ringturm, dessen Fassade neu gestaltet wurde und der Ausdruck des zögerlichen Wiener Umgangs mit hohen Häusern ist.

Caroline dreht sich nochmals um und nimmt jenes stimmige Wien-Bild auf, das man in der Welt kennt: Die Altstadt, dominiert vom Stephansdom, dem baulichen Manifest jahrhundertelanger geistig-kultureller Dominanz der katholischen Kirche in Wien.

Vienna's virtual Gaudí, Friedensreich Hundertwasser has also left his traces on the Danube Canal. The brightly-colored boat he designed takes insatiable admirers of his fantastic art from the Vienna Kunsthaus in the 3rd district (near the original "Hundertwasserhaus") to the district heating plant at Spittelau, also designed by him, and the office blocks adjacent to it, which are still to be decorated. The U6 will take us past this area later on.

Before leaving the Danube Canal, we should take a glance back at the first high-rise building constructed during the postwar period. This "Ringturm", whose facade was given a new look, has become a symbol of the hesitant Viennese approach towards high buildings. Caroline glances back at the view that has now become world-famous: the old city center, dominated by St. Stephen's Cathedral, the architectural manifestation of the spiritual and cultural dominance of the Catholic church in Vienna.

123

Auf der Mazzes-Insel

Wenige Schritte weiter findet sie sich auf historischem Boden des Wiener Judentums. Hier, auf der sogenannten Mazzes-Insel, jener uralten Insel zwischen den Armen der Donau, auch heute noch von Donaukanal und Donau umspült, befand sich Wiens Ghetto, hier lebten vor 1938 die meisten Wiener Juden, sie machten bis zu 20 Prozent der Leopoldstädter Bevölkerung aus. Hier blühte jüdisches Leben in einem Bezirk, der trotz seiner geographischen Nähe zum Zentrum immer noch als „Vorstadt" angesehen wird. Die brisante Mischung aus Altwiener Antisemitismus und dem Österreich-Export Adolf Hitler hatte jedoch nach dem Fanal der Kristallnacht die jüdische Bevölkerung in Wien fast ausgerottet.

Caroline sieht sich bei ihrer Wanderung durch die alten Gassen dieses Bezirkes in die jüdischen Viertel von Los Angeles oder New York versetzt: Im

On the Matzos Island

A few steps further along she finds herself on the historic ground of Vienna's Jewish culture. Here, on the so-called "Matzos Island", a very old island sandwiched between the Danube Canal and the main Danube, was Vienna's ghetto and, prior to 1938, most of Vienna's Jewish community lived here – up to 20% of the population of Leopoldstadt. Jewish life and culture flourished in this district which, despite its geographical proximity to the city center, is still regarded as a "suburb".

After the terror of the "Crystal Night", the explosive mixture of old Viennese anti-Semitism and the Austrian "export" Adolf Hitler almost eradicated Vienna's Jewish population.

During her walk through the old streets of this district Caroline is reminded of the Jewish quarters in Los Angeles and New York. Here in Vienna the signs of Jewish life are again becoming more visible.

Stadtbild ist jüdisches Leben heute wieder unübersehbar. Wesentlich dazu beigetragen hat die Tatsache, daß Österreich, ohne viel Aufhebens in der Welt zu machen, zusammen mit der damaligen Sowjetunion und Israel den aus dem Osten mehr oder weniger freiwillig abwandernden Juden Transit anbot auf dem Weg ins Gelobte Land. Viele der Ausgewanderten fanden dort aber nicht wie erwartet Milch und Honig und kehrten nach Wien zurück. Und die Leopoldstadt hat wieder jenes Flair zurückgewonnen, das die Ödnis der Nachkriegsjahre vertreiben half. Heute finden sich religiöse Einrichtungen und Schulen, Geschäfte jüdischer Kultur.

Beim nächsten Wien-Besuch, so hatte sich Caroline vorgenommen, würde sie auch ein Interview mit Leon Askin machen, jenem altösterreichischen Schauspieler, der in Hollywood in unzähligen Filmen mitgewirkt hatte und nach Jahrzehnten der Emigration wieder nach Wien zurückgekehrt war.

A strong contributory factor is that Austria, without making much publicity in this respect and after agreements made with the former Soviet Union and Israel, has become a transit country for Jews emigrating from Eastern Europe to the Holy Land. Many of the emigrants, however, did not find the anticipated milk and honey in Israel and returned to Vienna. And now Leopoldstadt has regained the characteristic atmosphere that was destroyed by the desolation of the postwar years.

Today, this district has Jewish religious institutions and schools, as well as shops with Jewish culture. During her next visit to Vienna, Caroline decides that she will arrange an interview with Leon Askin, the Jewish actor who made a name for himself in Hollywood and then, after years spent in exile, returned to live in Vienna.

Under Mayor Helmut Zilk, the City of Vienna decided to grant Austrian citizenship to Jewish emigrants and victims of

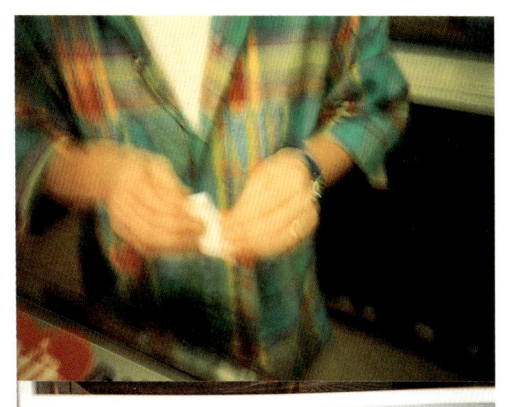

Wien hatte unter Bürgermeister Helmut Zilk beschlossen, den Emigranten der unseligen Hitler-Ära die österreichische Staatsbürgerschaft zu verleihen, wenn diese es wünschten.

Hollywood-Legende Askin genießt den Lebensabend nun in einem Leopoldstädter Seniorenheim. „Ein wirkliches Zuhause gibt es für einen Emigranten nicht mehr", sagte er in einem Interview und brachte auf den Punkt, was Felix Pollak, ein Lyriker, ein „Übersetzer zwischen den Kulturen" in seinem Gedicht „Wien: Die Straße" zum Ausdruck bringen wollte. Pollak – 1987 verstorben – war ebenfalls aus der Emigration heim(?)gekehrt und hatte hier Gedichte, die er im amerikanischen Exil in englisch geschrieben hatte, in deutsch nochmals geschrieben. Sein berührendstes Beispiel „Wien: Die Straße":

„Die Straße, die zur Grundschule führte,
ist groß geworden und breiter. Das Pissoir
fehlt. Obwohl ein Geruch nach Teer (und reifen
Delikatessen) noch in der Luft zu hängen scheint.
Die Schule steht noch. Sogar der muffige Raum 3a, in dem
 Erdkunde daheim war.
(Nur daß weitergeholte Namen – wie Kankakee –
ihre Distanz verloren haben.)

the Hitler regime if they should so wish.

The legendary Hollywood actor Leon Askin can now enjoy his final years in an old people's home in Leopoldstadt.

"An emigrant has no real home any more", he said in an interview and expressed the same views as Felix Pollak, a lyricist and "translator between cultures", in his poem entitled "Vienna: The Street". Pollak, who died in 1987, also returned to Vienna as an emigrant, and rewrote many of the poems he had written in exile in America in German. His most moving work is "Vienna: The Street":

The street that went to grade school has grown up and spread. The pissoir is missing. Though a scent of tar (and ripe delicatessen) seems to linger.

**The school still stands. Even the musty room 3A that housed geography.
(Except that far-flung names – like Kankakee –
have lost their distance.)**

**A different barber. Eyes my clothes and greets me in bad English.
 The manicurist
(face of a tired nurse) must be his wife. My best friend bit his nails.
Yes, cut my golden locks. He laughs**

Ein anderer Friseur. Beäugt meine Kleider
und begrüßt mich in schlechtem Englisch. Die Maniküristin
(Gesicht einer müden Krankenschwester) muß
seine Frau sein. Mein bester Freund kaute Nägel.

Ja, schneiden Sie meine goldenen Locken. Er lacht
beflissen. (Amis machen gern Witze.) Das Schaukelpferd ist weg. Die Uhr liest sich rückwärts im Spiegel voll blinder Flecken."

Caroline ist beeindruckt von der sichtbaren Lebendigkeit des Viertels um den Karmelitermarkt, wo gerade ein neues kleines Bezirkszentrum entsteht: Der Markt wird umgebaut, eine Tiefgarage und ein neues Marktamtsgebäude errichtet, der Platz um die alte Karmeliterkirche umgestaltet. Die Leopoldstadt lebt auf, das merkt Caroline auch bei ihrer Straßenbahnfahrt mit dem 21er Richtung Praterstern. Mit ein Grund dafür war auch die geplante EXPO 95, die zuerst in diesem Bezirk zu einer Spekulationswelle geführt hatte, sehr rasch unterbunden durch Intervention der Stadt: Eine Assanierungsverordnung wurde erlassen, die vor allem die ansässige Wohnbevölkerung vor drastischer Erhöhung der Wohnungskosten durch Spekulation schützen sollte.

obliging. (Amerikaner like to joke.).
The rocking horse is gone. The clock reads backward in a mirror full of blindspots."

Caroline is impressed with the vitality of the area round Karmelitermarkt, where a new small district center is being erected: The market is being rebuilt, a subterranean garage and an office building for the market are being constructed and the square round the old Carmelite Church is being redeveloped.
   Leopoldstadt is being revived. This is obvious to Caroline as she sits in tram 21 on her way to Praterstern. One of the reasons for this revival was the planned EXPO 95, which initially led to a wave of speculation in the area. However, this was soon put paid to by the municipality. An ordinance was issued which protected the residents of the area against the drastic increase in rents due to speculation.

128

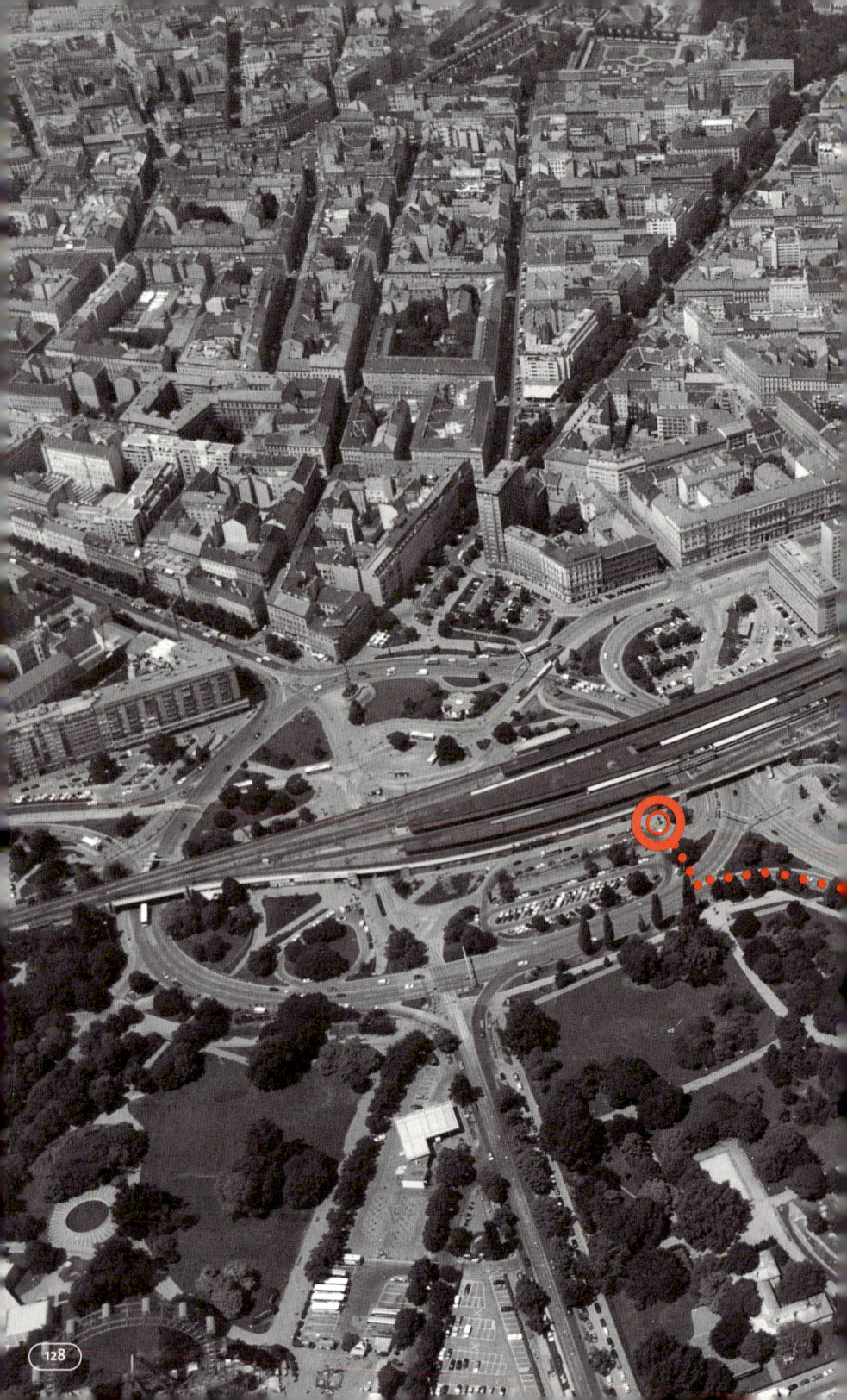

129

Auf der Suche nach der Stadt der Zukunft

Am Praterstern angelangt, macht Caroline einen Blick in die Praterstraße, die den Beginn jener „Entwicklungsachse" darstellt, die vom Zentrum über die Lassallestraße und die Wagramerstraße in die Erweiterungsgebiete der Donaustadt führt (erschlossen durch die U1). Auch hier werden Neugestaltungen für eine Aufwertung der Einkaufsstraße sorgen, der öffentliche Raum benutzerfreundlicher gestaltet.

Der Praterstern selbst mit seiner Verteilerfunktion für den Individualverkehr scheint Caroline nach ihrer Durchquerung der verkehrsarmen Innenstadt ein wenig störend, aber erstaunlicherweise scheinen es die Verkehrsplaner wenigstens geschafft zu haben, daß es hier selten Staus gibt. Baulich macht der Praterstern derzeit wenig her. Ein neues Projekt an der Ecke zur Nordbahnstraße könnte für ein wenig Belebung sorgen. Auf der anderen Seite der von der S-Bahn-Trasse zerschnittene Stadtlandschaft Praterstern beginnt ein neues Wien:

Hier hat der Prater, als eine der letzten Donauauen seinen letzten Ausläufer. Hier beginnt Wiens größter Vergnügungspark, unübersehbar markiert durch das Wiener Riesenrad. Ein Denkmal der Eisenarchitektur, das zwei Weltkriege überlebt und jetzt in London

In Search of the City of the Future

Having arrived at Praterstern, Caroline takes a look at Prater, which marks the beginning of the "development axis" that runs from the center through Lassallestrasse and Wagramerstrasse, following the route of the U1, to the urban expansion areas in Donaustadt. Here, too, there are redevelopment plans for upgrading the shopping street and making the public spaces more user-friendly.

Caroline finds Praterstern, with its roundabout for the dispersion of road traffic, rather busy after her walk through the inner city with its small streets and pedestrian zones. But at least there seem to be no traffic jams – that, *she had to hand to the urban planners. From the architectural point of view, nothing much is happening at Praterstern, with the exception of a new project at the corner of Nordbahnstrasse that could add some life to the area. But on the other side of the Praterstern junction, which is intersected by the tracks of the Schnellbahn, a new Vienna begins:*

Here we see the Prater, one of the last wetland areas along the Danube. It is also Vienna's largest amusement park, characterized by the Giant Ferris Wheel. This feat of iron architecture that has survived two world wars is now being emulated in London, where it will become one of the landmarks of the British capital.

Nachahmer gefunden hat, die der Themsestadt ein neues Wahrzeichen verpassen wollen.

Dahinter, von hier aus nicht sichtbar, das Messegelände. Jene letzte Erinnerung an die Weltausstellung 1873. Eigentlich hätte diese Wiener Messe ja im Zuge der EXPO-Planungen auf die Platte der heutigen Donau-City übersiedeln sollen und bis zuletzt hat man derartige Überlegungen gewälzt, nicht zuletzt, um das weitläufige Areal für stadtnahen Wohnbau zu nutzen. Status quo ist aber, daß die Messe am derzeitigen Standort verbleibt und nur in den Randgebieten Wohnhausanlagen entstehen.

Caroline macht sich auf den Weg durch die Lassallestraße und sucht die „Stadt der Zukunft", von der sie bei ihren Vorbereitungsarbeiten für das Wien-Feature gehört hatte.

Sie findet monumentale Bauten von Wilhelm Holzbauer: Eine Bank, eine Mineralölfirma und ein Computerkonzern haben ihre Verwaltungsgebäude bereits hier angesiedelt, ein weiteres Bürogebäude ist in Bau. Die neuentstandene Häuserfront verdeckt gnädig den Blick auf eine der letzten Stadtbrachen, das Gelände des alten Nordbahnhofes, seinerzeit nicht zuletzt für die Weltausstellung 1873 errichtet. Das heute von der Bahn fast nicht mehr benützte 49 Hektar große Areal ist Zankapfel zwischen der Stadt Wien und der Bahn. Seit Jahren wird über den Ankauf durch die

Behind the Prater, not yet visible from here, is the large fairground – the last reminder of the 1873 World Exhibition. In fact, it was planned that the Vienna Trade Fair and other exhibitions that are held here every year would move their venue to the Donau City, the area that was constructed with the EXPO 95 in mind. This would have freed the present site for urgently needed apartment blocks near the city center. The status quo is, however, that the trade fair will remain in the Prater and that further housing developments will only be built in peripheral areas.

Caroline starts making her way down Lassallestrasse, looking for the "City of the Future" that she has read about during her preparatory work for the feature film about Vienna.

She finds monumental buildings by Wilhelm Holzbauer: a bank, a mineral oil company and a computer concern have already moved their administration offices here, and a further office building is under construction. The new facades thankfully obscure the view onto the old North Railway Station, which was originally built for the 1873 World Exhibition. The 49 hectares of this site, which is hardly used by the railway today, are a bone of contention between the municipality and the railway authorities. For years, negotiations have been in process as to the purchase of this land by the City of Vienna, which needs it for further

131

Stadt verhandelt, die hier innerstädtische Stadterweiterung betreiben möchte. 20.000 Menschen sollen hier einmal wohnen, fast ebenso viele Arbeit finden. „Stadt der Zukunft" lautete denn auch einer der markantesten Projektnamen, und erst vor kurzem ist ein städtebaulicher Entwurf für die Nutzung fertiggeworden. Die Architekten Podrecca und Tesar haben eine unspektakuläre, dafür aber künftige Entwicklungen offenhaltende Rahmengestaltung erarbeitet, die in der Höhe der bereits bestehenden Bauten eine Art Makroform der künftigen Gestaltung vorgibt. Eine schräg verlaufende „Hauptstraße" soll bis zur Donau führen („Riesenradstraße"), volle städtische Infrastruktur ist vorgesehen. Bald soll auch mit einer ersten Wohnbebauung in der Nähe jener alten Straßenbahnremise begonnen werden, die am Rande des Areals in unmittelbarer Nähe der U1-Station Vorgartenstraße liegt. Diese ein-

redevelopment work. 20,000 people will one day live in this area and almost the same number find jobs here. "City of the Future" is one of the striking names given to this project and just recently urban planners drew up concrete plans for the utilization of the area. The architects Podrecca and Tesar have designed an albeit unspectacular basic model but one that leaves room for future developments, which presents a type of macroform of the future design at the height of the existing buildings. At a diagonal, a "main street" ("Riesenradstrasse") will lead down to the Danube and a complete urban infrastructure is foreseen.

The first building work for residential housing blocks near the old tram terminus located not far from the U1 subway station Vorgartenstrasse is scheduled to begin shortly. This unique wood and iron construction has managed to survive: for years there was an alternative cultural center here and the station was also the

malige Eisen- und Holzarchitektur konnte erhalten bleiben, jahrelang befand sich hier ein alternatives Kulturzentrum, die Remise war auch Heimat für das jährlich stattfindende Wiener Internationale Architekturseminar. Heute wird die Remise als erste europäische Inlineskater-Halle genützt. Das mit Internet-Terminals und Computerspielen ausgestattete Jugendzentrum entwickelt sich zum Hit für die Kids der Stadt.

In unmittelbarer Nähe betreibt ein Verein das „Wiener Integrationshaus". Das Wiener Musiker-Original „Ostbahn-Kurti" alias Willi Resetarits, bekannt geworden durch die besten Bruce-Springsteen-Interpretationen des deutschsprachigen Raumes, ist Motor und Aushängeschild eines von der Stadt unterstützten Projektes vor allem zur Integration der Flüchtlinge aus Bosnien. In einem hauseigenen Kindergarten lernen bosnische und österreichische Kinder-

venue for the annual Viennese International Architecture Seminar. At the moment it is being used as the first European inline skating hall. The youth center, which is equipped with Internet terminals and computer games, has become a hit for the city's young people.

Just nearby is the "Vienna Integration House". The Viennese musician "Ostbahn-Kurti", alias Willi Resetarits, who became known for the best Bruce Springsteen interpretations of the German-speaking area, is the engine and the figurehead of this project, which is backed by the City of Vienna, aimed at integrating refugees from Bosnia. In a kindergarten on the premises Bosnian and Austrian children learn to play and live together. In Lassallestrasse Caroline finds more traces of Vienna's connection with the former Eastern Bloc. Many of the shops bear the names of people from all over Eastern Europe and offer "all types of products" – cheap and from a possibly dubious source.

das Zusammenleben spielerisch ...
In der Lassallestraße findet Caroline zunehmend die Spuren der Ostverbindungen Wiens: Die Geschäfte tragen die Namen von Menschen aus aller Herren Ost-Länder und bieten „Waren aller Art" an. Billig und von nicht immer ganz geklärter Herkunft. Sie führen zum Mexikoplatz, jenem Ort an der Donau, der durch die Nähe zu den Schiffsanlegestellen seit jeher Umschlagplatz für alle erlaubten und verbotenen Waren und Dienstleistungen ist, die in Hafenstädten üblich sind. Für Wien ist es exotisches Gebiet, frequentiert hauptsächlich von Touristen aus den Reformländern. In den Zeiten der Aufweichung des Ostblocks herrschten hier Zustände wie auf einem Mega-Basar. Heute ist wieder beschauliche Ruhe eingekehrt.

Am Donauufer angelangt, öffnet sich der Blick in jenes Wien, das selbst für die meisten Wiener, die rechts der Donau leben, „terra incognita" ist.

Caroline and her companions continue on to Mexikoplatz. Situated next to the Danube and near the docks, it has always been a place of transshipment and a black market for all kinds of those permitted and forbidden wares and services that are characteristic of ports. For Vienna it is an exotic area, chiefly frequented by tourists from the former communist countries of the Eastern Bloc. When the Iron Curtain came down, it bustled with activity like a mega bazaar. Today, things have quieted down.

Having reached the Danube, Caroline is greeted with a view that was once only seen by tourists who came in by boat. For most of the Viennese who live to the right of the Danube it is still "terra incognita".

Die Donau
The Danube

137

139

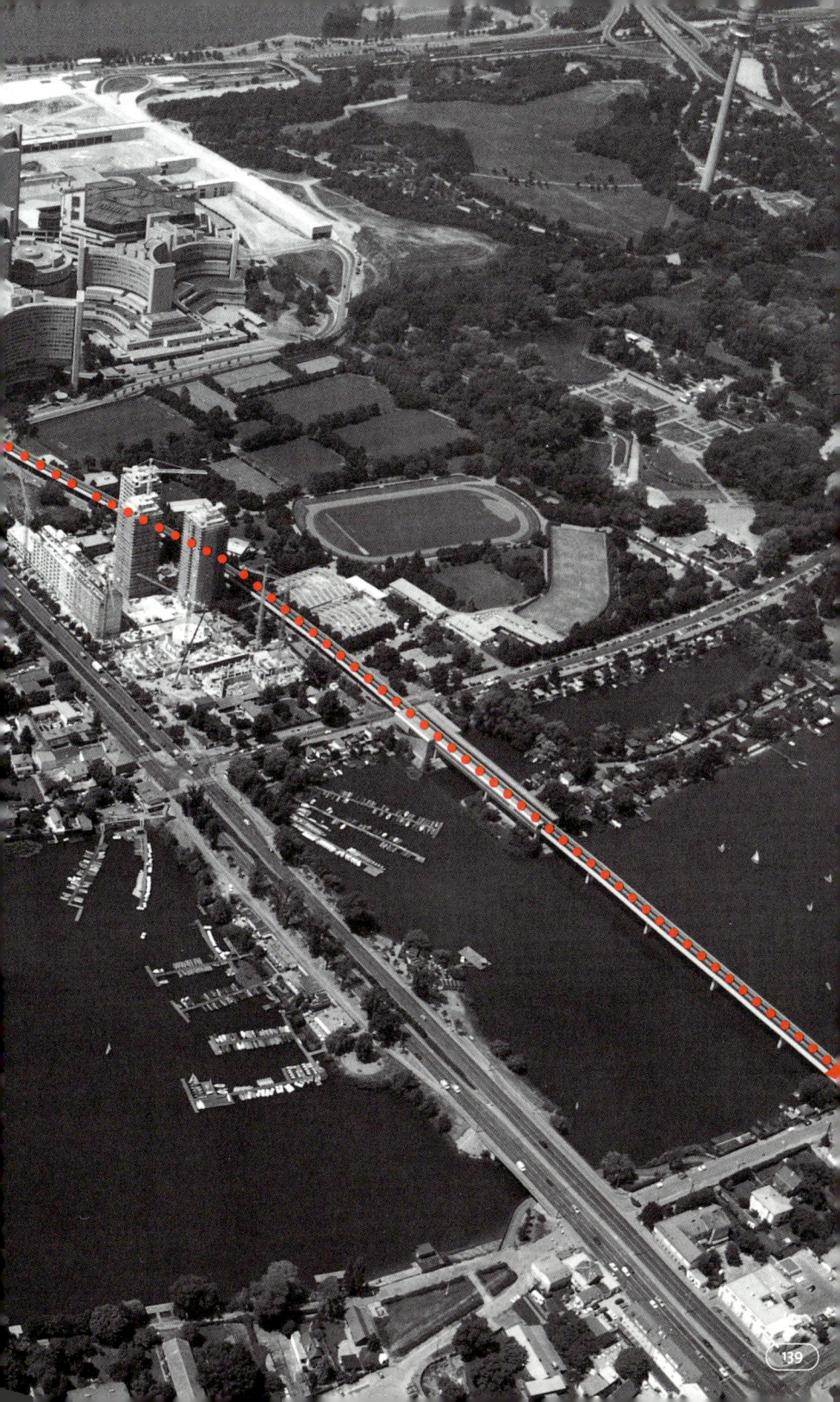

Hier stehen wir also mit Caroline an der „schönen blauen Donau", wie sie in der inoffiziellen Landeshymne, dem „Donauwalzer", poetisch besungen wird.

Blau? An manchen, ganz wenigen Tagen im Jahr. Wenn sich der Himmel im Wasser spiegelt. Und überhaupt: Das soll ein Fluß sein? Das Wasser scheint ja zu stehen. Richtig, im Frühjahr 1996 hat die Donau in Wien wieder einmal in ihrer langen Geschichte ein neues Outfit bekommen.

Von hier aus unsichtbar, staut einige Kilometer flußabwärts ein weltweit einmaliges Flußkraftwerk den Donaustrom. Dieser technische Eingriff ist sozusagen multifunktional: Die Donau wird im Wiener Bereich ganzjährig schiffbar gemacht, der Grundwasserhaushalt gesteuert, und Wien hat mit der Donauinsel ebenfalls weltweit einmaligen Freizeitbereich gewonnen.

Und die Stadt wächst endgültig an „ihren" Strom heran, betonen Carolines Begleiter.

Aber der Reihe nach. Dieser längste europäische Strom in west-östlicher Richtung war über Jahrhunderte eine natürliche Grenze. Damals, als er, noch wild und ungebändigt in viele Arme aufgeteilt, ein Areal durchfloß, das heute gleich mehrere Wiener Bezirke umfaßt.

In vergangenen Jahrhunderten war die Donau bei Wien fast unpassierbar. Brücken oder brückenähnliche Gebilde wurden von den jährlichen Hochwassern einfach weggeschwemmt. Die Römer hatten als erste die strategische Bedeutung dieser Gegend erkannt und eine Station ihres „Limes" hier errichtet. Jenseits der Donau lauerte damals das Unbekannte, das Wilde, die Völker, die später tatsächlich das römische Imperium zu Fall bringen sollten. Und irgendwie scheint sich dieses Unbehagen an „Transdanubien" über die Jahrhunderte erhalten zu haben.

Die Donau hat ihr heutiges Gesicht erst vor rund 120 Jahren verpaßt bekommen. In einem gigantischen, heute

Here we stand with Caroline looking at the "beautiful blue Danube", as it is so poetically described in Austria's unofficial national anthem, the "Donauwalzer".

Blue? Yes, on certain rare days in the year when the sky is reflected in the water. And anyhow: this is supposed to be a river? The water seems to stand still. Right, since the spring of 1996 the Danube in Vienna, once more in its long history, has got a new outfit.

From here, a few kilometers downstream and out of sight, is a universally unique power station that controls the flow of the river: when it is complete, it will also generate electricity.

But not just that. This technical installation is, so to speak, multifunctional: at one and the same time, the Danube in the Vienna region will become navigable for ships all the year round, the ground water in Vienna will be controllable and, with the Donauinsel, Vienna has gained a universally unique recreational area. And, in addition, the city will finally grow closer to "its" river, emphasize Caroline's companions.

But one thing after another. This river, the longest in Europe from east to west, was a natural border for hundreds of years. At one time it was wild and unruly, divided into many arms, and flowed through an area which today takes in several Viennese districts.

During the past centuries the Danube in Vienna was almost impassable. Bridges or bridge-like constructions were simply swept away by the annual high tides. The Romans were the first to recognize the strategic importance of this area and built a camp for their "Limes", or defense line. In those days, the other side of the Danube represented the unknown, the wild and there lurked the peoples that were later to cause the fall of the Roman Empire. And yet, somehow, this uneasiness surrounding "Transdanubia" has persisted for hundreds of years.

The Danube received its present face, so to speak, just 120 years ago. In a gi-

aus ökologischen Gründen und vor allem angesichts des entstandenen ökologischen Bewußtseins, unvorstellbaren Eingriff in die wildromantische Flußlandschaft wurde ein schnurgerades Bett gegraben, die Donau in einen Kanal gezwungen. Maschinen, die den Suezkanal errichtet hatten, gruben der Donau ihren neuen Lauf.

Europäische Hauptschlagader

Die Straßenbezeichnung Handelskai erinnert heute noch daran, daß in der damals geradezu explodierenden Hauptstadt der europäischen Großmacht Österreich-Ungarn vom Ausbau der Donau als internationalem Handelsweg geträumt wurde. Klar: Die Donau war immer Handelsweg gewesen, schon in Urzeiten. Aber sie war nie durchgehend schiffbar, vor allem nie durchgehend frei befahrbar gewesen. Die Donau hatte immer auch die politischen Verhältnisse in Europa im wahrsten Sinn des Wortes

gantic intervention, which would be virtually impossible today for environmental reasons and people's ecological awareness, in the wild, natural river landscape, a straight bed was dug and the Danube was forced into a canal. Machines that built the Suez Canal also dug the new course for the Danube.

European Main Arteries

The street name "Handelskai" still reminds us of the time when Vienna was virtually exploding as the capital of the Austro-Hungarian Empire, one of the great powers in Europe, and there were dreams of turning Vienna into an international commercial port. Of course: the Danube had always been a commercial transport route, even in primeval times. But it was not always navigable for ships and, above all, one could not always travel along it freely. For the Danube had always reflected the political situation in Europe in the true sense of the word.

widergespiegelt. Zuerst der Limes der alten Welt, die Trennung in Zivilisation und vermeintliche Barbarei. Dann ein Fluß, den sich zwei Welten teilten: Der Oberlauf gehörte dem Kaiser, der Unterlauf dem Sultan. Und Wien lag jahrhundertlang gar nicht weit von dieser europäischen Demarkation zwischen den Reichen des Christentums und des Islam. So wie es in diesem Jahrhundert fast fünfzig Jahre lang an der Demarkation zwischen der westlichen Welt und dem kommunistischen Einflußbereich gelegen war. Und heute droht das Schicksal einer Grenze zwischen dem reichen und dem armen Europa.

Seinerzeit mußte man nur eine Grenze passieren, wenn man die Donau befuhr. Heute sind es fast zehn Länder, durch die man fahren kann. Und auch das erst seit kurzem wieder. Denn obwohl mit der Fertigstellung des Kanals zwischen Rhein und Main seit Jahren mit dem irreführend so bezeichneten Rhein-Main-Donau-Kanal eine durchge-

First of all the limes of the ancient world, the dividing line between so-called civilization and the barbarians. Then it became a river that separated two worlds – one side belonged to the Emperor and the other to the Sultan. For hundreds of years, Vienna lay not far off this demarcation line between the realms of Christianity and Islam. Just as in this century when, for almost 50 years, Vienna was sandwiched between the demarcation of the western and the Communist world.

Formerly, there was only one border to pass when using the Danube. Today, there are almost ten countries that one can travel through. But this has only been since recently. With the completion of the canal between the Rhine and the Main, misleadingly referred to as the Rhine-Main-Danube Canal, a continued stretch of water has become passable for ships between the North Sea and the Black Sea but this has only become free again since the end of the war in former Yugoslavia.

hende Schiffahrtsstrecke zwischen Nordsee und Schwarzem Meer besteht, kann man den Kontinent erst wieder queren, seit der Krieg in Ex-Jugoslawien beendet ist. Mit ein Grund, warum es heute (noch?) nicht vor Schiffen wimmelt auf der Donau in Wien. Für Wien ist die Donau immer schon die europäische Lebensader gewesen. Im Mittelalter etwa, als mit dem Stapelrecht die Stadt zu einem Handelszentrum nahe der europäischen Transportwegekreuzung wurde. Heute bemüht sich Wien in der ARGE Donauländer, einem Interessenszusammenschluß aller Regionen, durch die die Donau fließt, Gemeinsamkeiten zu fördern und im neuen Europa die Ost-West-Schnittstelle zu spielen.

Caroline fällt ein Zitat von Elias Canetti ein, der im heute bulgarischen Rustschuk geboren worden war: „Alles was ich später erlebt habe, war in Rustschuk schon einmal geschehen. Die übrige Welt hieß dort Europa, und wenn jemand die Donau hinauf nach Wien fuhr, sagte man, er fährt nach Europa ..."
Canetti später: „Wie viel ich Wien und Österreich geistig schulde, dafür legt, so hoffe ich, jede Seite Zeugnis ab, zu der ich mich bekenne."

Und wieviel schuldet, Wien, schuldet Österreich, seinen Nachbarn am Strome? Caroline hat sich zum Thema Donau den hervorragenden Katalog zur Wiener Milleniumsausstellung „Die Donau, 1.000 Jahre Österreich – eine Reise" mitgenommen, in dem die Bedeutung dieses Stromes für Wien in den verschiedensten Facetten und Dimensionen behandelt wird.

Wien an die Donau

Der Handelskai war also ein Versuch, auch städtebaulich Wien an die Donau zu bringen. Im Jahr 1873 sah Wien eine Weltausstellung, für die ein großer Teil der einstmaligen Insel zwischen dem heutigen Donaukanal und der Donau erst zu Bauland gemacht wurde. Bau-

Another reason why the Danube is still not very full of ships in Vienna.

The Danube has always been the main European lifeline for Vienna; as in the Middle Ages when the city became a trading center along the European transport route. Today, Vienna is endeavoring, within the ARGE Danube countries, to act as a focal point for all the regions through which the Danube flows, to promote common ground and to act as a pivot between East and West in the new Europe.

Caroline is reminded of a quotation by Elias Canetti, who was born in what is today Rustschuk (Ruse) in Bulgaria: "Everything which I later experienced had already happened in Rustschuk. From there, the rest of the world was referred to as Europe, and when someone traveled up the Danube to Vienna, one said he was traveling to Europe ..."
Canetti later: "Every page I have written hopefully bears witness to how much I owe Vienna and Austria intellectually."

And how much does Vienna and Austria owe its neighbors along the Danube? In any case, Caroline had brought with her the excellent catalogue for Vienna's Millennium Exhibition: "The Danube. 1,000 Years of Austria – A Journey", in which the importance of the river for Vienna is described in all its different dimensions and facets.

Vienna on the Danube

The Handelskai was an attempt to extend building in Vienna right up to the Danube. In 1873 a World Exhibition was held in Vienna. This was the first attempt to turn the one-time island that lay between the present Danube Canal and the Danube into building land. So the tourist attraction of looking at buildingsites did not originate in Berlin, after all. At the 1873 World Exhibition one could admire and marvel at the building construction along the Danube from an observation tower.

stellenschauen ist nicht erst in Berlin als Tourismus-Attraktion erfunden worden: bei der Weltausstellung 1873 konnte man von einem Aussichtsturm den Bau des neuen Donaulaufes bestaunen.

Das Gesicht Wiens von der Donau aus wurde jedenfalls für Jahrzehnte geprägt. Und es war kein einladendes Gesicht. Hafengegend eben. Heute ist der Hafen flußabwärts gerückt, unsichtbar sozusagen, aber mit größerer Bedeutung denn je. Denn als der Handelskai fertig war, schlitterte die Monarchie in Schwierigkeiten und zerbrach schließlich. Das Rumpfstück der Republik Österreich brauchte damals keinen Welthafen mehr. Heute hat der Wassertransport aus anderen Gründen wieder an Bedeutung gewonnen und Wien ist der größte Binnen-Containerhafen Europas. Der Handelskai verfiel über die Jahrzehnte. Die damals angestrebte Hochwassersicherheit hatte sich als trügerisch erwiesen. Der ins enge Bett gezwängte Strom suchte die Stadt immer wieder mit verheerenden Hochwässern heim. Doch zwei Weltkriege und die finanzielle Aushungerung Wiens in der ersten Republik ließen alle Wasserbaupläne in weite Ferne rücken. Erst in den sechziger Jahren konnte man wieder investieren und plante den „absoluten Hochwasserschutz" für den Strom, der übrigens durch die Regulierung die Fließgeschwindigkeit eines Gebirgsflusses erreicht hatte! Ein technisches Projekt sah ein „spaghettiförmiges Entlastungerinne" vor. Auf 20 Kilometer Länge sollte die Donau ein Parallelbett bekommen. Als die Bauarbeiten begannen, keimte auch Umweltbewußtsein, keimten bürgerinitiativenähnliche Bewegungen auf. Das Projekt wurde vor allem in den Medien in der Luft zerrissen und zum politischen Zankapfel ersten Grades, an dem eine Jahrzehnte während große Koalition zerbrach. Die Diskussion hatte ihr Gutes: Die damaligen Planungsverantwortlichen starteten ein Verfahren, das als Wiener Modell in die Planungs-

The face of Vienna from the Danube remained the same for decades; and it was certainly not an inviting face, but simply a dock area. Today, the docks are located downstream, out of sight, so to speak, but have assumed more importance than ever. As the Handelskai reached completion, the Monarchy got into difficulties and finally collapsed. The rump of the former empire that became the Republic of Austria no longer needed an international port. Today, water transport has regained importance but for other reasons and Vienna is now the largest inland container port in Europe.

Over the years, the Handelskai fell into decline. The precautions taken against flooding proved deceptive. The river that had been forced into a narrow bed often flooded over, causing havoc in the city. But two world wars and the weak financial position of the First Republic of Austria put paid to any thoughts of new hydraulic constructions for the time being. Only in the 1960s could investments again be made and plans drawn up for complete protection against the dangers of flooding, although with its regulation the Danube had reached the speed of a mountain river!

A technical project produced a spaghetti-like rivulet to relieve the strain. Over a stretch of 20 kilometers the Danube should receive a parallel river bed. As the construction work started, environmental considerations suddenly became apparent and a public campaign was launched. The project was torn to pieces, especially in the media, and became a political issue of the first order, destroying in its wake the political "great" coalition that had been laboriously built up over the past decade.

Of course, the issue was not without its good points. The planning authorities then started a procedure that was to go down in history as a Viennese planning model. The dominance of technology was broken and an interdisciplinary basis created. Open competitions should

geschichte eingehen sollte. Die Vorherrschaft der Technik wurde gebrochen, erste „interdisziplinäre" Ansätze wurden geschaffen, Wettbewerbsverfahren sollten für eine möglichst qualitätvolle Gestaltung des gesamten Donauraums in Wien sorgen. Und auch wenn es aus dem Volksmund nicht mehr wegzubringen ist: Aus dem „Entlastungsgerinne" wurde die Neue Donau. Und es entstand die Donauinsel. 20 Kilometer frei zugängliche Erholungs- und Freizeitlandschaft mitten in der Stadt. Unterschiedlich gegliedert finden sich auf der „Insel" naturnahe Räume, städtische Bereiche (manche meinen, die seien zubetoniert und zu stark verbaut, zu stark kommerzialisiert) und einige „Naturreservate" im Süden der Insel.

Mitten in die Bauarbeiten platzte eine Katastrophe. Am 1. August 1976, an jenem Tag, als Österreichs damaliger „Nationalheld" Niki Lauda in einem Rennwagen fast verbrannt wäre, stürzte in den frühen Morgenstunden die

create the highest quality design for the whole Danube area. Out of the "spaghetti-like" rivulet developed the Neue Donau and, more importantly, the Donauinsel, or "Danube Island", creating 20 kilometers of recreation and leisure terrain in the middle of the city. Differently structured, the "Island" consists of open areas, municipal areas (criticized by some as being too built-up and too commercialized) and, to the south, a nature reserve.

But in the middle of the building work a catastrophe occurred. On 1 August 1976, the day on which Austria's former national hero Niki Lauda was almost burnt to death in a car racing accident, the Reichsbrücke collapsed into the water in the early hours of the morning. Fortune in misfortune: apart from a bus which, thankfully, was without passengers, there was only one car on the bridge at the time. Unbelievable what would have happened had the bridge collapsed in rush hour.

Reichsbrücke ins Wasser. Glück im Unglück: Es war nur ein Bus ohne Passagiere unterwegs, der einzige Autofahrer fand allerdings beim Einsturz den Tod. Unvorstellbar, wenn die Brücke während des Stoßverkehrs eingestürzt wäre. Dem baulichen und politischen Skandal folgte eine unglaublich schnelle Neubauaktion. Das Tempo, in dem diese wichtige Verkehrsader wiederhergestellt werden mußte, und finanzielle Engpässe führten zu einem Brückenbauwerk, über dessen Ästhetik geteilte Meinung herrscht. Die neue Reichsbrücke erfüllt aber ihre Funktionen: Getrennt voneinander können Autos, U-Bahn und Fußgänger und Radfahrer nicht nur die Donau überqueren, die Donauinsel erhielt einen direkten Zugang, eine eigene U-Bahn-Station.

Aus der Insel wurde der städtebauliche Hit dieser Zeit. Die WienerInnen „be-

The building and political scandal was followed by an unbelievably fast rebuilding action. The speed at which this important traffic link had to be rebuilt and the lack of sufficient finances led to a bridge whose aestheticism is a debatable matter.

In any case, more important and successful is its functionality. Separated from one another, cars, subway, pedestrians and cyclists can not only cross over the Danube but the Donauinsel was also supplied with a direct approach with its own subway station.

The Island was the city planning hit. The Viennese occupied the Island as their main recreational area, which saved them the trouble of fleeing from the city at weekends. Up to 300,000 people occupy the Island on sunny weekends and millions visit it for the festivals that take place each year. On a normal working

setzten" die Insel als ihr Haupterholungsgebiet, das einem Wochenend-Stadtfluchten ersparte. Bis zu 300.000 Menschen strömen an schönen Wochenenden, mehrere Millionen zu den jährlichen Festen auf die Insel. Auch an einem ganz normalen Arbeitstag genießen hier tausende Menschen ihre Mittagspause oder nachmittägliche Freizeit.

In den sechziger und frühen siebziger Jahre hätte aus der Insel auch Bauland werden sollen, inzwischen sind größere Bauvorhaben undenkbar geworden. Die finden jetzt in „Transdanubien" statt. Denn die Umgestaltung des Donauraumes hat es auch ermöglicht, daß die Stadt links des Stromes heranwächst. Im Vorfeld des im Wiener Volksmund UNO-City genannten Sitzes der Vereinten Nationen, entsteht die Donau-City. Und die hat eine kurze, aber bewegte Geschichte.

day, thousands of people enjoy there their lunch time break or their free time after work.

According to the planning mentality of the 1960s and early 1970s the area should have been used for building, but meanwhile the idea of large constructions has become unthinkable. These are now taking place in "Transdanubia". The remodeling of the Danube area has allowed building to take place on the left side of the river. In front of the UNO City, the home of the United Nations, the Donau City is coming into being. Its history is short but eventful.

Brücken in die Zukunft

Womit wir wieder bei der internationalen Bedeutung der Donau für Wien wären: Als von einem Fall des Eisernen Vorhanges nicht einmal geträumt werden durfte, was kaum mehr als 10 Jahre her ist, kamen weitsichtige Denker in Wien und der Schwesterstadt Budapest auf die Idee, eine gemeinsame Weltausstellung zu veranstalten. 1995 hätte sich die Welt in Wien und Budapest ein Stelldichein geben sollen und über „Brücken in die Zukunft" sinnieren (so das offizielle Motto der geplanten EXPO.) Für dieses Vorhaben wurde in einem weiteren aufwendigen Planungsverfahren ein Standort gesucht. Unter dem Titel „Chancen für den Donauraum Wien" wurde 1985 ein Ideen- und Planungsverfahren gestartet, das so unterschiedliche Projekte wie das Kraftwerk, die EXPO, aber auch die gesamte Entwicklung im Donauraum unter einen Hut bringen sollte. Für die EXPO wurde dabei das Areal vor der UNO-City gefunden. Ein eigener Wettbewerb brachte unterschiedlichste Gestaltungsvarianten, die vor allem auch bereits die Nutzung des Areals nach der EXPO vorsahen.

Doch die heute Geschichte gewordenen Ereignisse machten allen Planungen einen Strich durch die Rechnung. Wie aus heiterem Himmel fiel der Eiserne Vorhang, es waren keine Brücken mehr zu schlagen zwischen unter-

Bridges into the Future

Which brings us again to the international significance of the Danube for Vienna. Before one ever dreamt that the Iron Curtain would fall, and hardly more than 10 years ago, visionary thinkers in Vienna and its sister city, Budapest, came up with the idea of organizing a World Exhibition. 1995 should have been the year when the world came together in Vienna and Budapest to brood over the "Bridges into the Future"(this was the official motto of the planned EXPO). In an extensive planning period, suitable terrain was sought for the fulfillment of the project. In 1985, under the title "Chances for the Vienna-Danube Area", an idea and planning process was started that would bring the various projects, such as the power station, the EXPO and as the title indicates, the whole development of the Danube area together. For the EXPO the ground in front of the UNO City was found. A competition brought forth many different layout variations for the area which also took into consideration the use of the ground after the EXPO had finished. But the changing face of history thwarted the plans. As if from heaven, the Iron Curtain fell – there were no bridges to be built anymore between two different systems. The much debated EXPO project was clearly shattered in Vienna by a referendum and later in Budapest.

schiedlichen Systemen. Das ohnehin nicht unumstrittene Projekt der EXPO wurde in Wien bei einem Volksentscheid klar abgeschmettert, später sagte auch Budapest das Fest ab.

Die rückblickend gesehen eher negativen Erfahrungen mit der EXPO in Sevilla und die heftigen Diskussionen um die EXPO in Hannover lassen auch in Wien die Meinung aufkommen, daß die beiden Städte vielleicht gar kein Unglück erlitten haben: Großereignisse wie EXPOs sorgen offenbar eher für Irritation in der Bevölkerung und bringen nicht immer den gewünschten Stadtentwicklungsschub. Was in Wien vor allem in intellektuellen Kreisen bedauert wurde und wird, ist die Tatsache, daß die EXPO als Motor und Impulsegeber für eine umfassende Modernisierung der Stadt abhanden gekommen ist. Bis dato konnte kein „Ersatzmotor" aufgetrieben werden.

Nicht verloren waren jedenfalls die Planungsanstrengungen:

Aus dem EXPO-Projekt wurde unmittelbar die sogenannte „Nachnutzung". In der Donau-City soll ein zweites, neues Zentrum fachnutzung". In der Donau-City soll ein zweites, neues Zentrum für Wien entstehen, das den alten Stadtkern entlastet, es auch ermöglicht, diese großartige historische Substanz zu erhalten und zu schützen. Allerdings ist auch das Projekt der Donau-City in Turbulenzen geraten: Die Winde der

The EXPO in Seville and the hotly-discussed EXPO in Hanover helped Vienna draw the opinion that perhaps the two cities were saved a misfortune: huge events such as EXPOs people often find irritating and do not always bring the desired urban development.

What was, and still is, regretted in the intellectual circles of Vienna is that the EXPO would have served as an engine and impulse for a modernization of the city. Until now no new "engine" has been found.

However, all the planning was not in vain: out of the EXPO-project a so-called "after-use" project came into being. In the Donau City, a second, new city for Vienna should come into being which would relieve the old city center and protect its historic substance. However, the Donau City project also came into turmoil. The winds of change within Europe have blown strongly over Vienna, taking with them some ideas. The economic results of Austria joining the EU and, above all, the opening of the Eastern bloc have not been as quick and extensive as hoped for such a project to be worth its while for private investors. At least, not immediately and to the full extent. The competition on the European real estate market has also had its effect: The Donau City can only grow slowly. Which on the other hand increases the chances that a second La Defense on the banks of the Danube will not

Veränderung in Europa haben auch heftig über Wien geblasen und so manche Idee verweht. Die wirtschaftlichen Auswirkungen des EU-Beitrittes Österreichs und vor allem die Ostöffnung haben sich nicht im erwarteten Tempo und Umfang niedergeschlagen. Noch „rechnet sich" das Projekt für private Investoren nicht. Jedenfalls nicht sofort und in vollem Umfang. Die Konkurrenz auf dem europäischen Immobilienmarkt tut ein übriges: Die Donau-City kann nur langsam wachsen. Was auf der anderen Seite die Chance erhöht, kein zweites La Defense am Donauufer zu bekommen. Keine von Riesenhand hingewürfelte Architekturspielzeugstadt, sondern ein harmonisch wachsendes städtisches Ensemble.nicht sieht, ist die gewaltige Infrastruktur, die bereits geschaffen worden ist: Die Donauuferautobahn, Wiens wichtigste Autobahndurchfahrung, wurde auf einer Länge von mehreren Kilometern eingedeckt, Bauland für ein zweites Wiener Zentrum geschaffen und vor allem: Auch Transdanubien rückt an den Strom heran. Die im planerischen Jargon „Entwicklungsachse" genannte Straßenverbindung, die vom Praterstern bis Kagran reicht, ist dem Reißbrett entsprungen und wird gerade bauliche Wirklichkeit.

Ohne daß Wien Ähnlichkeiten mit amerikanischen oder deutschen Metropolen wie Frankfurt anstrebt: Zusätzlich zur klassischen Erscheinung bekommt es

come about. No architectural toy city thrown together by a giant's hand, on the contrary, a harmoniously growing city. Already one can see traces of Vienna's new skyline: what can not be seen is the tremendous infrastructure that has already been created. The Danube riverfront highway, Vienna's most important highway thoroughfare has been covered for several kilometers, building land for a second Vienna center created and, above all: Transdanubia also moves up towards the river. The connecting street from the Praterstern to Kagran was planned at the drawing board and is presently being realized.It is not that Vienna strives to compete with American or German metropolises such as Frankfurt: in addition to its traditional appearance, Vienna is getting a skyline of the 21st century.

A few years ago a hot discussion in Vienna regarding high-rise buildings was carried out. Out of the ideological arguments concerning the height of houses, which often do not exceed the height of church towers, a moderate, pragmatic development has come about. The many architectural competitions and public opinion have also played their part.

Now Caroline has crossed over the Danube. Below left she can see the Copa Kagrana, a city recreation and amusement center with an international atmosphere. For warm summer nights an absolute must! Before her lies the old Danube, an old arm of the Danube river

auch eine Skyline des 21. Jahrhunderts.

Noch vor wenigen Jahren tobte in Wien eine Hochhausdiskussion. Aus dem ideologischen Streit um die Höhe von Häusern, die nur allzuoft das Kirchturmniveau nicht überschritt, ist eine moderate, pragmatische Entwicklung geworden. Wozu sicherlich auch die vielen Wettbewerbsverfahren und die begleitende öffentliche Meinungsbildung ihren Beitrag geleistet haben.

Caroline hat also die Donau überquert und sieht die Copa Kagrana, ein städtisches Erholungs- und Vergnügungszentrum mit internationalem Flair, dessen Gesicht sich allerdings stark ändern wird. Heute für sommerliche Nachtschwärmer ein absolutes Muß.

Vor ihr liegt dann noch die Alte Donau: jener Altarm, der im Zuge der großen Baulandbeschaffung im vergangenen Jahrhundert zu unserem heutigen Glück nicht mehr mit dem Aushubmaterial der Donauregulierung aufgefüllt werden konnte. Ein eindringliches Beispiel dafür, daß auch nicht fertiggestellte Projekte positive Auswirkungen auf das Lebewesen Stadt haben können.

which in the process of creating building land in the last century (to our good fortune today) could not be filled up with the material dug out of the Danube regulation.

A classical example of how incomplete projects can have a positive effect on a city.

Querungen

Es sind zwar keine „tausend Brücken", über die man den engeren Donauraum überqueren kann oder muß, aber das Anwachsen Wiens im Norden hat auch das Brückennetz in den letzten Jahren dichter werden lassen.

Während der Neubau der Reichsbrücke wie bereits erwähnt eine rasche Fertigstellung erforderte und eher zum reinen Zweckbau wurde, während die Brigittenauer Brücke, die durch ihre orangerötliche Färbung auffällt, eine heute noch umstrittene Realisierung eines letzten Teiles des ursprünglich vorgesehenen Wiener Stadtautobahnnetzes (heute ohne Autobahn-Anschluß am rechten Donauufer) darstellte, konnten die weiteren Brücken sorgfältig geplant und auch architektonisch anspruchsvoller gestaltet werden. Beschleunigt wurde das Brückenschlagen im Donauraum vor allem durch die Errichtung des Donaukraftwerkes Freudenau, dessen Aufstau auch die Hebung mehrerer Brücken erforderte.

Die dringend notwendig gewordene Sanierung der Nordbrücke erforderte eine Ersatzbrücke, die nach den Umbauarbeiten als Fußgänger- und Radfahrverbindung mit dem Namen „Nordsteg" erhalten bleibt.

Der U6-Brückenschlag über die Donau erfolgte unmittelbar neben der bestehenden Schnellbahn-Brücke und bietet ebenfalls für Fußgänger und Radfahrer einen separierten Übergang.

Die Hebung, Instandsetzung und Verbreiterung der Praterbrücke schließlich erforderte ein Ausweichbauwerk, das als Donaustadtbrücke für Schnellbusverbindungen über die Donau und als Querung für eine mögliche U-Bahn-Verbindung dienen kann.

Architektonisch gesehen ist die Donaustadtbrücke als Schrägseilbrücke die augenfälligste neue Donauquerung. Sie hat übrigens eine kleine „Schwesterbrücke" für die U6 über den Donaukanal.

Crossings

It isn't really a thousand bridges one has to, or even can, cross, to get across the narrow Danube area. However, the expansion of Vienna in the north has resulted in an increase in bridges over the last few years.

Whereas the new Reichsbrücke which, as already mentioned, had to be built at a fast tempo, is purely functional and the Brigittenauer Brücke, which sticks out on account of its orange-red color and still remains a heavily disputed realization of the last part of the planned Vienna City Highway (without connecting to the right side of the Danube), other bridges could be planned with more care and, from the architectural standpoint, are far superior. Above all, the construction of bridges in the Danube area was speeded up by the construction of the Danube power station in Freudenau whose dam made it necessary to heighten a number of bridges.

The urgently needed renovation of the Nordbrücke called for a temporary replacement, which, once the building work will be completed, will remain as the "North sidewalk" for pedestrians and cyclists. The bridge for the U6 subway crossing the Danube was built directly alongside the existing bridge used by the city metropolitan trains and offers a separate means of crossing for pedestrians and cyclists alike.

The raising, maintenance and widening of the Prater bridge finally called for an alternative construction. The Donaustadtbrücke serves as a fast connecting road over the Danube for buses and could also serve as a possible connecting road for the subway.

From an architectural standpoint, the Donaustadtbrücke with its oblique cables, out of all the Danube bridges, is the bridge that most catches attention. It also has a smaller "sister bridge" for the U 6 subway that crosses the Danube canal.

Einige Fußgängerverbindungen von den Donauufern zur Donauinsel lassen heute schon fast die einstige schwere Passierbarkeit des Donauraumes vergessen.

Stichwort Brücken: Auch fernab der Donau, am Wienfluß, wurde eine bemerkenswerte Brücke neu gebaut: Der „Hackinger Steg" ist nicht nur ein funktionell gelungener Brückenschlag für die Fußgänger, die das Wiental überqueren wollen, er ist auch ein städtebaulicher Akzent des späten zwanzigsten Jahrhunderts an der Westeinfahrt Wiens.

Kraft, die Freude schafft

Das Kraftwerk Freudenau, dessen Lage außerhalb des dichtbebauten Stadtgebietes es sozusagen „unsichtbar" macht, hat weithin sichtbare Folgewirkungen.

Die bauplanende und -ausführende „Donaukraft" hat, wie in allen Stauräumen an der Donau, in engster Zusammenarbeit mit der Stadt Wien fast ein-

On account of the numerous pedestrian crossings available between the river banks of the Danube and the Donauinsel, the once difficult crossing has become a thing of the past.

On the subject of bridges: Far away from the Danube, in fact over the Wien River, a remarkable bridge was newly constructed. The "Hackinger Steg" situated at the west entry to the city is not just a functionally successful bridge for pedestrians crossing from one side of the Wien valley to the other, but also a highlight of late 20th century urban planning.

Power that gives Pleasure

The Freudenau power station whose position beyond the densely built up area of the city makes it "invisible" so to speak, actually has widely visible consequential effects.

"Donaukraft", the company responsible for the planning and building, as with all the dams along the Danube,

dreiviertel Milliarde Schilling in die Ausgestaltung des rechten Donauufers gesteckt.

Von Nußdorf bis zur Freudenau erstreckt sich ein mehrere Kilometer langer neuer Ufer-Park, der insbesondere der Bevölkerung der donaunahen Gebiete der Leopoldau und der Brigittenau dient. In diesen Gebieten rückte und rückt Wien ja auch verstärkt durch Wohnbauten an die Donau. Im gesamten Staubereich wurden auch die Uferwege neu gestaltet, man kann nun tatsächlich wieder „am Wasser" spazieren oder radfahren. Auch das südliche Donauinselufer wurde naturnahe neu gestaltet, insgesamt wurden an der Donau in Wien im Zuge des Kraftwerksbaus 200.000 neue Bäume und Sträucher gepflanzt.

Und auf der Insel selbst wurde ein 1,5 Kilometer langer Umgehungsbach für die Fischwanderung geschaffen, der nach der Erstbepflanzung ein wertvolles neues Biotop darstellt, das dem freien

worked closely together with the City of Vienna and invested almost one and three quarter million Austrian schillings in constructing the right side of the Danube riverbank.

From Nussdorf all the way to Freudenau there is a long, new river bank park. This serves as a place of recreation particularly for the citizens of the Leopoldau and Brigittenau areas which lie next to the Danube. In these regions, on account of the increased building of apartments, Vienna is also moving closer to the Danube.

The river sidewalks throughout the whole dam area were newly constructed. One can now walk, or ride a bike along the side of the water. Altogether there were 200,000 new trees and bushes planted along the Danube in the process of building the power station.

On the island itself a 1,5 kilometer long auxiliary stream was created for fish migration, which after the first planting produced a valuable new biotope. This

Spiel der Naturkräfte überlassen wird. Der Kraftwerksbau bietet auf der Staumauer einen neuen Fußgänger- und Radweg und damit eine neue attraktive autofreie Verbindung aus Simmering zur Donauinsel. Das Projekt Freudenau erzeugt somit nicht nur Kraft (aus Strom), sondern schafft auch Freude für die Menschen, die den Donauraum als Freizeit- und Erholungsgebiet nutzen. Bemerkenswert ist, daß aus heutiger Sicht das Planungsverfahren für diese gravierende Neugestaltung des Donauraumes unter starker Einbeziehung der mitbestimmungswilligen Bürger in jeder Hinsicht erfolgreich und störungsfrei verlaufen ist. Anders als beim Fast-Bürgerkriegsanlaß Hainburg bewies das Wiener Modell, daß die Umsetzung von Großprojekten heute noch möglich ist – wenn auch langwierig und nicht unkompliziert. Unverzichtbar sind dabei entsprechende Umweltverträglichkeitsprüfungen und intensive Bürgerbeteiligung geworden.

Einen nächsten Testfall wird Wien und das angrenzende Umland im Süden übrigens beim Bau der für Wien so dringenden Verbindungsstraße zwischen Ost- und Südautobahn (B 301) zu bewältigen haben. Dabei geht es um die Abwägung zwischen Umweltschutz und der Notwendigkeit, weite Wohngebiete vom bereits vorhandenen schweren Transitverkehr zu entlasten.

biotope has been left to the free forces of nature. The dam wall of the power station serves as a new pedestrian and cycle track and offers an attractive car-free connection between Simmering and the Donauinsel. The Freudenau project not only produces power from electricity but also creates pleasure for the Viennese, who use the Danube area as a place of relaxation. It's quite remarkable from today's point of view that the planning process of this serious new layout of the Danube area was done with the participation of the inhabitants of Vienna. The involvement of the interested citizens in the planning process was in every way successful and trouble-free. In comparison to the Hainburg atomic power station that had almost been the cause of a civil war, the Viennese model proves that the realization of large-scale projects, even when long and complicated, are possible with the relevant environmental protection and the intensive involvement of the citizens.

The next testing case for Vienna and the surrounding area in the south will be to cope with the construction of the urgently needed connecting highway between the east and south freeway (B301). This involves considerations both of environmental protection and the necessity of relieving living areas on the periphery of the city of heavy transit traffic.

Terra incognita
Unknown Land

157

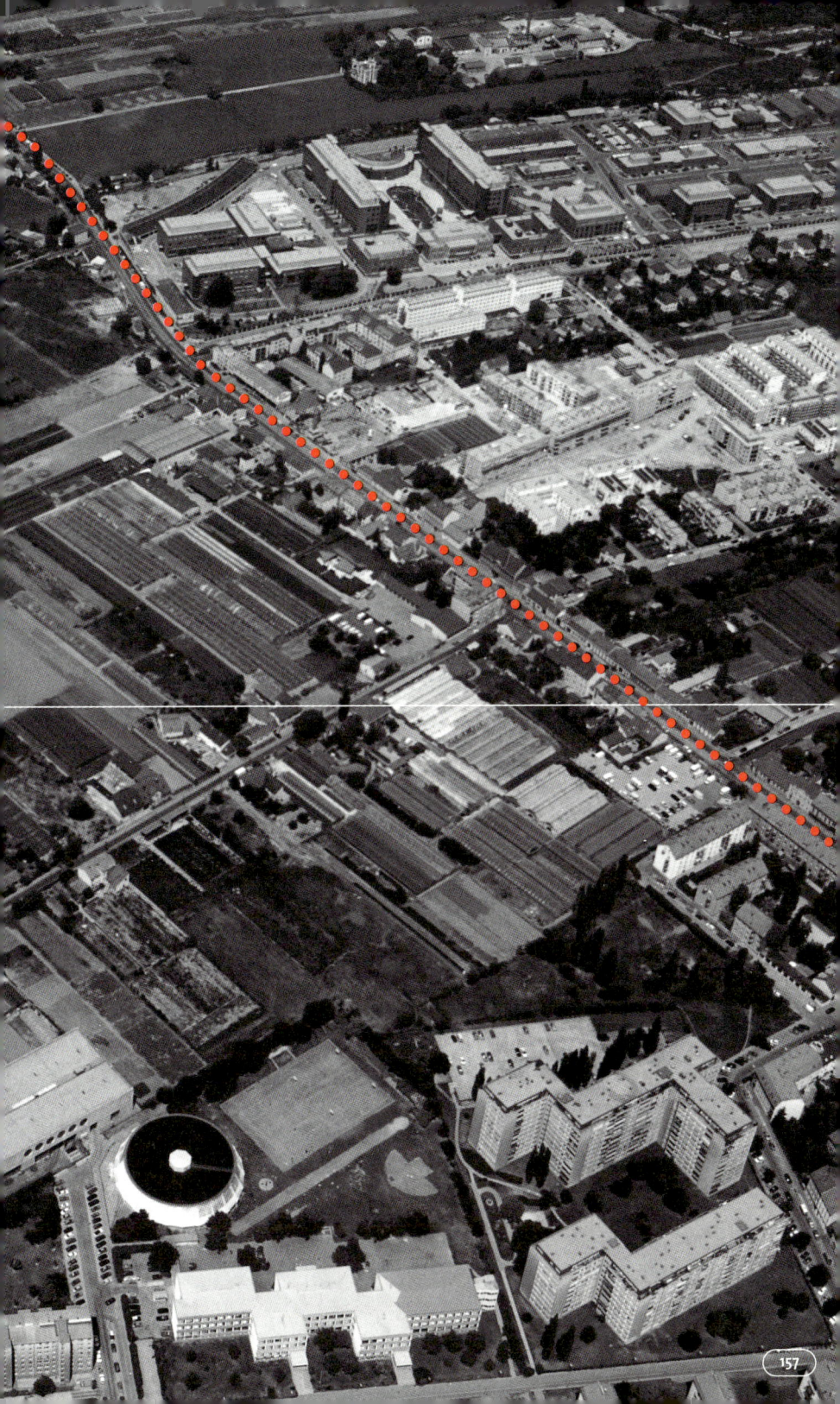

Caroline ist überrascht von der neu sich entwickelnden Skyline jenseits des großen Stromes, die ein Gegengewicht zur „alten" Stadt zu bilden beginnt.

„Über die Donau hinweg, dort ist die Stelle, auf welcher unsere Stadt in nicht allzu ferner Zukunft zu großen Schöpfungen schreiten muß", formulierte Otto Wagner bereits 1930 seine Vision für die Wiener Stadtentwicklungsstrategie.

Otto Wagner hatte richtig vorhergesehen. Die Stadt entwickelte sich in dieser Ebene, in dieser „terra incognita". Donaustadt und Floridsdorf gehören heute zu den größten Wiener Bezirken, nicht nur flächenmäßig.

Und dennoch: Bis heute ist dieses Gebiet nicht richtig „Stadt" geworden. Man muß gar nicht bis an den nordöstlichen Rand Wiens reisen, um festzustellen, daß dort die gebaute „Stadt" weit, weit weg liegt. Die Dörfer inmitten weiter Felder legitimieren sozusagen auch den Status des „Landes", den Wien innerhalb Österreichs auch hat. Und nur langsam arbeitet sich die „Stadt" vor in Richtung Weite.

Caroline läßt sich die Hintergründe dafür erklären: Der starke Bevölkerungszuwachs der letzten Jahre und der erhöhte Wohnflächenbedarf der Wiener führten in den neunziger Jahren zu einem erhöhten Wohnbaubedarf, der in der ersten Welle in den Stadterweiterungsgebieten zu befriedigen war.

Parallel dazu wurde die Stadtverdichtung kontinuierlich weitergeführt, und wenn heute gelegentlich von einem Planungs- oder Baustop auf der grünen Wiese die Rede ist, werden gerne Begriffe und Dimensionen verwechselt. Tatsache ist, daß Wien in den neunziger Jahren die Zahl seiner Wohnungsneubauten auf rund 10.000 jährlich hochgefahren hat und daß dabei fast alle mobilisierbaren innerstädtischen Flächenreserven aufgebraucht wurden. Allein im letzten Jahr erfolgten zwei Drittel der neuen Wohnwidmungen im gut erschlossenen Gebiet.

Caroline is quite surprised by the newly developing skyline which is springing up on the other side of the Danube creating a strong counterbalance to the "old" part of the city.

"Beyond the Danube lies the place where our city must stride, in a not too far distant future for its great creations" was how Otto Wagner in 1930, expressed his vision for the strategy of Vienna's city development.

Otto Wagner was right. The city developed in this plain, in this "terra incognita". Today the Donaustadt and Floridsdorf belong to count among the biggest and most important districts.

Nevertheless, even until today, this area has still not really become part of the "city". One does not have to travel to the north-east edge of Vienna to realize that the "city" built there lies far, far away. The villages in the middle of wide open fields justify so to speak, the definition of countryside, land/state, an attribute which Vienna also enjoys within Austria. It is only slowly that the "city" is working its way into the distance.

Caroline is interested to know the reasons for this development and has it explained to her: the strong population growth over recent years and the increasing need for living space has led to a necessity for residential housing in the 1990s. This need was satisfied by the expansion of the city into these areas.

Parallel to the building activities in the Danube area the intensification of building in the city continued. Today, now and then when there is talk of a planning or building stop in the open countryside, quite often terms and dimensions are confused. The truth of the matter is that Vienna in the 1990s increased its number of new apartments by about 10,000 per year. Every conceivable expanse of ground in the inner city has been used. In the last year alone two thirds of all new apartment buildings where built in well-developed areas.

Wenn nun die Bevölkerungszahl sich zu stabilisieren scheint, hat Wien sozusagen vorgebaut: In den klassischen Stadterweiterungsgebieten wurde widmungsmäßig Vorsorge für künftigen Baubedarf geschaffen. Die nötige Infrastruktur (vor allem leistungsfähige öffentliche Verkehrsmittel) vorausgesetzt, können ohne Vorlaufzeiten qualitätvoll geplante Stadtteile errichtet werden.

If the size of the population seems to have stabilized for the time being, Vienna, so to speak, has taken precautions for the future. In the classical areas of city expansion precautions have been taken for any future building needs. The necessary infrastructure, above all, efficient public transport, could reach the well-planned parts of the city without any problems whatsover.

Architekturmeile

Caroline will sich noch am „Eingang" in die neue Donaustadt umsehen: Wien solle nicht Chicago, nicht Manhattan werden, lauten die (politisch motivierten) Slogans gegen eine bauliche Modernisierung Wiens, von denen sie gehört hatte. Ihr Eindruck: Die unbestimmte Angst vor dem Fremden, dem Anderen, dem Neuen wird dabei auch mit der Höhe von Bauwerken vermantscht. Die Hochhausdiskussion vor einigen Jahren war eine eher irrationale. Ihre Begleiter erzählen ihr: Ein damals unter Mitwirkung von COOP Himmelblau erarbeiteter „Hochhauskriterienkatalog", der möglichst objektiv prüfbare Voraussetzungen für die „Stadtverträglichkeit" hoher Bauten (die in Wien bei 26 Meter beginnen!) definierte, blieb über Jahre mangels konkreter Nachfrage unbenutzt. Umso bemerkenswerter, daß es jetzt gelungen ist, Wien eine neue Architekturmeile zu verpassen, die ohne die

Architectural Mile

Caroline still wants to take a look around the "entrance" to the Donaustadt. Vienna should not turn into Chicago or Manhattan proclaim the politically motivated posters opposing a modernization of Vienna of which Caroline had heard. Her impression: The uncertain fear of something strange, something different, something new is all part of the same syndrome as with the height of buildings. The discussion about high-rise buildings that took place a few years ago was, as already mentioned somewhat irrational. Her companions explained: at that time a catalogue was worked out with the collaboration of COOP- Himmelblau to discuss the criteria for multistory building. It objectively aimed to define the prerequisite for the city's "tolerance" of high buildings(which in Vienna starts at 26 meters!) and remained unused for many years for lack of demand.

gewohnte Proteste der Modernisierungsängstlichen entsteht.

Im Zuge der Donauraumplanungen war das Kerngebiet dieser im Entstehen begriffenen Architekturmeile – wie bereits erwähnt – als Gelände einer geplanten EXPO 95 herausgefiltert worden. Dort wo über Jahrzehnte das Monumentalbauwerk der UNO-City aus der Ebene ragte, das durch seine Solitärwirkung irgendwie auch das Exterritoriale der UNO-Einrichtungen unbeabsichtigt unterstrich, befindet sich Bauland, das bis in die späten achtziger Jahre kaum verwertungswürdig erschienen war. Auf einer alten Deponie gelegen, scheinbar eingezwängt zwischen Alter und Neuer Donau, zwischen Kleinhaussiedlungen und der fast dörflichen Struktur des alten Stadtteils Kaisermühlen, war es kaum Gegenstand baulicher Begehrlichkeiten.

Doch der zunehmende Flächenverbrauch führte auch hier zum Umdenken. Und zur Entwicklung „dichter"

Strukturen. Wo, wenn nicht hier, sollte Wien in die Höhe wachsen? Schmale Grundstücke, hervorragende Verkehrsaufschließung über U-Bahn (10 Fahrminuten bis ins Zentrum) und Autobahn, die Nähe höchstwertiger Freizeitgebiete ließen auch hochwertige Wohnprojekte entstehen. Und die Stadtplanung legte Wert darauf, daß diese markante Bebauung auch höchsten architektonischen Maßstäben gerecht wird.

Die „Neue Donaustadt" kann, erfährt Caroline, auf dem Umweg über diese Bebauung nicht nur baulich an die Donau und damit an das „alte" Wien herangeführt werden, sie kann auch zur „Adresse" werden. Und so drängte sich die österreichische und internationale Architektenelite, als es um die einzelnen Projekte ging. Einen gebot es, aus der fremden Heimat Australien heimzuholen für ein besonders sensibles Projekt: Dort, wo heute die drei hohen Gemeindebauten der Nachkriegszeit zwischen dem Kern von Kaisermühlen und der

Therefore, it's even more remarkable that Vienna has succeeded in building an architectural mile without the usual protests against modernization.

In the planning process of the Danube area the central point for the emergence of this architectural mile, as already mentioned, was an exhibition center for a planned EXPO 95. There, where over a period of decades the monumental building of the UNO City has loomed, which somehow through its solitary position unintentionally emphasizes the exterritoriality of the UN, is building land which until the late 80s was considered unusable. Situated between the old and new Danube on an old disposal site between small housing estates and the almost village-like structure of Kaisermühlen, the ground was hardly desirable building land.

However, with the extensive increase of construction in the area opinion begun to change. Now "denser" planning was in the air. Where, if not here should

Vienna build up into the sky? Small plots of land, excellent transport possibilities through the extension of the subway (10 minutes traveling time to the center) and the highway. Furthermore, the excellent possibilities for free time activities in the area led to the emergence of high quality building projects. The urban planners were particularly eager that the highest architectural standards should there be observed.

Caroline hears that the new Donaustadt, where the Danube connects with the "old" Vienna can become quite a fashionable place to live as a result of the high quality building. The Austrian and international architectural elite showed their eagerness to plan for the various projects as they occurred. One architect (Harry Seidler a Viennese who went to live in exile in Australia) returned from his new-found homeland, Australia to his Austrian roots to work on a particularly sensitive project: where the three high municipality-owned post-

Donau in den Himmel ragen, wird Harry Seidler, Wiener Exilant der Zwischenkriegszeit in Australien, die bauliche Verdichtung herstellen: 600 Wohnungen mit einem signifikanten Hochhaus bilden auf 50.000 Quadratmeter dereinst den „Wohnpark Neue Donau".

Seidler, der etwa die Skyline der Olympiastadt Sydney wie kein anderer Architekt geprägt hat, plant für Melbourne einen mit 500 Metern in der Spitzenklasse der Hochhäuser angesiedelten Turm. Für Wien will er nicht so hoch hinaus, aber „in Wien fühle ich mich nach wie vor zu Hause. Ich liebe diese Stadt. Für mich ist es eine Ehre, an die Tradition des weltberühmten Wiener Wohnbaus anzuknüpfen. In Australien gibt es eigentlich keinen städtischen Wohnbau. Da werden fast alle Wohnanlagen von Privaten gebaut."
Die besondere Faszination für Seidler: „Auch wenn der Grollo Tower eines der höchsten Gebäude der Welt sein wird, ist für mich das österreichische Projekt

war apartment blocks stand, between the center of Kaisermühlen and the Danube, is where Harry Seidler will realize his next project: 600 apartments that will create a significant high-rise building on a space of 50,000 square meters, namely the "New Danube Residential Park".

Seidler, who has influenced the skyline of the Olympia City Sydney more than any other architect is planning a 500 meter top-class, high-rise apartment tower for Melbourne. He doesn't wish to build quite so high for Vienna, but "As always, I feel at home in Vienna, I love this city. It is an honor for me to continue the tradition of the world famous Vienna residential building. In Australia there are hardly any residential buildings councilbuilt. Nearly all residential parks are privately built." The special fascination for Seidler: "Even if the Grollo Tower is going to be one of the highest buildings in the world, the Vienna project is more interesting for me. The fact is, that amongst architectural peers the Vienna

wichtiger: Der Wiener Wohnbau ist in Fachkreisen weltberühmt. Ich bin stolz, mit dem ersten Projekt in meiner Geburtsstadt Teil dieser Tradition zu werden." Daß dies ein Mann sagt, der 1938 nach dem Einmarsch der Hitlertruppen seine Heimat fluchtartig verlassen hatte müssen, darf auch als Zeichen gewertet werden, daß das Wien des ausgehenden zwanzigsten Jahrhunderts erfolgreich daran gearbeitet hat, eine seiner dunkelsten Phasen im Umgang mit einzelnen Bevölkerungsgruppen zu bewältigen.

An der Reichsbrücke wächst auch der erste Hochbau der Donau-City: Wilhelm Holzbauer errichtet hier den „Andromeda Tower". Hans Hollein zeichnet für den künftigen Schulbau in der Donau-City verantwortlich. Und Gustav Peichl und der japanische Stararchitekt Tara Isozaki planten einen Zwillings-Hochhausturm. Diese Türme und der rund 100 Meter hohe Turm des Harry Seidler-Projektes werden dereinst das „Tor" zur

building tradition is world famous. I am proud to be involved in this first major project in the city of my birth and to become part of this tradition."

That these comments should be made by an individual, who in 1938, after the invasion of Hitler's troops had to flee the city of his birth is of special note. Furthermore, it is a sign how Vienna towards the close of the 20th century has successfully worked on getting over one of the darkest phases in its dealings with individual sections of the population.

By the Reichsbrücke can be found the first example of building construction in the Donau City: Wilhelm Holzbauer is building the "Andromeda Tower" here. Hans Hollein is responsible for the plans of the future school building and Gustav Peichl and the Japanese star architect, Arata Isozaki, have planned a twin highrise apartment block.

These twin apartment blocks and the circa 100 meter high block from Harry Seidler will form the "gateway" to the

Donaustadt bilden und für Orientierung wie für urbane Identität in der heutigen „terra incognita" sorgen.

Ein Stück stadtauswärts nach der UNO-City ist eine weitere Hochhausgruppe fast fertiggestellt. Im anschließenden Wohnpark Alte Donau werden drei Gebäude von Gustav Peichl (zusammen mit Rudolf Weber), von NFOG (Nigst-Fonatti-Ostertag-Gaisrucker) und von Coop Himmelblau – übrigens der erste Wohnbau in ihrer Heimatstadt Wien – für futuristische Akzente sorgen.

Wenn Wien also auch keinerlei Absicht hat, hinsichtlich der Sicherheitsverhältnisse mit amerikanischen (oder anderen) Großstädten verglichen zu werden: Hinsichtlich der neuen modernen Architektur an der Hochhausmeile zwischen Alter und Neuer Donau ließe es sich etwa einen Vergleich mit der amerikanischen Architekturmetropole Chicago durchaus gefallen.

Caroline möchte sich diese wachsende Hochhauslandschaft aus einer anderen Perspektive ansehen und tut dies am besten vom höchsten bestehenden Gebäude dieser Gegend aus: Auf dem einst als Wahrzeichen der Wiener Internationalen Gartenausstellung 1964 errichteten Donauturm befindet sich eine Aussichtsterrasse und ein sich drehendes Restaurant, von dem man nicht nur die „Neue Donaustadt" gut beobachten, sondern fast ganz Wien überschauen kann.

Kagran: Auf dem Weg zum Zentrum

Eine Großstadt braucht ein Zentrum. Soweit, so einfach und selbstverständlich. War es aber in dieser neuen Donaustadt bis vor gar nicht allzulanger Zeit keineswegs. Eingefleischte Wiener vom rechten Donauufer rümpften bereits angesichts der U1-Endstationsanzeige „Zentrum Kagran" die Nase ob derartiger innerstädtischer „Provinzialität". Tatsächlich war auch über viele Jahre ein Einkaufszentrum („Donauzentrum") neben

Donau City and will serve as points of orientation and urban identity in the present "terra incognita".

A stretch further outwards from the city beyond the UNO City building a further high-rise block is almost completed. In the connecting "Old Danube Residential Park" three buildings by Gustav Peichl (together with Rudolf Weber), NFOG (Nigst-Fonatti-Ostertag-Gaisrucker) and COOP Himmelblau – by the way, their first building in their hometown Vienna, will be highlights of futuristic building.

Whereas Vienna has no intention of being compared to American, or other large cities as far as security goes, concerning its architecture along the architectural mile between the old and new Danube it would be quite happy to be compared with the architectural metropolis Chicago.

Caroline would like to see this developing area of high-rise-story buildings from another perspective and does this from the highest building in the region: from the Danube Tower that was built for the Vienna International Garden Exhibition in 1964. Here from the observation terrace and the rotating restaurant it is possible not only to see over the new Donau City but over almost the whole of Vienna.

Kagran: On the Way to the Center

Every city simply needs, quite understandably, a center. This was not the case in the new Donau City until recently.

The deep-rooted Viennese from the right side of the Danube River started to turn up their noses at the inner city "provinciality" when the terminus of the U1 subway was called "Kagran Center". The truth of the matter is that the only prominent construction in the district of Donaustadt for many years was a large shopping center.

Caroline discovers that even here a tremendous change is taking place and

der U1-Endstelle der einzige markante Ort im Bezirkszentrum der Donaustadt. Caroline stellt fest, daß auch hier eine gewaltige Veränderung und städtische Verdichtung einsetzt. Sind es einerseits die zuvor erwähnten Stadterweiterungsgebiete in der östlichen Donaustadt (Donauspital, Langobardenstraße, Erzherzog-Karl-Straße, Aspern), wächst die Donaustadt auf der anderen Seite mit Floridsdorf zusammen.

Als Beispiel empfehlen ihre Begleiter Caroline (diese Gebiete liegen nicht an der Reiseroute) die östlichen Teile der Donaustadt. Man kann dorthin einen Ausflug mit der Straßenbahnlinie 26 vom Zentrum Kagran aus machen. Richtung Aspern, entlang der Langobardenstraße und angrenzend an das Donauspital („Sozialmedizinisches Zentrum Ost") findet man einen von Anfang an voll funktionsfähigen Stadtteil. Weiter östlich davon liegen die größten Reserveflächen auf dem Areal des einstigen Flugfeldes Aspern, die erst erschlossen werden können, wenn das „Rückgrat", ein leistungsfähiger S-Bahn-Betrieb auf der vorhandenen S80-Strecke möglich ist. Während Carolines Besuch in Wien hatten die Republik Österreich und das Land Wien über die Finanzierung dieser Ausbaumaßnahme in den kommenden Jahren verhandelt. Erfolgreich, aus Wiener Sicht.

Noch weiter „draußen" bilden die alten Ortskerne von Eßling und Süßenbrunn (wo ein bemerkenswertes Wohnprojekt an einem Golfplatz entstanden ist) gewachsene Kristallisationspunkte für neue Stadtteile. Hier, im Nukleus dieser Entwicklungen, stellt die Albert-Schultz-Eishalle den ersten sichtbaren architektonischen Akzent (Architektenteam Müller, Berger, Krismer) dar. In unmittelbarer Umgebung wird ein multifunktionales Zentrum mit einem Multiplex-Kino und einer Parkgarage das Gebiet weiter aufwerten.

Und weil Caroline vorher die entstehende Wiener Architekturmeile bewun-

an increase of building activity is the result: on the one hand in the above-mentioned expansion areas in the east of Donaustadt ("Sozialmedizinisches Zentrum Ost" hospital, Langobardenstrasse, Erzherzog-Karl-Strasse, Aspern) and on the other hand in those parts where Donaustadt is coalescing with the district of Floridsdorf.

By way of an example, Caroline's companions recommend the eastern parts of Donaustadt (which are not part of the itinerary). They can be reached from Kagran Center by the no. 26 tram. In the direction of Aspern, along Langobardenstrasse and bordering on the "Sozialmedizinisches Zentrum Ost" hospital can be found a fully-functioning new district. Further eastward lie the largest expanses of land still unused, on the former Aspern airfield. These can only be developed once an efficient Schnellbahn link-up via the existing S80 line is put in place. During Caroline's visit to Vienna, the Austrian Government and the province of Vienna had been negotiating over the financing of this future extension. With great success, from the Viennese point of view.

Even further "out", the old centers of Essling and Süßenbrunn (where a remarkable residential project on the edge of a golf course had been completed), form natural points of crystallization for new districts.

Here at the nucleus of this development the Albert Schultz ice-stadium is the first noticeable architectural highlight (built by the team of architects Müller, Berger, Krismer). In the nearby vicinity a multifunctional center with a multiplex movie-house and a huge parking garage will further increase the area's value.

Because Caroline had admired the emergence of the architectural mile mention must be made of the activities further outwards on Wagramerstrasse. At the intersection between Wagramer/ Eipeldauerstrasse a vision of city shaping

dert hatte: Weiter draußen an der Wagramer Straße (im Kreuzungsbereich mit der Eipeldauerstraße) besteht die Vision eines Stadtteilvorhabens, das von den Planungen der Architekten Eric Moss, Michael Sorkin, Mark Mack, COOP Himmelblau, Raimund Abraham, Carl Pruscha, Thom Mayne und Martha Schwartz getragen ist.

Für Wien war es ein toller Erfolg, einige der innovativsten jungen Architekten der USA für ein soziales Wohnbauprojekt zu gewinnen. Andererseits stellte das Planungsverfahren aber auch für die Jungstars der amerikanischen Architekturszene eine besondere Herausforderung dar, weil es sozialen Wohnbau in den USA in dieser Form nicht gibt.

Rund 500 Wohnungen, Geschäfte und andere Infrastruktureinrichtungen wurden in diesem Verfahren für das an der künftigen U1-Verlängerung gelegene Projekt geplant.

Wien innovativ

Caroline besteigt jetzt die Straßenbahnlinie 26 Richtung Floridsdorf und unternimmt eine Reise zu neuen Universitäten und innovativen Wohnbauprojekten.

Die Donaufelderstraße, durch die sie der 26er schaukelt, hat ihren Namen nicht zufällig. Hier befanden sich bis vor kurzem ausgedehnte Felder, Reste davon sind noch sichtbar. Was daran erinnert, daß Wien einen für eine Großstadt ungewöhnlich hohen Landwirtschaftsanteil hat und sich theoretisch autark versorgen könnte. In Zahlen: 1.560 Hektar landwirtschaftlich genutzter Fläche findet man innerhalb der Stadtgrenzen, fast 1.300 landwirtschaftliche Betriebe wurden noch 1990 registriert. Insgesamt werden mehr als die Hälfte der 42.000 Hektar großen Bundeshauptstadt land- und forstwirtschaftlich genutzt. Neben dem klassischen und weltberühmten Weinbau wird in Wien vor allem Gemüse angebaut.

is coming about with planning done by the architects Eric Moss, Michael Sorkin, Mark Mack, COOP-Himmelblau, Raimund Abraham, Carl Pruscha, Thom Mayne and Martha Schwartz.

To win some of USA's young, innovative architects for a municipality housing project was a great success for Vienna. On the other hand, it was rather a challenge for the young stars of the American architectural scene because municipality housing complexes in this form do not exist in the USA.

Around 500 apartments, stores and other infrastructural facilities were planned for this area, which in the future will be reachable by the extension of the subway U1.

Innovative Vienna

Caroline boards the no. 26 tram in the direction of Floridsdorf and makes an excursion to the new universities and innovative housing projects.

Donaufelderstrasse, through which the tram rocks, did not get its name by sheer coincidence. Until a short while ago the area was surrounded by fields, the remains of which can still be seen. This reminds us of the fact that Vienna, as a major city has an unusual high proportion of farming land and could theoretically, provide for itself. In figures: 1560 hectares arable land lie within the city borders, almost 1,300 farms were registered in 1990. Altogether more than half of the 42,000 hectares federal capital is used for agriculture and forestry. Besides the world-famous wine production Vienna mainly grows vegetables.

Caroline passes extensive housing estates. She realizes that the old university City of Vienna now has a faculty on the ìotherî side of the Danube. Long before the discussion started whether the University for Economics or part of the University for Technical Sciences should be moved to the Donau City, the building of the University for Veterinary Medicine

Künftige Generationen werden in diesem neuen Stadtteil aber nur mehr vom Namen an das Donau-"Feld" erinnert werden. Schon heute fährt Caroline an ausgedehnten Wohnanlagen vorbei. Und registriert, daß die alte Universitätsstadt Wien auch diesbezüglich über die Donau gewachsen ist. Lange bevor es Diskussionen darüber gab, ob etwa die Wirtschaftsuniversität oder Teile der Technischen Universität in die Donau-City übersiedeln sollten, hatte der Bau der Veterinärmedizinischen Universität hier an der Donaufelderstraße begonnen. 1996 wurde diese ausgedehnte Anlage, die sich nach einigen kosmetischen Veränderungen auf Betreiben der Stadtplanung heute als campusähnliches Areal gut in die Umgebung einfügt.

Stichwort Campus: In Wien ist der Campus-Gedanke bisher nicht wirklich heimisch geworden, wie Caroline erfährt, und es mag auch an der Streuung der universitären Einrichtungen über

had already begun in Donaufelderstrasse. In 1996 this widespread complex, after a few minor cosmetic changes instigated by the urban planners, fits well into the surrounding region, the area having a campus-like atmosphere.

Keyword Campus: In Vienna the idea of a campus is something not really familiar as Caroline discovered. It could be due to the fact that the various faculties of the university are situated in different parts of the city that many Viennese do not realize. Vienna, with more than 200,000 people actively, or passively involved in university education, represents a true metropolis of learning.

Further plans with a promising future in the Donaufeld region concern the area referred to as "Sun City". Here 700 apartments for almost 2,000 people are being built designed by the architect team "Atelier 4". With this European-wide, outstanding ecological housing project 70% of the energy for warm water and 20% of heating energy will be gained through

weite Teile der Stadt nie ins Bewußtsein der Wiener gedrungen sein, daß Wien mit rund 200.000 Menschen, die im Bereich der höheren Bildung „passiv" oder aktiv beteiligt sind, eine wahre Bildungsmetropole darstellt.

Zukunftsträchtig sind auch die anderen Vorhaben im Bereich des Donaufeldes: Sun City nennt sich die „Sonnenstadt Donaufeld". Hier werden nach Plänen des Architektenteams „Atelier 4" 700 Wohnungen für fast 2.000 Menschen gebaut. Insgesamt werden bei diesem europaweit herausragenden ökologischen Wohnbauprojekt 70 Prozent der Energie für Warmwasser und 20 Prozent der Raumwärme durch insgesamt 6.000 Quadratmeter Sonnenkollektoren auf den Dächern gewonnen.

Die Vergabe an insgesamt sieben Bauträger sorgte für architektonische Vielfalt und soziale Durchmischung. Neben den Wohnungen entsteht ein Seniorenzentrum, ein Studentenheim und Nahversorgungseinrichtungen.

6,000 square meters of solar collectors placed on the roof.

The allocation of the work between seven building contractors provides architectural variety and social diversity. Besides the apartments there will be a senior citizens' center, a students' residence and general grocery stores.

As in other new parts of the city there will be a special transportation concept evolved to keep the housing project free from traffic as far as possible.
At the present time in the Donaufeld area a project is in progress, the largest in Europe, planned solely by women. Especially over the last few years female architects have shown how successful they are. The housing project situated at Donaufelderstrasse/Carminweg represents so to speak "a part of the city made by woman's hand". The ultimate aim: to create new and better everyday living standards for everyone based on the experiences of women.

Wie auch bei den anderen neuen Stadtteilen wird ein spezielles Verkehrskonzept für möglichst viele verkehrsberuhigte Bereiche innerhalb der Anlage sorgen.

Im Wiener Donaufeld entsteht gerade der europaweit größte von Frauen geplante Stadtteil. Gerade in den letzten Jahren sind zunehmend auch weibliche Architekten siegreich aus verschiedenen Verfahren hervorgegangen. Die „Frauen-Werk-Stadt" an der Donaufelderstraße/Carminweg soll aber sozusagen „ein Stück Stadt aus Frauenhand" darstellen. Vordringlichstes Ziel dabei ist, auf Grundlage der Erfahrungen von Frauen neue Alltagsqualitäten für alle Bewohnerinnen und Bewohner zu schaffen. Auf 2,3 Hektar entstehen 350 Wohnungen für rund 1.000 Menschen.

In dem auf Initiative des Wiener Frauenbüros durchgeführten Verfahren ging das städtebauliche Leitprojekt von Franziska Ullmann (die auch im Süden Wiens, „In der Wiesen", plant) siegreich hervor. Mit ihr planen Gisela Podreka, Elsa Prochazka und Liselotte Peretti. Jede Architektin betreut 80 bis 100 Wohneinheiten.

Die Frauen-Werk-Stadt setzt einige Akzente wie das Wohnen und Leben „zwischen Drinnen und Draußen", transparente, also einsehbare Stiegenhäuser zur Vermeidung von Angsträumen, die Renaissance der Wiener „Pawlatschen", Kommunikationsräume und vor allem variable Wohnungen, die die Küche als Arbeitsplatz und Aufenthaltsort berücksichtigen. Wert legten die Planerinnen auch auf besonders demokratisches Planen und Bauen.

On 2.3 hectares, 350 apartments for around 1,000 people will be built.

The building project initiated by the Vienna Office of Women's Affairs was triumphantly won by Franziska Ullmann (who is also responsible for the planning of the "In der Wiesen" project in the south of Vienna). Gisela Podreka, Elsa Prochazka and Liselotte Peretti are planning with her. Each architect will be responsible for 80–100 apartments.

The women's housing project aims to highlight the quality of living and life, between "outside and inside", clear, transparent, visible staircases, the avoidance of closed-in rooms and the rebirth of the Viennese "Pawlatschen"(a balcony going round the inner walls of a building). Emphasis is laid on rooms that promote communication – the kitchen is a place of relaxation, as well as work and above all, variety within the apartments themselves. The architects have also laid great emphasis on democratic planning and building.

Auto-los

Immer wieder ist Caroline fasziniert von der „autofreien" Planung: Auch hier wird der Autoverkehr weitestgehend aus der Anlage verbannt.

Besonders „radikal" das nächste Vorhaben: bei der Fultonstraße entsteht der „Autofreie Stadtteil". Auf Initiative des Grünen Stadtrates und Planers Christoph Chorherr werden rund 250 Wohnungen für bis zu 800 Menschen entstehen, die bereit sind, ohne eigenes Auto zu leben. Statt wie in Wien üblich 1 Stellplatz pro Wohnung werden hier höchstens 10 Prozent davon errichtet.

Der Standort befindet sich zwischen der U1-Station Kagran und der U6-Station Franz-Jonas-Platz und wird durch die Straßenbahnlinie 26 und den neuen 27er erschlossen.

Einkaufsmöglichkeiten sind in unmittelbarer Nähe vorhanden, vor der Haustür liegt das Erholungsgebiet Alte Donau. Für jene, die auf das Auto nicht

Car-free

Caroline is continually fascinated by the "traffic-free" planning. Once again in the above-mentioned project cars are mostly not allowed in the residential area.

One quite "radical" intention is the development of a traffic-free part of the city at Fultonstrasse. At the initiative of the City Councillor and planner Christoph Chorherr, 250 apartments for around 800 people are being built for those who are prepared to live without a car.

Instead of providing one parking lot for each apartment as is the norm in Vienna, this project at the utmost will only provide 10% parking ground.

This project is located between the U1 subway station Kagran and the U6 Franz Jonasplatz and will be served by the no.26 and the new no. 27 tram.

Shopping possibilities are available in close proximity as well as the recreational area of the old Danube. For those who cannot do without a car completely a

ganz verzichten wollen oder können, ist car-sharing vorgesehen.

Stichwort Erholung: Wesentlicher Bestandteil der auch im Wiener Stadtentwicklungsplan festgeschriebenen Stadtverdichtungs-Philosophie ist die Grünversorgung. Gerade weil dicht und kompakt gebaut wird, keine Flächenverschwendung, wie etwa im Wiener Umland mit seiner Einfamilienhaus-Struktur, betrieben wird, kann Grünraum gesichert werden. Müssen etwa in manchen Teilen agrarisch genutzte Flächen der Stadterweiterung weichen (Ersatzflächen werden selbstverständlich angeboten), wird gleichzeitig Wiens Grüngürtel geschlossen und Grünkeile werden Richtung Zentrum gezogen.

Mittlerweile nähert sich der 26er dem Zentrum von Floridsdorf, Caroline entdeckt wieder alt-gewachsene Stadt.

Das Hoch im Norden

Der 26er setzt die kleine Reisegesellschaft am Franz-Jonas-Platz ab (benannt nach einem legendären Wiener Bürgermeister der Nachkriegszeit und österreichischem Bundespräsidenten). Hier bietet sich Caroline das Paradebeispiel für die Gestaltung eines der höchstrangigen Verkehrsknotenpunkte Wiens im Zusammenhang mit dem städtebaulichen Umfeld. Im Zuge der U6-Verlängerung hierher wurden nicht nur die Bahnhofsanlagen, sondern der gesamte Vorplatz neu gestaltet. Floridsdorf, das in seinem Zentrum unter einer wahren Verkehrslawine litt, wird schrittweise vom Verkehr befreit. Die U6-Anbindung ist ein erster wichtiger Schritt, nach der U1-Verlängerung in den Norden ist die Verlängerung der U6 bis Stammersdorf vorgesehen.

Und auch der Individualverkehr soll um das Zentrum Floridsdorf geführt werden. Die Verlängerung des Auto-

form of car sharing is being planned.

Key word relaxation: An important part of the Vienna city development philosophy is the provision of sufficient green area. Because of the compact way buildings are erected, no area is wasted as is the case in the surrounding countryside with its individual house structure and it is possible to secure that adequate green is left. Although certain agricultural areas have had to give way to urban development (naturally replacement areas were offered) at the same time Vienna's green belt will be joined-up and green corridors will cut into the direction of the city center.

Meanwhile the no. 26 tram approaches Floridsdorf and Caroline discovers another part of the city which has grown "old".

Northern Highs

The 26 tram stops at the Franz Jonas Platz and the small group of passengers alight. (This square was named after the legendary post-war Viennese mayor who was also the President of the Austrian republic.) Here Caroline sees a superb planning example of a Viennese traffic junction designed in combination with the urban surroundings. In the process of the U6 subway extension not only was the train station completely newly laid out but the whole forecourt as well. The center of Floridsdorf that suffered heavily under congestion is gradually being freed from traffic. The U6 connection is the first important step in this direction. After the further extension of the U1 to the north the U6 will be extended as far as Stammersdorf.

It is also aimed to relieve the center of Floridsdorf from private transport as well. The extension of the expressway feeder over Brünnerstrasse in the direction of

bahnzubringers über die Brünner Straße Richtung Leopoldau war ein erster Ansatz, um eine weitere Verlängerung als Bundesstraße Richtung Donaustadt wird noch heftig diskutiert. In Floridsdorf soll auch ein weiteres „transdanubisches" Hochhaus entstehen: Die „Florido-Plaza".

Caroline nimmt jedenfalls den 31er Richtung Stammersdorf und gleitet unbehelligt vom Autoverkehr in den Norden Wiens. Gleich zu Beginn passiert die „Bim", wie sie in Wien liebevoll genannt wird, den Schlinger-Hof, einen der Parade-Gemeindebauten des Roten Wien, der sich frisch renoviert präsentiert. Hier sorgt auch einer der vielen Wiener Märkte für gute Nahversorgung.

Nach der Querung des Autobahnzubringers und der Schnellbahn kommt das Betriebswirtschaftliche Zentrum der Universität Wien in Sicht, das zum Kern der „Universitätsstadt Floridsdorf" werden soll. Die gesamte Sozialwissenschaftliche Fakultät der Uni Wien soll hier auf den ersten Wiener Campus übersiedeln. Bis zu 8.000 Studenten könnten hier leben und studieren, 800 Arbeitsplätze im Gefolge.

Kurz danach eines der letzten Großwohnbauprojekte der siebziger Jahre: Der Heinz-Nittel-Hof. Heinz Nittel war jener Wiener Stadtrat, der am 1. Mai 1981 von einem Terroristen, erschossen worden ist. Die monumentale Anlage mit Trutzburg-Charakter markiert das vor-

Leopoldau was the first step. It is still a matter of hot debate whether to extend it further as a federal highway in the direction of the Donaustadt. A further high-rise, "transdanubia" apartment block is planned for Florisdorf: the "Florido-Plaza".

Caroline in any case takes the 31 tram in the direction of Stammersdorf and travels unmolested by traffic to the northern part of Vienna. Straight away the tram, referred to as the "bim" in Vienna, passes one of the most foremost examples of municipal buildings built in "Red Vienna" between the two world wars which has just undergone complete renovation. Here, one also finds one of the many Viennese markets that provide excellent products for local inhabitants.

After crossing the expressway feeder and the high-speed railway one catches sight of the Business Management Center of the University of Vienna that will be the core of the "University town Florisdorf". The complete social sciences faculty of the University of Vienna plans to move here forming the first Vienna Campus. Up to 8,000 students will be able to live and study here and the campus will also create 800 new jobs. A little further still Caroline comes across one of the last large building projects of the 1970s: the Heinz Nittel-Hof. Heinz Nittel was the Vienna City Councillor who was shot dead by a terrorist on 1 May 1981.

läufige Ende der „alten Besiedlungspolitik" im Norden Wiens.

Ab der Gerasdorfer Straße beginnt ein Mustergebiet für das Neue Wien. Eine alte Planung aufgreifend, wurden und werden hier fast viertausend Wohnungen errichtet, was der Dimension einer Kleinstadt entspricht. Caroline stellt fest, daß die Straßenfronten der kilometerlangen Bebauung an beiden Straßenseiten beim Erstbesucher für unangenehme Assoziationen sorgen, daß sich aber dahinter eine neue Wohnlandschaft auftut, die durch bauliche Vielfalt, eine schon heute funktionierende Infrastruktur und einen unmittelbaren Zugang zu Erholungsräumen (Marchfeldkanal, Bisamberg) besticht.

The monumental building with its character of defiance marks the end of the "old settlement policy" in the northern part of Vienna.

Gerasdorferstrasse is a perfect example of the "new Vienna". Taking up an old plan, almost 4,000 apartments were, and are being built, taking on the dimension of a small city.

The kilometer-long apartment building project, which covers both sides of the street can occasionally create unpleasant associations for someone seeing it for the first time, but Caroline soon realizes that behind these fronts, a new form of residential living has been created. This residential living area is interesting because of the variety of the buildings themselves, a well- functioning infrastructure and an easy accessibility to recreational areas (Marchfeld canal, Bisamberg).

Wien macht Schule

Caroline findet in diesem Siedlungsgebiet im Bereich der Ocwirk-Gasse auch ein Vorzeigebeispiel für die neue Wiener Schulbaukultur: Ein Bau von Gustav Peichl, mustergültig für die neue Architektur einer Schule als Lern- und Lebensraum. Hier verbringen die Schüler den größten Teil des Tages. Verschiedene Vereine haben Mitnutzungsmöglichkeiten, sodaß die Schule nahezu rund um die Uhr in Betrieb ist. Ein Kommunikationszentrum für diesen neuen Stadtteil also und ein Beispiel für die neue Wiener Schulgesinnung. Identitätsstiftend auch für das „Viertel", das in einem Zug errichtet wurde. Architektonisch markant ist der zentrale elliptische Baukörper. „Zu schön um wahr zu sein" übertitelte die kritische Wiener Stadtzeitung „Falter" einen Beitrag über den neuen Wiener Schulbau der letzten Jahre und vermerkt, daß es gelungen ist, einige renommierte Architekten dafür zu gewinnen. Hans Hollein war der erste gewesen, der aufgrund der komplexen und komplizierten Situation am Bauort (in Währing, Köhlergasse) in einer Planungszeit von 11 Jahren einen heute weltweit beachteten neuen Schulbau konzipiert hatte.

Christian Zillner schreibt im „Falter" aber auch über die gesellschaftlichen Dimensionen des Schulbaus: **„Billig, häßlich, einfallslos und weder auf die**

Viennese Schools

In the housing scheme, situated in Ocwirk-Gasse Caroline also finds a noteworthy example of the new way in which Viennese schools are being built. The building by Gustav Peichl is a prime example of new school architecture creating a place of learning and living. Here, pupils spend most of the day while different organizations and clubs have an opportunity of using the property for their activities in the evenings. In this way the school is almost in use 24 hours a day, a new communication center for this part of the city and an example of a new educational policy in Vienna. Furthermore, the building has given an identity to a district that sprang up almost in one go. Architecturally, the central oval-shaped building is heavily interesting.

"Too beautiful to be true" was the headline of the critical Viennese city newspaper "Falter" in an article concerning the building of schools in Vienna over the last few years, and commenting upon the success of winning renowned architects for these projects. Hans Hollein was the first architect, who over a planning period of 11 years (as a result of the complex and complicated situation on the building site in Währing, Köhlergasse) created a new school building concept which has received notable consideration world-wide.

Menge der Schüler und Lehrer, noch auf deren Bedürfnisse abgestimmt – unsere allgemeine Schularchitektur ist das Ebenbild unseres Bildungswesens. Gebäude und Lehrer sorgen für einen bleibenden schlechten Eindruck. Und anderswo? In New York beispielsweise hätte der republikanische Bürgermeister Giuliani gern beinharte Burschen aus der Wirtschaft als Leiter des kommunalen Schulsystems, um das für seine Begriffe überbordende Bildungsbudget nach privatwirtschaftlichen Gesichtspunkten einzudämmen. Tatsächlich gibt es aber seit zwei Jahren ein unabhängiges Komitee aus New Yorker Geschäftsleuten, das sich mit dem Problem des kommunalen Schulwesens befaßt. Seine Mitglieder besuchten Schulen, analysierten den Zustand der Gebäude und der Lehrverhältnisse und kamen zu folgendem Urteil: Wenn nicht sofortige und weitreichende Maßnahmen zur Instandsetzung der Gebäude getroffen werden, ist anzunehmen, daß in naher Zukunft Schüler, Lehrer oder Verwaltungspersonen getötet werden. Für solche Endzeitprophezeiungen hat Giuliani freilich kein Gehör. Die Wiener Stadtregierung ist glücklicherweise zarter besaitet als der Chefzyniker des Big Apple."

Caroline muß schmunzeln beim Vergleich mit dem Big Apple und läßt sich erklären, daß man in der Stadtplanung zwar Herrn Zillners Meinung über das Wiener Schulwesen nicht ungeteilt

Christian Ziller writes in the "Falter" also about "the social dimensions of school building":
"Cheap, ugly, lacking creativity, and not conceived for the number of pupils or teachers and their needs – our general school architecture is a reflection of our education system. Buildings and teachers ensure a permanent bad impression. How is it elsewhere? In New York for example, the republican mayor, Giuliani, would like to have hard business men from the world of commerce as leaders of the communal school system. These leaders should check the, in his opinion, overstrained budget for education along private economic lines. Actually, for the last two years there has been a private independent committee of New York business people looking into the problems of the communal school system. Its members visited various schools, analyzed the conditions of the buildings and the teaching environment and came to the following conclusion: when immediate and adequate measures are not undertaken to renovate school buildings, then it can be assumed that some time soon, pupils, teachers or running staff will be killed. Naturally, Giuliani shows no interest for such prophecies of the final days. The Vienna city government is fortunately more sensitively strung than the chief cynic of the Big Apple".

Caroline can't help smiling at the comparison with the Big Apple. She is

übernehmen will. Immerhin ist das österreichische Bildungssystem trotz aller Verbesserungsnotwendigkeiten im internationalen Vergleich hervorragend, und gerade in Wien bemüht sich ein innovativer und engagierter Stadtschulrat um noch mehr Qualität. Aber die Absicht hinter dieser auch architektonisch markanten Schulbauoffensive liegt auf der Hand: Den Schülern einen Lebens- und Arbeitsraum zu schaffen, der möglichst wenig Streß und Aggression aufkommen läßt. Und sie in diesem Lebensalter qualitätvolle Architektur auch im wahrsten Sinne des Wortes erleben zu lassen. Sozusagen als außerschulischer Lebensbildungs-Auftrag. Mündige Menschen, so die Maxime, lassen sich auch keine totalitäre, menschenverachtende Architektur bieten.

Das Schulbauprogramm umfaßte unter anderem auch die ebenfalls von Gustav Peichl geplante Schule im Stadterweiterungsgebiet Wienerberg (Favoriten), die Hauptschule Absberggasse in Favoriten, von Rüdiger Lainer inszeniert, oder Boris Podreccas Ganztagesschule in der Liesinger Dirmhirngasse sowie die Projekte einer ganzen Reihe junger Architekten.

Besonders bemerkenswert findet Caroline die Bilder von der gläsernen Schule von Helmut Richter in der Penzinger Waidhausengasse. Die deutsche Fachzeitschrift „Transparent" beschreibt sie als **„implantierten ... gläsernen Kri-**

told that in the Urban Planning Department, not everyone is prepared to adopt Mr. Ziller's opinion about the Viennese school system. At any rate the Austrian educational system, despite improvements that might be necessary, is excellent by international standards. In Vienna in particular, a committed and innovative Board of Education is continually looking for improved quality. The intention behind this architectural offensive in school building is quite clear: to present the pupils with a living and working ambiance where as little stress and aggression as possible can arise. To offer them already at this age the experience of quality architecture. In other words, responsible human beings, so the maxim, will not accept a totalitarian and inhuman architecture.

The school building program involves, the school in Wienerberg (Favoriten) also planned by Gustav Peichl, the junior high school in Absberggasse in Favoriten planned by Rüdiger Lainer and the school in Dirmhirngasse in Liesing by Boris Podrecca, as well as a whole series of further buildings by young architects.

Caroline finds the pictures of the school made of glass, designed by Helmut Richter and situated in Waidhausengasse in the Penzing district quite remarkable. The German Architectural magazine "Transparent" describes the building as an **"implanted glass crystal which is an incredible provocation for**

stall, der für die Gemeinschaft der Wiener Hausmeister, Baubeamten und die ansässigen Grantler eine Wahnsinns-Provokation bedeutet". Und bezogen auf die unmittelbare Nähe eines Friedhofes: „Es prallt ein Organismus aus verglasten, also offenen und fließenden Räumen auf die statische Archaik des Wiener Totenkults." Und: „In der Tat sind die Coolness und die meist eben glatten technischen Oberflächen gewöhnungsbedürftig, gerade dann, wenn man selbst in Schulen mit rauher Ziegelschale groß geworden ist."

the Viennese mentality" *and refers to the cemetery which lies directly opposite the school* "It collides as a glazed organism of open rooms flowing one into another against the static archaic reality of the Viennese cult of the dead. In fact the coolness and for the most part smooth, technical surfaces of the building do take some getting used to, especially when one grew up in schools which were constructed of raw red brick."

Erweiterte Stadt

Zurück zur Stadterweiterung Brünner Straße. Stadterweiterung stand einige Zeit im Geruch, billige Wohnungsversorgung bar jeglicher Infrastruktur zu liefern. Verkehrsmäßig isoliert, mithin auch in gesellschaftlicher Isolationslage. Auch Wien hat seine einschlägigen Erfahrungen mit derartigen Projekten, wobei man bei aller gebotenen Selbstkritik behaupten kann, daß etwa das bereits erwähnte „Schöpfwerk" in Meidling oder die Großfeldsiedlung in Floridsdorf schon zur Zeit ihrer Fertigstellung in den siebziger Jahren deutlich mehr Qualität hatten als vergleichbare Quartiere in anderen Städten.

Dennoch: Es gehört zum Credo der heutigen Stadtplanung, Widmungen nur mehr dann zuzulassen, wenn entsprechende Infrastruktur gewährleistet ist. Selbst das Vorzeigeprojekt der Stadterweiterung, der Wienerberg, litt in den ersten Phasen aufgrund zu geringer Dichte und daher marktwirtschaftlich zu geringer Nachfrage an einer Unterversorgung an Einkaufsmöglichkeiten.

Hier, in der Brünner Straße, wurden die bereits vorhandenen Grundsatzplanungen daher in dieser Hinsicht genauestens überprüft und adaptiert, sodaß sich diese Kleinstadt am Großstadtrand heute voll funktionsfähig präsentiert. Caroline findet in den Planungen Volksschulen und eine Hauptschule und meh-

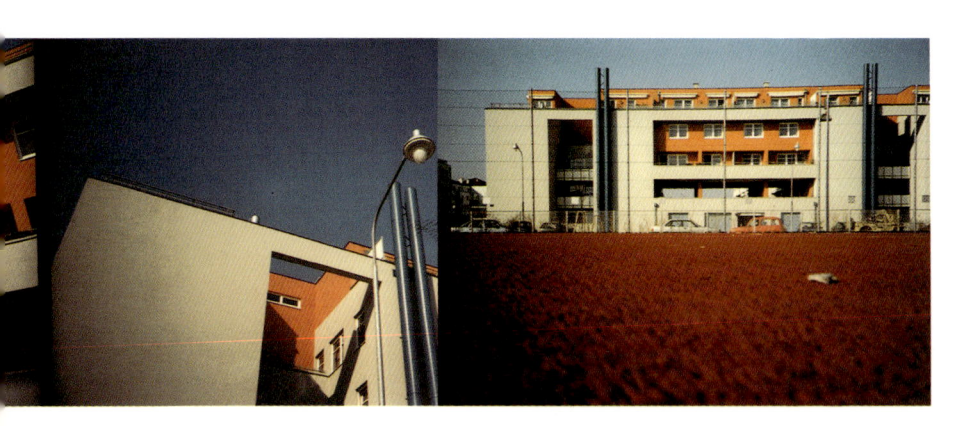

Expanding City

Back to the expanding city in Brünnerstrasse. For a while the city extension plans stood in a bad light and it was rumored, living quarters were being provided without the necessary infrastructure. An area isolated from society and transportation. Vienna has had its appropriate experiences with projects of that kind. However, it must be said, even with the necessary self-criticism, the already-mentioned "Schöpfwerk" in Meidling or the Grossfeld housing estate in Floridsdorf, at the time of their construction in the 1970s had clearly more living quality than comparative buildings in other cities.

Nevertheless, today part of the creed of urban planning is always to guarantee an optimum of infrastructure. Even Vienna's prime building project, the Wienerberg, suffered in the first phase because it wasn't compact. Economically, small businesses were not prepared to invest in the area and consequently this led to a lack of shopping facilities.

In Brünnerstrasse these aspects were looked into, given utmost consideration and plans adopted accordingly so that this "small city" bordering on the periphery of the city functions perfectly. Caroline finds elementary schools, a junior high school and kindergartens to be in agreement with Vienna standards. Shopping possibilities are numerous.

rere Kindertagesheime. Für die Versorgung gibt es ein Nahversorgungszentrum mit Supermärkten und Einzelgeschäften und dem für Wien so wichtigen Kaffeehaus. Zwei Nebenzentren und ein Wochenmarkt ergänzen das Angebot. Ein Jugendzentrum, eine Außenstelle der Volkshochschule und eine Musikschule stehen zur Verfügung. Arztordinationen, eine Apotheke und Einrichtungen der sozialen Erwachsenenbetreuung sind bereits vorhanden.

Besonderes „Zuckerl" für die Stadtrandbewohner ist das ausgedehnte Freizeit- und Erholungsgebiet des Marchfeldkanals, der sich zwischen den großen Bauteilen hindurchschlängelt. Wegen der Senkung des Grundwasserspiegels im Marchfeld (der Kornkammer Österreichs), die aufgrund der vergangenen Donauregulierungen und der intensiven Bewässerung der Felder eingetreten war, mußte eine künstliche Wasserzufuhr geschaffen werden. Der Marchfeldkanal „verläßt" die Donau etwa auf der Höhe des Einlaufbauwerkes der Neuen Donau und durchquert den 21. Bezirk bis hinaus in das Marchfeld, wo er in den Rußbach mündet. Bei der Gestaltung dieses „Kanals" wurde auf Naturnähe großer Wert gelegt, und diese „Natur aus zweiter Hand" liefert sozusagen im Nebeneffekt Erholungswert für die Neu-Städter an der Brünner Straße.

There is a large shopping center with supermarkets, grocery stores and the obligatory coffee house as well as a weekly fruit and vegetable market. Furthermore there is a youth center, evening classes, a music school, doctor's surgeries, a drug store and a social service's center helping grown-ups.

A tremendous plus-point for the local inhabitants is the wide variety of free-time and recreational possibilities on offer along the Marchfeld canal. Because of the sinking of the ground-water level in the Marchfeld, which occurred on account of the regulation of the Danube and the intensive irrigation of the fields, an artificial water supply had to be made. The Marchfeld canal "leaves" the Danube approximately at the level of the dam on the new Danube and crosses the 21st district until it reaches the Marchfeld when it flows into the river Russbach. As this canal was being planned special attention was given to creating a construction as close to nature as possible. An excellent side effect of the canal is the recreational value for the "new city" dwellers of Brünnerstrasse.

181

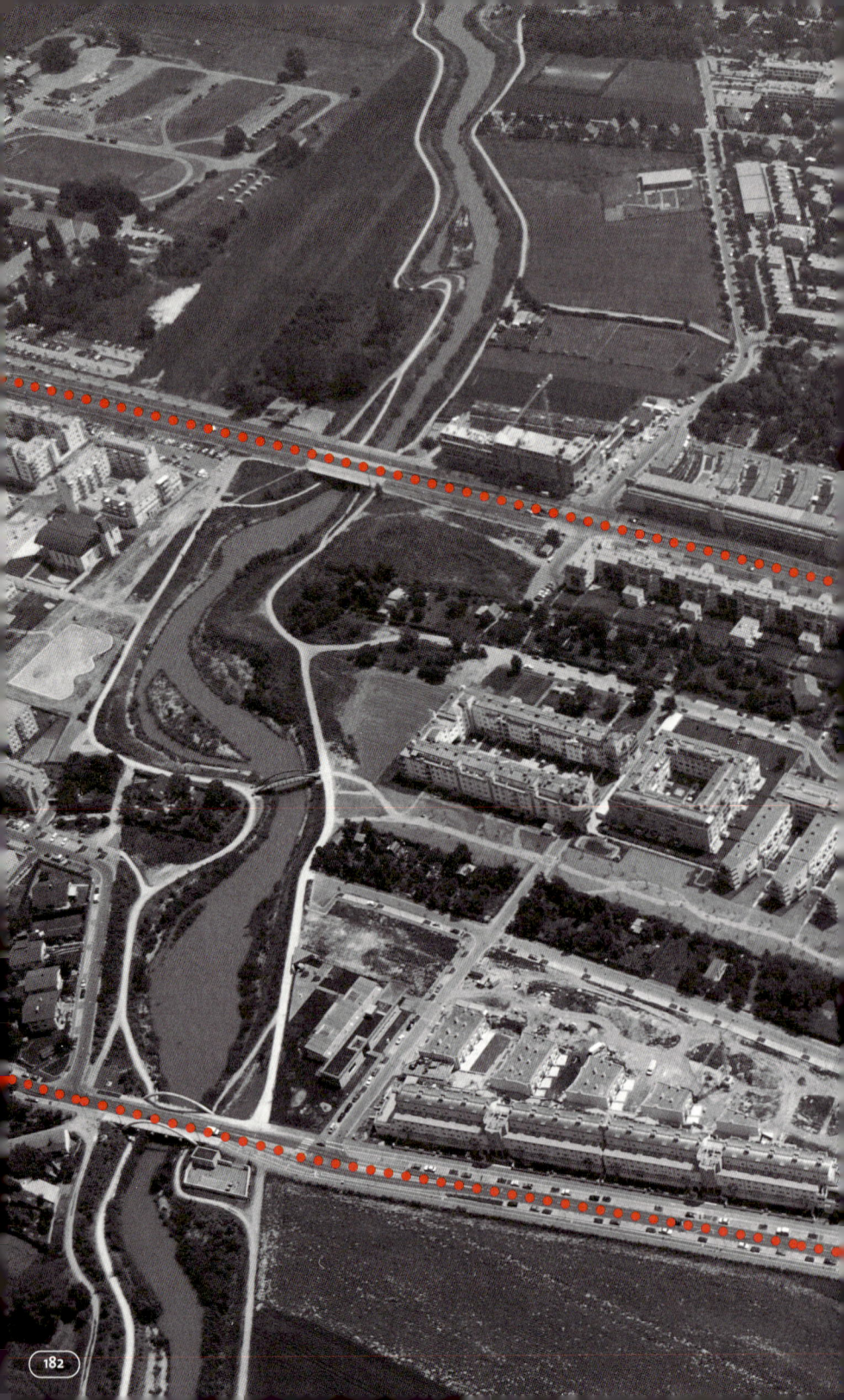

183

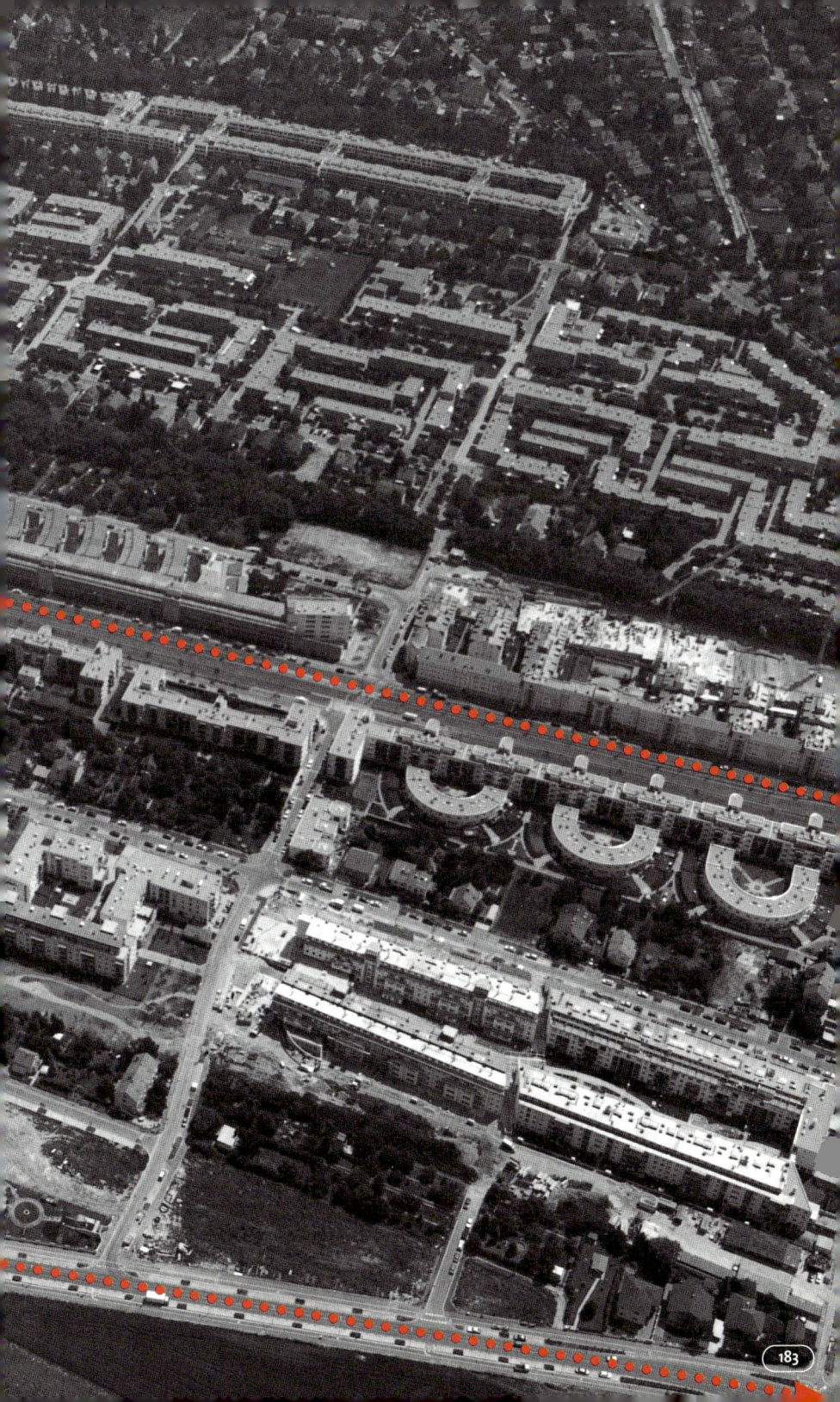

Die vergessenen Dörfer

Diesen Titel gab der bereits zitierte „Falter" einer Story über die sogenannten alten Ortskerne in Wien. Einen solchen Ortskern haben wir als nördlichsten Zielpunkt unserer Wien-Reise gewählt. Von der Endstation der Straßenbahnlinie 31 sind es nur mehr wenige Schritte in das alte Stammersdorf, eines jener Dörfer, die sich auf Wiener Stadtgebiet noch sichtbar erhalten haben. Für die Bewohner der neuen Stadtteile ist es eine nahegelegene gastronomische Bereicherung ihres Alltages: Hier finden sich traditionelle „Heurige", die im Gegensatz zu ihren touristisch überschwemmten Pendants in den klassischen Heurigenorten im Westen Wiens (etwa Grinzing) sich ihre Originalität weitestgehend bewahrt haben.

Deutlich erkennbar ist hier noch die dörfliche Siedlungs- und Baustruktur. Unangenehm, den dörflichen Charakter beinahe schon zerstörend, ist der durchflutende Verkehr. Eine der wenig spektakulären, aber dringend notwendigen Aufgaben der Stadtplanung war es daher in den letzten Jahren, Orte wie dieses Stammersdorf in ein Schutzzonenprogramm aufzunehmen, das sowohl die identitätsbewahrende Unterstützung und Beratung bei Bauvorhaben beinhaltet wie auch die Reduzierung des Schwerverkehrs zum Ziel hat. Tempobegrenzungen sind erste Schritte zur Verkehrsberuhigung, angestrebt werden, wo möglich, Umfahrungen.

Diese Dörfer bilden in den Stadterweiterungsgebieten auch hervorragende Kernzonen für eine behutsame Verdichtung (Beispiele: Süßenbrunn, Eßling oder Aspern). Wenn auch in den kommenden Jahren die Stadterweiterung aufgrund stagnierender Bevölkerungszahlen nicht im gleichen Tempo wie bisher weitergeht, wird man diesen Dörfern in der Stadt besonderes Augenmerk schenken müssen. Und vielleicht tut ihnen diese Pause auch ganz gut.

The forgotten Villages

This was the title given to a story that appeared in the already quoted newspaper "Falter" about the old village centers on the outskirts of Vienna. We have chosen one of these old town centers as the most northern point of our Vienna journey. From the 31 tram terminus one only has to go a few meters on foot to reach the old center of Stammersdorf, a place within the boundaries of Vienna which has still retained its originality. For the inhabitants of the new parts of the city it is a near-by gastronomic enrichment of their everyday life. It is here that one finds the traditional "Heurige" still in their original state as opposed to the "Heurige" in Grinzing, in the West of Vienna visited by many tourists.

The village housing and building structure is clearly recognizable here. The traffic which flows through almost destroys the village-like character. One of the least spectacular, but most urgent and necessary tasks for the city planners over the last few years was to place villages such as Stammersdorf under a protective program. The aim, of course, being the protection of the village identity. A further task is the reduction of heavy traffic. Strict tempo restrictions are already in force. The City Council is striving for alternative bypass roads as far as this is possible.

These village regions provide excellent centers for a cautious expansion of the city, Süssenbrunn, Essling and Aspern are good examples. When the city extension into these regions does not take place at the same tempo as earlier, basically on account of the stagnation of total population, one would be wise to give these small villages in the city one's special attention. Anyhow, perhaps the ease in building construction is good for them.

Even further north still, and difficult to reach with public transport, lies an especially significant area for Vienna's green belt: the "Rendezvous Berg". Caro-

Noch etwas nördlicher und mit öffentlichen Verkehrsmitteln noch nicht gut zu erreichen, liegt ein für die Sicherung des Wiener Grüngürtels besonders bedeutsames Gebiet: Der Rendezvous-Berg. Caroline läßt sich seinen Namen erklären: Er geht auf eine denkwürdige Begegnung („Rendezvous") zwischen Napoleon, der vor der Einnahme Wiens stand, und dem Erzherzog Karl zurück. Für Wien brachte das Rendezvous nichts – Napoleon nahm die Stadt, um hier aber auch erstmals mit Mißerfolgen konfrontiert zu werden. Dieses Areal ist für Caroline aber aus einem anderen Grund interessant. Sie will Informationen zum Thema „Grün in Wien".

line has its peculiar name explained: it leads back to a memorable meeting between Napoleon, who was about to seize Vienna, and the Archduke Karl. The rendezvous was unsuccessful for Vienna – Napoleon seized the city – only to be confronted, for the first time with failure.

This area is of interest to Caroline for another reason – the theme "Green in Vienna".

Grüner Gürtel

„Zur Wahrung der sanitären Interessen der Bewohner" hatte der Wiener Gemeinderat 1905 die Schaffung eines Wald- und Wiesengürtels beschlossen.

Damit war vor allem der Wienerwald unter einen Schutz gestellt, der ihn letztlich auch zwei Weltkriege und die damit verbundenen Brennholz-Schlägerungen der notleidenden und frierenden Wiener Bevölkerung überleben ließ.

Mit dem Wiederaufbau Wiens nach dem Zweiten Weltkrieg machte Wien städtebaulich den ersten großen Schritt über die Donau, wo scheinbar unbegrenzte Flächen zur Verfügung standen. Mit immer größerem persönlichen Anspruch auf Wohnraum (1910 waren es noch 10 Quadratmeter pro Einwohner, 1991 verfügte jeder im Schnitt über 33 Quadratmeter) wuchs auch der Flächenbedarf für den Wohnbau. Dazu kamen noch die notwendigen Betriebsbaugebiete.

The Green Belt

"To protect the sanitary interests of its inhabitants" the Vienna Council in 1905 decided to create a belt of forests and meadows around the city.

Above all, the Vienna woods were placed under protection. During two world wars the trees were chopped down to help the suffering and freezing Viennese inhabitants survive.

With the rebuilding of Vienna after World War II the first steps were taken to build on the other side of the Danube where unlimited area was available. With the continual increase in living space demanded by the individual (in 1910 it was 10 square meter per person, in 1991 on average 33 square meters per person), the need for more building space grew. This also led to the necessary building of industrial areas.

Whereas Vienna perhaps no longer grows at the tempo and to the extent that was predicted a few years ago, it has

Auch wenn Wien nicht in jenem Tempo und Ausmaß wächst, wie es noch vor wenigen Jahren prognostiziert wurde, stößt es bald an seine nachhaltig verträglichen Grenzen im Flächenverbrauch.

Hätte Wien im Wohnbau ähnlich „großzügig" agiert wie andere österreichische Bundesländer, gäbe es heute keinen unverbauten Fleck mehr innerhalb der Stadtgrenzen. Dazu kam ein neues Verständnis der Menschen für den Umgang mit der Umwelt, mit dem erlebbaren Grün. Als sich vor fast einem Vierteljahrhundert ein Politstreit um den „Sternwartepark" (im grünreichen Villenbezirk Währing) entzündete, war das der Auftakt für eine neue politische Disziplin. In einer Abstimmung entschied die Mehrheit der Wiener, daß dieser Park nicht verbaut werden dürfe (geöffnet, wie dies damals gefordert worden war, wurde der Park aber für die Öffentlichkeit bis heute nicht). Aufgrund dieser Abstimmungs-„Niederlage" nahm damals übrigens ein Bürgermeister seinen Hut ...

Den Höhepunkt der neuen Bürgerbewegung im Kampf ums Grün erlebte Österreich Mitte der achtziger Jahre, als wenige Kilometer von Wien entfernt an der Donau bürgerkriegsähnliche Auseinandersetzungen um die Errichtung eines Donaukraftwerkes tobten. Die damals auf politischer Ebene angesagte Nachdenkpause führte zu nachhaltigen Veränderungen in der Planungshaltung.

Für Wien selbst bedeutete es nicht zuletzt eine Wende in der Stadtentwicklungspolitik. Stand noch Anfang der achtziger Jahre eine geplante Wohnbebauung auf den grünen Steinhofgründen im Westen Wiens am Rande des Wienerwaldes im Mittelpunkt einer Volksbefragung, wo das Projekt eine klare Abfuhr erlebte, sind die Anrainer (im weiten Sinne) heute schon von allem Anfang an in die Widmungs- und Entscheidungsverfahren miteinbezogen.

Caroline wird später in den planerischen Unterlagen blättern: Im Stadtentwicklungsplan von 1994 findet diese

almost reached the limits it is bound to by contract.

If Vienna had built as "generously" as other states in Austria then there would not be any unused area within the city borders.

Additionally, people began to be aware of the environment and to understand how it should be treated. As a political battle started almost 25 years ago regarding the "Sternwartepark" (situated in the green villa district of Währing) this was the impulse for a new political discipline. After a referendum the Viennese population decided that the park area should not be built upon (incidentally, the park is still not open for the general public). As a result of the referendum defeat the then mayor of Vienna resigned. The climax of the Viennese battle to conserve green areas occurred in the 1980s as a few kilometers from Vienna, on the Danube, a power station was to be built. There was almost a revolt among the Viennese. Since then the promised

"rethink" has led to lasting changes.

For Vienna itself it meant a turning point in urban development policies. At the beginning of the 1980s a planned building development on the grounds of the green Steinhofgründe, situated in the West of Vienna, on the border of the Vienna woods was the central theme of a referendum. The project was rapidly abandoned. Nowadays, people in the neighborhood are involved in the decision making from the very start.

Later on Caroline will take a look at the planning documents. In the 1994 Urban Development Plan Vienna's new environmental awareness finally found its expression. Its aims and principles are set down in this plan.

Exactly 90 years after the Vienna Woods were placed under protection, the city planning commission decided upon a "green belt for Vienna".

Within the framework of a green security program for the South and West, after the "1,000 Hectare Program North-

„Wienerische" Grün-Bewußtseinsänderung ihren deutlichen Niederschlag. Die wesentlichen Grundsätze und Ziele sind darin enthalten.

Genau 90 Jahre nach Unterschutzstellung des Wienerwaldes präsentierte die Stadtplanung den „Grünen Gürtel für Wien". Im Rahmen eines Grün-Sicherungsprogrammes für den Süden und Westen wurden- nach dem „1.000 Hektar-Programm Nord-Ost" die Voraussetzungen für die Schließung dieses Grüngürtels geschaffen.

Über die Grünversorgung in den inneren Bezirken hat Caroline bereits am Beispiel des Bezirkes Neubau erfahren, vor allem von der diesbezüglichen Änderung der Wiener Bauordnung. Sie soll die Sicherung und Ausweitung von Grün im dichtbebauten Gebiet gewährleisten. Hier, am Rendezvous-Berg, beginnt auch ein Grün-Zug, der hin bis zur Alten Donau führt. Ein Wiener Charakteristikum: Grün soll nicht nur „portionsweise" in der Stadt (etwa in Parks) vorhanden sein oder am Stadtrand zur Verfügung stehen, sondern möglichst auch zwischen den Stadtentwicklungsachsen vernetzt werden.

Der Landschaftsplan für den Rendezvousberg sieht eine vielfältige Ausgestaltung und inhaltlich naheliegende Nutzung vor: Sozusagen reanimiert soll die Natur hier werden, um in diesem Biotop die ortstypische Vegetation wieder sichtbar und erlebbar zu machen. Daneben sind aber auch Forschungseinrichtungen vorgesehen. Die Deponien sollen landschaftsgestalterisch eingesetzt werden. Das künftige Naherholungsgebiet für die Bewohner an der Brünner Straße ist von dort aus entlang des Marchfeldkanals verkehrsfrei zu erreichen.

Caroline gefällt die Wiener Vision: Die Windverhältnisse auf dieser Anhöhe bieten sich für die Errichtung von Windrädern zur Energieerzeugung an. Möglich, daß hier Wiens erstes Windkraftwerk entsteht.

East", the prerequisites for the closing of this green belt were created.

Caroline had already found out through the example of the district of Neubau about the provision of green areas in the inner city and the changing of the Viennese building regulations. These changes should secure the continuance and the extension of green areas in densely built-up districts.

Here on the Rendezvousberg, a green section starts that extends to the old Danube. A Vienna characteristic: green should not just be available in "portions" throughout the city (in parks for example), or on the city borders, but as far as possible through the whole of the inner city districts.

The landscape plan for the Rendezvousberg shows a varied design, and obvious utilization. In other words, nature should be re-encouraged in this biotope, in order to make the typical vegetation of the region visible again. Alongside this, there are plans for research installations and disposal sights integrated into the landscape. The future recreational area from here along the Marchfeld canal is to be reached traffic free for the local inhabitants of Brünnerstrasse.

Caroline is quite impressed with the Viennese vision: the wind conditions at this altitude offer the possibility of constructing wind generators for the production of energy. It is possible that Vienna's first wind power plant will be constructed here.

Caroline would like to visit a "Heurigen" in Stammersdorf and will take a cab back to the U6 subway station Floridsdorf – on the way, she will ask the cab driver to go via Strebesdorf in order to see a further old town center, but also, to take a look at city extensions that had been made in the early years of expansion. In Floridsdorf she continues her journey, where she takes the subway to return to the city center.

Caroline würde gerne einen „Heurigen" in Stammersdorf besuchen und wird mit dem Taxi zurückfahren zur U6-Station Floridsdorf und den Taxifahrer bitten, über Strebersdorf zu fahren, um einen weiteren alten Ortskern, aber auch Beispiele der Stadterweiterung der frühen Jahre zu sehen.

In Floridsdorf nimmt sie dann ihre Reise per U-Bahn wieder auf, um in die „Stadt" zurückzukehren.

Sightseeing im Donauraum
Sightseeing in the Danube Are

191

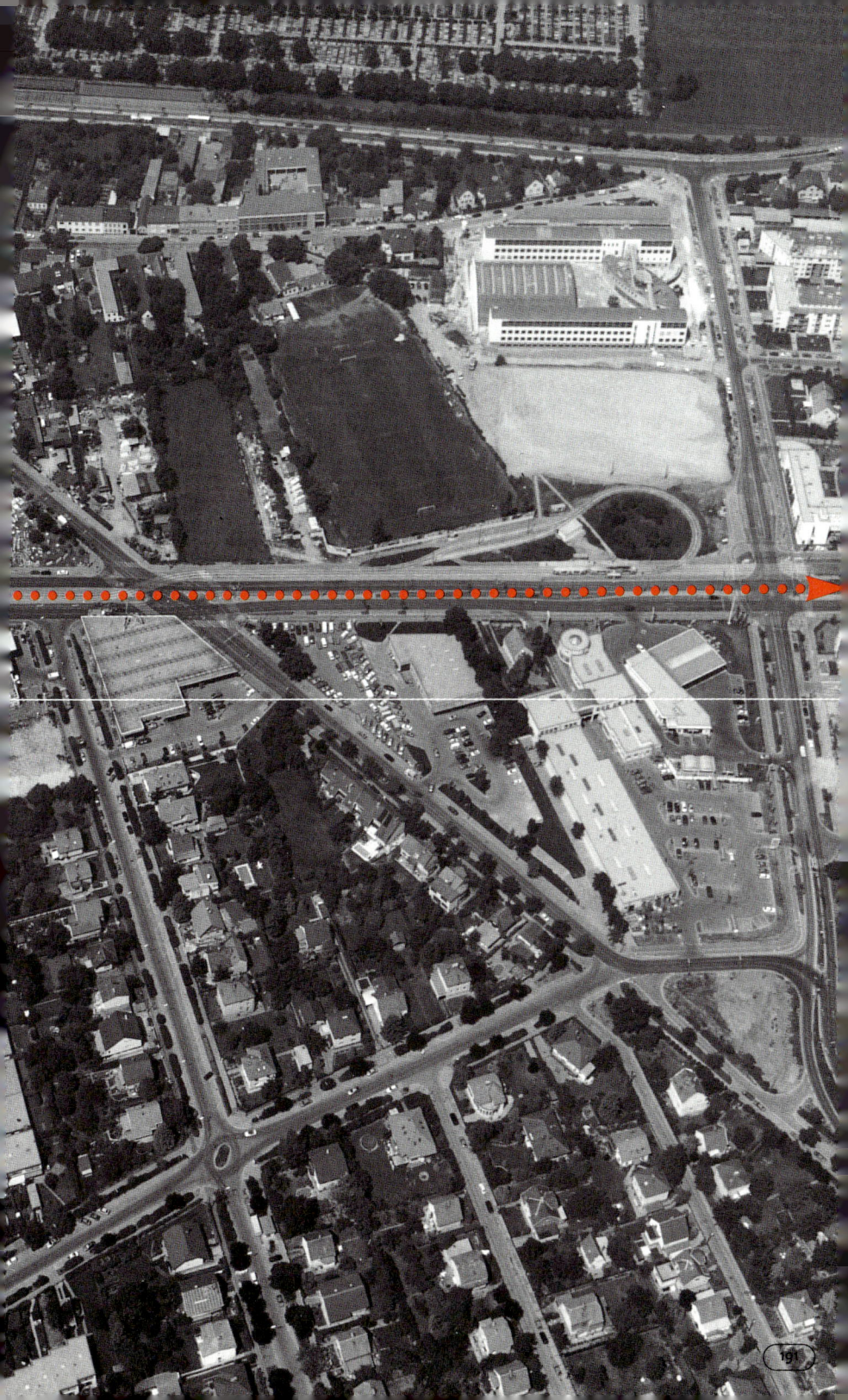

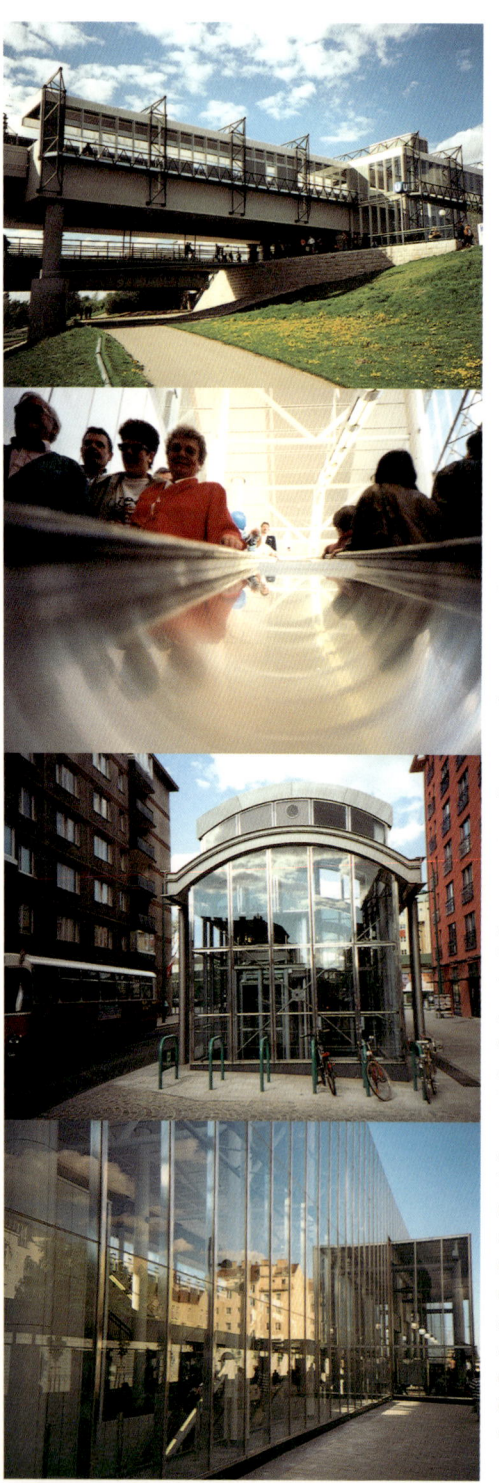

Beim Betreten des neugestalteten Bahnhofes Floridsdorf, der von der U6 und den Stammstrecken des S-Bahn-Netzes im Raum Wien bedient wird, fällt nicht nur Caroline die Helligkeit, Transparenz des Baus auf. Sie soll sich in den oberirdischen Stationen der U6 bis zur Spittelau fortsetzen und bietet neben einem erhöhten Sicherheitsgefühl im Vergleich zu älteren dunklen und verwinkelten Bahnhofsbauten phantastische Möglichkeiten zum Sightseeing im Donauraum.

Es empfiehlt sich auch für alteingesessene Wiener, in den einzelnen Stationen auszusteigen, sich umzusehen und den nächsten Zug zu nehmen. Zuerst gleitet die U6 über den Beginn der Alten Donau mit dem Wasserpark, um dann die Donauuferautobahn zu queren und an der Neuen Donau zu halten. Hier bieten sich das wohl aufregendste Panorama und ein perfekter Überblick über die baulichen Veränderungen in diesem Gebiet. Ein städtebauliches Panoramafenster sozusagen.

As Caroline enters the newly-designed Floridsdorf train station, which is used by the U6 subway and the high-speed railway serving the surrounding area of Vienna, she notices how light, spacious and transparent the station is. The same transparent effect will be continued in the U6 stations above ground along the line to Spittelau. It offers a feeling of security in comparison to the older, dark, meandering stations and a marvelous way of sightseeing in the area.

It is also recommendable for the Viennese to go to the trouble of alighting at the various stations, taking a look around, and then to continue their journey. Firstly the U6 glides over the start of the old Danube with its water park before crossing over the Danube highway and reaching its first stop at the new Danube. Here one has the most exciting panorama and a perfect view of the building changes in this area. In other words, an urban panorama window so to speak.

Die Silhouette der UNO-City, der künftigen Donau-City und des Donauturms wird noch durch die Wiener Moschee ergänzt: Ein weiteres Symbol für die Multikulturalität und die Vielfalt auch der Religionen dieser Stadt. War es den Türken vor mehreren Jahrhunderten in zweimaligem Anlauf nicht gelungen, den Halbmond über Wien aufzupflanzen, ist heute der Islam in Wien als Religion ebenso vertreten und anerkannt wie die christlichen Religionen, der jüdische Glaube oder die Glaubensphilosophien des Fernen Ostens (am rechten Donauufer, bereits in der Nähe des Kraftwerkes Freudenau findet sich auch ein buddhistisches Zentrum).

Das Panorama läßt noch das „alte" Wien erkennen, vor allem aber auch die immer dichter werdende Bebauung am rechten Donauufer. Fast bei allen Lichtverhältnissen erstrahlt bis hierher auch der Glanz der Hundertwasserschen Vergoldung des Fernwärmewerkes Spittelau. Deutlich zu erkennen auch die topographische Situation: Die Donau zwängt sich zwischen den nördlichsten Ausläufern der Alpen (hier sichtbar sind der Leopoldsberg und der Kahlenberg) und dem Bisamberg durch.

Caroline erblickt unterhalb der Station den im Vergleich zur aufgestauten Donau reißenden Verkehrsstrom der Donauuferautobahn, wobei Staus auch hier nicht ausgeschlossen sind ...

Von hier aus läßt sich auch erkennen, welche Bauleistung und Baulandgewinnung die Überplattung dieser Autobahn für die Donau-City und bei Kaisermühlen bedeutet.

Caroline wird empfohlen, den Weg zur nächsten U-Bahn-Station auch zu Fuß zurückzulegen und ein klein wenig die Atmosphäre zu erleben, die die Donauinsel prägt. An „Venice Beach" fühlen sie sich erinnert, jenen legendären Küstenstrich von Los Angeles, und die Wiener Copa Kagrana will nicht zufällig an südliches Lebensgefühl appellieren.

In addition to the silhouette of the UNO City, the future Donau City and the Danube Tower is the Vienna Mosque that serves as a symbol of the multi-cultural character, and the variety of religions practiced in the city. Whereas the Turks many hundred years before had tried to hang the half moon over Vienna, today, Islam as a religion, is represented, and recognized as much as the Christian faith, Judaism or the philosophies of the Far East. On the right bank of the Danube near the Freudenau power station a Buddhist center stands).

This panorama still allows a glimpse of "old" Vienna but even more, the ever-increasing building construction on the right side of the Danube. From this point, almost by any light conditions, the golden shine reflected from the roof of the heating station in Spittelau can be seen. One also recognizes quite clearly the topographical situation: the Danube squeezes through the most northern foothills of the Alps (here one can see the Leopoldsberg and the Kahlenberg) and the Bisamberg.

Caroline catches sight of the traffic congestion below the station on the Danube riverfront highway. Even here traffic tailbacks are not out of the question.

From this position one recognizes the fantastic building achievements and the gain in building land for the Donau City and Kaisermühlen made through building over the Danube riverfront highway.

Caroline is recommended to walk to the next subway station taking in some of the atmosphere that makes the Donauinsel so special. Along the "Venice Beach" she is reminded of the legendary stretch of coast in Los Angeles and it is not just by chance that Vienna's "Copa Kagrana" tries to create a southern atmosphere. The modes of transport that dominate here are bikes, inline-skaters and pedestrians!

To describe the "island", as it is referred to by the locals, would take up too much space. Caroline would be better off taking

Die sanften Verkehrsmittel der Gegenwart dominieren hier: Radfahrer, Inlineskater – und Fußgänger.

Die „Insel", wie sie im Volksmund heißt, zu beschreiben, würde den Platz sprengen. Caroline würde sich am besten einen Tag Zeit nehmen, um sie zu Fuß, per Rad, oder eben skatend zu erforschen. Mit öffentlichen Verkehrsmitteln ist die Insel aus fast allen Teilen der Stadt in kurzer Zeit zu erreichen. Mit ein Grund dafür, daß die Wochenend-Stadtfluchten abgenommen haben.

Diese Passage der Reise zeigt Caroline aber auch, welche Schneise seinerzeit die Donauregulierung geschlagen hat und wie schwierig und langwierig es ist, die Stadt tatsächlich an die Donau zu bringen. Die Städter selbst haben die Gegend ja schon in Beschlag genommen, die Bauten folgen etwas langsamer.

Caroline kommt am mittlerweile über die Landesgrenzen hinaus bekannten, unterhalb der Floridsdorfer Brücke verankerten „Schulschiff" vorbei, benannt nach der Friedens-Aktivistin Berta von Suttner. Obwohl in jeder Hinsicht eine Verlegenheitslösung (es war damals kein rasch verfügbarer Baugrund für eine Schule am linken Donauufer vorhanden und es bestand die Notwendigkeit, einer Schiffswerft unter die Arme zu greifen), ist das Schulschiff heute eine Attraktion geworden.

In unmittelbarer Nähe erinnert der „Weg des Friedens" nach einer Idee des früheren Belgrader Bürgermeister Bogdan Bogdanovich, der wie so viele Dissidenten aus dem früheren (politisch gesehen) Osten Europas in Wien eine Wahlheimat gefunden hat, daran, daß wenige hundert Kilometer stromabwärts der scheußlichste und unverständlichste Krieg auf diesem Kontinent (nach dem Zweiten Weltkrieg) stattgefunden hat und heute mannigfaltige Wiederaufbauarbeit zu leisten ist. Und wie sensibel man in Wien aufgrund der geopolitischen Lage für eine neue

a free day to discover its delights by bike or on foot. The island can be reached quite easily from all parts of the city by public transportation. The island and its recreational opportunities is now one reason why people remain in the city at the weekend as opposed to fleeing to the country.

This part of the journey also shows Caroline what path the regulation of the Danube took, and how difficult and what a lengthy procedure it actually is, to bring the city up to the Danube. The city dwellers already occupy the area, building follows somewhat slower.

Caroline reaches the "school ship" (well known beyond the borders confines of Vienna) which is anchored below the Floridsdorf Bridge and named after the peace activist, Berta von Suttner. The school ship was the solution to an awkward situation. At the time there was no ground available on the left bank of the Danube for the construction of a school and a shipyard needed supporting. Today the school ship is quite an attraction.

In the nearby vicinity we come across the "Way of Peace" street which was built according an idea of Bogdan Bogdanovich, the former Mayor of Belgrade. Bogdanovich like so many dissidents from the former (politically) east of Europe has found a new home in Vienna. The "Weg des Friedens" reminds us that a few hundred kilometers downstream the most terrible and incomprehensible war on this continent (after World War II) has took place. Today enormous reconstruction work has to be done. Because of its geopolitical position Vienna is particularly interested in securing a framework of security within Europe, based on the stability of peace and the necessary economical situation in the countries that are susceptible for crises. The Friedensweg incidentally was designed by Vienna schoolchildren based on an idea of Bogdanovich's.

„Sicherheitsarchitektur" in Europa sein muß, die auf der Stabilisierung des Friedens und der dazu notwendigen wirtschaftlichen Situation in den krisenanfälligen Ländern bauen muß. Den Friedensweg gestalteten übrigens Wiener Schüler nach den Ideen Bogdanovichs.

Waterfront

Nochmals quert Caroline die Donau und sieht vor sich die künftige „waterfront" und die neue Ufergestaltung.

Auch das rechte Donauufer bildet noch immer eine Barriere zwischen den Wohngebieten und dem Strom: Der Handelskai ist nach wie vor eine stark befahrene Durchzugsstrecke, daneben liegen die Gleise der Verbindungsbahn, auf der Wiens S-Bahn-Ring geschlossen werden wird und heute schon die S45 bis zur Station Handelskai verkehrt.

Caroline nimmt nun wieder die U6 und taucht in den Untergrund, es lohnt sich aber, jedenfalls ab der Station Dresdner Straße kurz „aufzutauchen" an die Oberfläche: Hier wird deutlich, welche Folgewirkungen der U-Bahn-Bau für den Stadtraum, für die Wohnumgebung hat. Entlang der gesamten Trasse der U6 ist im 20. Bezirk die Oberfläche neu gestaltet worden. Ein Radweg verbindet die Gürtelbezirke über die Spittelau und eben die Brigittenau mit dem Donauraum, im Bereich Leipziger Platz ist ein neuer Park entstanden, neue Bebauung verleiht der alten Wohngegend frische „Farbflecken". An der „Uferkante" des Donaukanals, den die U6 wieder im Tageslicht überquert, entstehen in der Brigittenau neue Stadtteile. Der Kornhäuselpark ist in seiner bunten Vielfalt besonders auffällig, in der Forsthausgasse und auf den sogenannten Hofbauergründen wird noch gebaut. Spannend findet Caroline das Panorama, das sich

Waterfront

Again Caroline crosses the Danube and takes a look at the future "waterfront" and the new layout of the bank side.

The right side of the Danube bank forms a barrier between the living area and the river. The Handelskai is still a much-used road for traffic along the river bank. The tracks of the connecting railway, to which Vienna`s Schnellbahn will be eventually connected, lie alongside this road and serve the S45, which runs as far as Handelskai station.

Caroline takes the U6 again which at this point travels underground. However, it is worthwhile to alight at the Dresdnerstrasse station. It is quite clear what consequences the construction of the subway has had for the city and the surrounding living area. In the 20th district the whole stretch of the U6 has been newly designed. A bike route connects the districts along Vienna`s Gürtel with the Danube area, passing through the Spittelau and Brigittenau neighbourhoods. Around Leipziger Platz a new park has been formed brightening up the old living area. On the edge of the Danube canal where the U6 crosses at ground level new parts of the city are being built in the Brigittenau district – the Kornhäuslpark is particularly attractive. In Forsthausgasse and on the so-called Hofbauergründen new buildings are still being constructed.

in der Umgebung der Station Spittelau bietet und auch Wiener entdecken einen bisher verborgenen Stadtteil neu: Der optisch alles dominierende Bau der „Fernwärme Wien" mit dem (Geßler?) Käppchen von Meister Hundertwasser, lenkt von der kilometerlangen gebirgsartigen Baumasse der Bahnüberbauung ab, die den neuen Franz-Josefs-Bahnhof, die Wirtschaftsuniversität und das Verkehrsamt beherbergt. Mitten in diesem alles in allem spannenden architektonischen Chaos entsteht als besonderer Akzent ein kleiner, aber feiner Bau nach Plänen von Zaha Hadid, einer irakischen Architektin, die mit ihren alle herkömmlichen baulichen Grenzen sprengenden Plänen weltweit für Aufsehen sorgt! Sie plante einen die Stadtbahnbögen „umklammernden" Baukörper mit Geschäften, Ateliers, Gastronomiebetrieben, Büros und Lofts. Erhalten werden dabei die alten Stadtbahnbögen Otto Wagners, die der neuen Umgebung zusätzliche Spannung verleihen. Ein wenig unterhalb am Donaukanal schmiegt sich elegant ein Versicherungsgebäude nach Plänen von Boris Podrecca fast ans Ufer. Auch die Station Spittelau lädt zum kurzen Aussteigen ein: der innerstädtische Norden Wiens ist hier fast total zu überblicken. Die U6 ist hier mit der U4 verbunden und an die Regionallinien der Bahn sowie die Franz-Josefs-Bahn angebunden. Der bedeutende Verkehrsknoten bietet mit seiner Transparenz hervorragende Einblicke ins innerstädtische Stadtwachstum.

Caroline finds the panorama around the Spittelau station exciting and even the Viennese are rediscovering a former hidden part of the city: The landmark building of the "Vienna district heating station", with its gold cap designed by Hundertwasser, distracts from the kilometer long mass of building that houses the new Franz Josefs Railway station, the University of Economics and the divisional traffic office.

In the middle of all this exciting architectural chaos a special highlight, the project by the Iraqi female architect, Zaha Hadid. Her highly original and unusual plans are always the cause of sensation. She is busy planning new bridges for the city railway line complete with shops, studios, restaurants, offices and lofts. The old railway bridges designed by Otto Wagner will be maintained giving the project and the surrounding an added excitement. Below, along the Danube Canal an elegant insurance building designed by Boris Podrecca, nestles up to the banks of the Danube.

The Spittelau Station invites one to alight for a moment to take a look around. From this point out the northern part of the inner city can be seen almost completely. The U6 connects here with the U4 and the regional railway, as well as the Franz Josef Railway – in other words, quite an important railway junction offering an excellent insight into how this urban area has expanded.

199

Wo bitte, geht's hier zu den S
Can you tell me, how to get to

ms?

e slum?

202

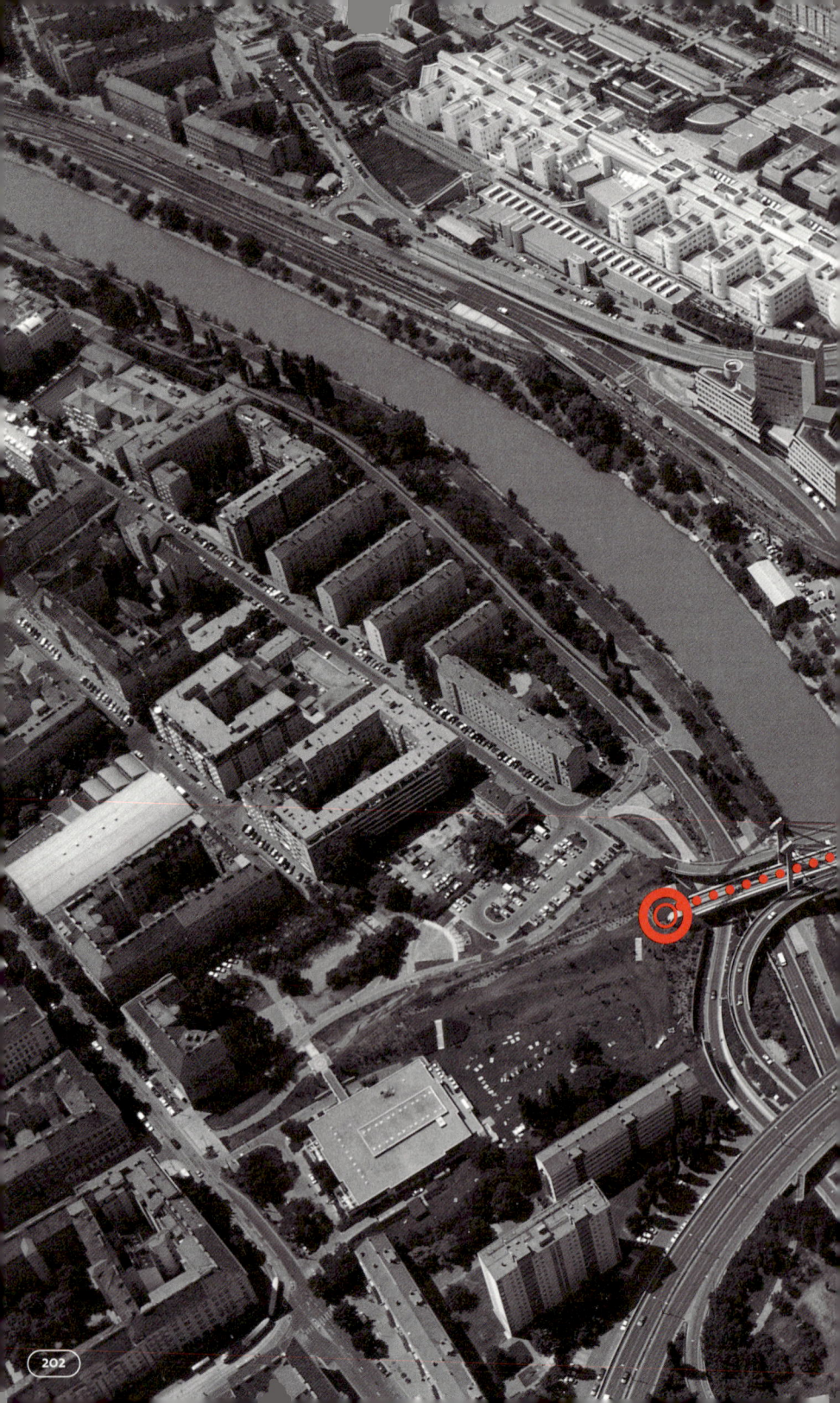

203

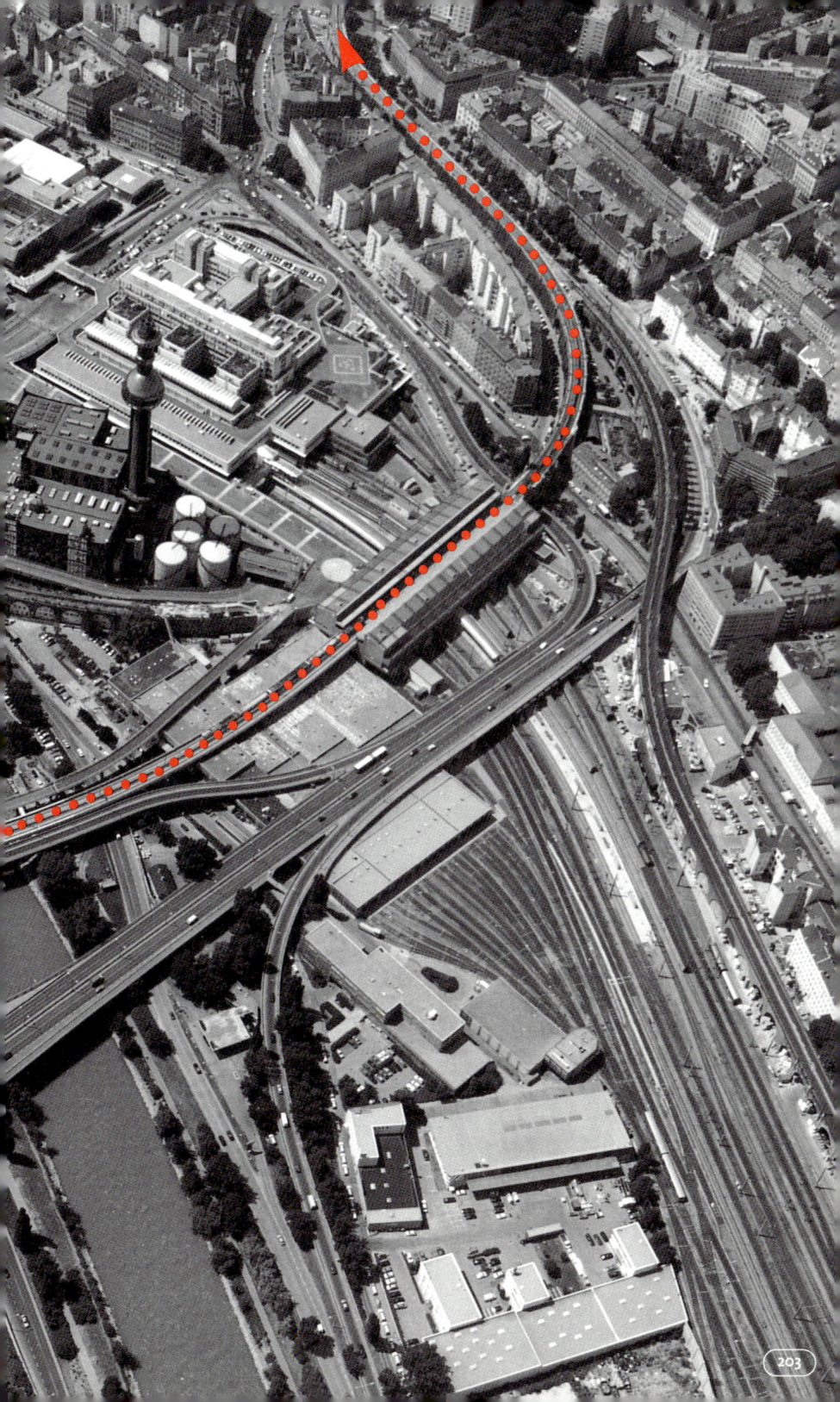

Bereits auf den alten Bögen der Otto-Wagner-Stadtbahn geht es jetzt weiter in die Stadtlandschaft des Gürtels, die wir erstmals im Gebiet von Gumpendorf berührt haben.

Kurz nach der Station Nußdorfer Straße findet sich ein Beispiel für die alten Straßenbahn-Betriebsgebäude, in Wien „Remisen" genannt. Viele sollen neu genutzt werden. Die Remise Kreuzgasse, ein besonders repräsentatives Exemplar der alten Ziegelbauweise, soll neu genutzt werden. Ein wesentlicher Teil dieses einzigen noch erhaltenen Betriebsbahnhofes aus dem letzten Viertel des vorigen Jahrhunderts steht unter Denkmalschutz und muß in die geplanten Überbauung integriert werden. Die Kreuzgasse, merken Carolines Begleiter an, ist demnach nicht nur ein Stadtentwicklungs-, sondern auch ein klassisches Stadterneuerungsprojekt. Rund 100 Wohnungen, soziale und kulturelle Einrichtungen werden dem Bezirksteil einen wichtigen Impuls und neue Attraktivität geben. Ein ähnliches Projekt mit stärkerem Wohnanteil wird im Bereich der Remise Maroltingergasse in Ottakring realisiert.

Kurz hat Caroline noch einen Blick auf das „Allgemeine Krankenhaus" (AKH), ein in den sechziger Jahren geplantes Großspital.

Heute würde man ein derart großes Spital, das auch der Forschung und Lehre ein gewaltiges Dach über dem Kopf bietet, kaum mehr derart zentral planen. Dennoch: Es handelt sich dabei um eines der modernsten und bestausgerüsteten Spitäler Europas.

Caroline ist von seinen Auswirkungen auf das Stadtbild ein wenig irritiert: Fast von jedem Punkt der Stadt rechts der Donau drängt sich der aus der Ferne viel dunkler wirkende Bau ins Bild.

Hinter dem neuen AKH verbirgt sich übrigens so etwas wie eine historische Stadtbrache, die sich langsam zum kulturellen und Freizeit-Biotop entwickelt hat. Die weitläufige Anlage des alten

From the old Otto Wagner bridges the metropolitan railway travels along the cityscape of the inner city, which Caroline first met in the "Gumpendorf" area.

Shortly after the Nussdorferstrasse station there is an old tram depot called "Remise" in Vienna. Many of these old depots are to be put into use again. The depot situated in Kreuzgasse, a fine example of an old brick building is going to be reused. Many of these buildings from the last century, which belong to the Vienna Transport Board, are under protection and have to be integrated into planning schemes. Caroline's guide mentions that Kreuzgasse is not just a city development project but an urban renewal project. Around 100 apartments, social and cultural meeting places will give the district an important impulse and make it more attractive. From 5 teams who submitted plans for this project the winners were Karla Kowalski and Michael Szyskowitz. A similar project with a stronger proportion of living accommodation is to be carried out with the depot situated in Maroltingergasse in Ottakring. Before we turn to the central area of the "Gürtel plus URBAN Project", we have a first-class view of the AKH – a huge hospital that was planned in the 1960s. Today, one would not plan such a centralized hospital (which also functions as a teaching and research hospital). However, we are concerned with one of the most modern and well-equipped hospitals in Europe.

Caroline is slightly irritated by the effect the building has on the overall view of the city. From almost every point of the city, right of the Danube, the hospital building, pushes its way through the skyline.

By the way, hidden behind the new AKH hospital something like a historic city area lies inactive. But slowly it has developed into a cultural and recreational "reserve". The spacious area of the old AKH hospital is waiting to be used by the University. Plans for a small university

AKH harrt einer Nutzung durch die Universität, Pläne für eine kleine Universitäts-Stadt liegen vor, ebenso teilweise kommerzielle Nutzung in den Randbereichen.

Carolines U6-Fahrt endet schließlich bei der Station Josefstädter Straße, von wo aus sie das URBAN-Gebiet erforschen wird.

Über den Gürtel

Caroline erfährt, daß es sich beim URBAN-Projekt Gürtel Plus, das die EU mitfinanziert, sozusagen um die Sanierung von slum-ähnlichen städtischen Lebensräumen handelt. Caroline ist ein wenig irritiert, als sie im Zusammenhang mit der Gegend, die sie sieht, den Begriff Slums hört und denkt an die US-Städte, die sie kennt.

„In Los Angeles wurden die Territorialkämpfe der Latinos und Afroamerikaner in den heruntergekommenen Stadtteilen treffend nicht als ‚class struggles' sondern als ‚Breadwar' bezeichnet, da die Spannungen weit eher durch die sozialen und finanziellen Nöte der Beteiligten erklärt werden können als durch die Unterschiedlichkeiten der Lebensstile. Alteingesessene Mieter in Wien beklagen sich oft über die kulturelle Andersartigkeit der ‚Ausländer', die sich in Sprache, Musik, Essensgerüchen und ähnlichem äußert. In Wahrheit bilden wohl auch hier die gemeinsame Not, sich kein besseres Quartier leisten zu können, und ein Kampf um den öffentlichen Raum in der hohen Dichte dieser Stadtteile den eigentlichen Hintergrund", hatte die Architektin Silja Tillner Caroline bei einem Vorbereitungsgespräch zur Wien-Reise erzählt.

Tillner hatte lange in Los Angeles gelebt und gearbeitet, als sie von der Stadtplanung Wien eingeladen wurde, gemeinsam mit Kurt Puchinger unkonventionelle Konzepte für den Gürtel zu entwickeln. „Der Gürtel stellt durch die räumlich großzügige Konzeption und

city exist as well as for buildings on the outskirts to be put to commercial use.

Caroline's journey on the U6 finally ends at the Josefstädterstrasse station from where she will explore the URBAN area.

Beyond the Vienna Gürtel

Caroline discovers that the "Gürtel plus URBAN Project", which is partly financed by the EU, is concerned with the renovation of slum-like city living areas. Caroline is irritated when she hears the word "slums" used in connection with the area which she sees, and thinks of the slums in the cities of the USA.

"In Los Angeles the territorial struggles of the Hispanics and Afro-Americans in the down and out parts of the city are not described as 'class struggles' but rather as 'bread war'. The tension is caused more by the social and financial needs of the people involved rather than the differences in the style of life. Old Viennese tenants often complain about the cultural differences of the 'foreigners' which express themselves through language, music, smells of food and similar things. The truth of the matter is, that the common poverty and not being able to afford better living accommodation, as well as the struggle for dominance on the street are the real reasons behind this tension". This was how the architect, Silja Tillner explained the matter to Caroline in a conversation they had before she set out on her Vienna journey.

Tillner had lived and worked in Los Angeles for a long time before she was invited by the Vienna urban planning authorities to develop an unconventional concept for Vienna's Gürtel area together with Kurt Puchinger.

"The Vienna Gürtel, with its spacious, generous conception and its mass of buildings in many different styles next to the Danube canal and the Wiental, represents one of the most important roads for the structure of the city.

seine die Bebauungsdichte widerspiegelnde, abschnittsweise unterschiedliche Gestaltung neben dem Donaukanal und dem Wiental einen die Stadtstruktur bestimmenden Straßenraum dar. Ursprünglich war der Gürtel als repräsentativer Straßenzug mit mehreren Baumreihen nach dem Vorbild der Pariser Boulevards und der Wiener Ringstraße gedacht. Durch die Dominanz des Verkehrs ist er heute in seiner Funktion als Freiraum und klimawirksame Grünschneise weitestgehend eingeschränkt. Eine seinerzeit relativ günstige Wohnlage ist heute schwer beeinträchtigt", lautete die lapidare Beschreibung der „Ausgangslage" in einem Abschlußbericht jener Projektleitung, die Ende der achtziger Jahre ein Entwicklungsprogramm für den Gürtel vorgelegt hatte.

Die „Ringstraße der Proletarier" bezieht heute bei Tag ihre Identität über Verkehrsstaus, bei Nacht über das Rotlichtmilieu. Nach Aussage von Verkehrsexperten ist sie die lauteste Straße

Originally, the Gürtel was planned as a representative street with rows of trees modeled on the Paris boulevards and the Vienna Ring. Dominated by traffic, the Gürtel is very much restricted in its function as an effective lane of green trees. Living accommodation which was relatively cheap is heavily affected by the flow of traffic". This is how the Gürtel's condition is described in a report produced at the end of the 1980s concerned with a redevelopment program.

"The Ringstrasse of the Proletarians" is identified with traffic chaos by day and prostitution by night. According to traffic experts the Gürtel is the noisiest road in Austria. The local residents speak of a *"traffic-hell"*.

The extensively calculated plans from the 1980s could not be carried out: it's true that already at the beginning of the 1980s, the consideration of building underground tunneling was decided against. This plan fell through not just on account of the huge financing in-

Österreichs. Die Anrainer sprechen schlicht von einer Verkehrshölle.

Die groß angelegten Planungen der achtziger Jahre hatten nicht realisiert werden können: Zwar hatten sie schon den zu Beginn des vergangenen Jahrzehnts angestellten Überlegungen über eine weitestgehende Untertunnelung eine Absage erteilt: Nicht nur an den Finanzen sollten diese Pläne scheitern, auch verkehrsorganisatorisch wäre eine solche Tieflegung des Verkehrs mit allen nötigen Auf- und Abfahrten eher negativ gewesen.

Aber auch die vorgeschlagene Verlegung der Fahrbahnen in die Mitte des Gürtelverlaufes hin zur früheren Stadtbahn, auf der heute die U6 fährt, ließ sich nicht realisieren. Wie bereits am Beispiel des Südgürtels im Bereich des Gaudenzdorfer Knotens erwähnt, hat die Republik Österreich bis dato keine Budgetmittel dafür freigemacht.

Außerdem, erklären die Experten Caroline, stünden die Kosten für eine Verlegung der Fahrbahnen in keiner Relation zur erzielbaren Verbesserung für die Anrainer. Zu allem Überdruß ginge ein beträchtlicher Teil des alten Baumbestandes verloren.

Tillner stellte daher im Auftrag der Stadtplanung eine „Urban Design-Studie für den Gürtel im Planungsbereich von Josefstädter Straße bis Gaudenzdorfer Knoten an", die 1994 abgeschlossen wurde und einer der Grundsteine für das URBAN-Projekt Gürtel Plus wurde.

Caroline, die bei der Station Josefstädter Straße die U6 verlassen hat und zu Fuß unterwegs ist, geht es wie Bernd Zimmermann, dem Planungsdirektor der New Yorker Bronx, der auf Einladung des Europaforum Wien und der Stadtplanung seine Erfahrungen mit der Sanierung des weltweit berüchtigten New Yorker Stadtteiles mit dem Gürtel-Vorhaben verglichen hatte: „Wo bitte geht's hier zu den Slums?" hatte er gemeint. Nun, die Slums im klassischen Sinn gibt es in ganz Wien nicht, aber Wien ist

volved, but also of the organization of the traffic such a tunneling would involve. The project would have required so many tunnel entrances and exits that it would have had a negative influence.

The proposed moving of the traffic lanes to the middle of the Gürtel up to the tracks of the U6 subway couldn't be realized. As already mentioned with the example of the South Gürtel in the region of Gaudenzdorfer junction, the Austrian Government has until today not allocated money from its budget for the realization of such a project.

Incidentally, the experts explain to Caroline that the actual costs of moving the lanes have no relationship to the actual gains for the local residents. Besides, a considerable stretch of trees would be lost. Tillner was given the job by the Vienna Urban Planning Department of producing an "Urban Design Study for the Gürtel in the region between Josefstädterstrasse and Gaudenzdorfer junction" that was accepted in 1994 and

forms part of the basis for the "Gürtel plus URBAN Project".

Caroline who got out of the subway at Josefstädterstrasse and is now underway on foot has the same impression as the planning director of the New York Bronx, who was invited to Vienna by the Europaforum Wien. The purpose of the visit was to share his experiences of redeveloping the world-famous Bronx with the Gürtel project. He asked "How do I get to the slums".

In the classical meaning of the word slums do not exist in Vienna. Vienna is a European city with different standards of living and therefore, is already sensitive to the matter of what are comparatively insignificant slum tendencies.

Caroline has the situation on the Gürtel explained: at the present time 130,000 people live in the "Gürtel plus" area, a third of whom are foreigners. The quota of foreigners here is double that of the Vienna average. The unemployment rate of the 70,000 inhabitants who are

eben eine europäische Stadt mit anderem Anspruchsniveau und daher sensibel bereits bei vergleichsweise geringfügigen Verslumungstendenzen.

Caroline läßt sich daher die Situation am Gürtel schildern: Derzeit leben in der Zone Gürtel Plus 130.000 Menschen, von denen ein Drittel Ausländer sind. Der Ausländeranteil ist hier doppelt so hoch wie im Wiener Durchschnitt. Die Arbeitslosigkeit der 70.000 Einwohner im erwerbsfähigen Alter liegt um 2 Prozent höher als im Wiener Durchschnitt. Und von den Menschen mit Beschäftigung ist ein Drittel in einkommensschwachen Berufsgruppen tätig, 10 Prozent mehr als im Wiener Durchschnitt.

In den letzten 20 Jahren gingen 10 Prozent der Arbeitsplätze verloren, in manchen Teilgebieten bis zu 35 Prozent. Während in anderen Teilen Wiens der Anteil der Jugendlichen in den letzten zwanzig Jahren um etwa zweieinhalb Prozent gesunken ist, stieg er im Bereich Gürtel Plus um 1,3 Prozent.

Und die Anzahl der Wohnungen der schlechtesten Kategorie ist hier doppelt so hoch wie im Wiener Durchschnitt. Von den rund 77.000 Wohnungen in der Gürtelzone stammen zwei Drittel aus der Zeit vor 1919, fast doppelt soviel wie im Wiener Durchschnitt.

Und schließlich die mangelhafte Grün-Versorgung: Während in Wien insgesamt jedem Bewohner 23 Quadratmeter Grünfläche zur Verfügung stehen (in den dichtverbauten Gebieten immerhin noch 6 Quadratmeter), müssen sich die Gürtelbewohner mit 1 Quadratmeter begnügen.

Wozu noch kommt, daß sich entlang des Gürtels das Rotlicht-Milieu breitgemacht hat. Zwar war durch eine gravierende Änderung des Wiener Prostitutionsgesetzes vor einigen Jahren der Straßenstrich in der Umgebung von Schulen, Kindergärten, Kirchen und öffentlichen Einrichtungen drastisch unterbunden worden, gerade im Gürtelbereich wurden aber von Großspekulanten

still capable of work lies 2% higher here than the Vienna average. From the people who are in employment one third belong to a low income group – again 10% more than the Vienna average.

Over the last 20 years there has been a 10% loss of jobs and in certain regions of the area as much as 35%. Whereas in other parts of Vienna the proportion of youngsters over the last 20 years has declined by circa 2.5%, in the "Gürtel plus" area it has risen by 1.3%.

The number of apartments in the worst category is twice as high here than the Vienna average. From around 77,000 apartments in the Gürtel zone two thirds were built before 1919 – almost twice the Vienna average.

Lastly, the lack of green areas is also a problem: whereas in the rest of Vienna around 23 square meters of green area are available per person – in the densely built-up areas, 6 square meters, the local inhabitants of the Gürtel have to be content with 1 square meter.

Furthermore, prostitution has opened its doors along the Gürtel and the area is the prime red-light district address. Through the changes in the Vienna prostitution laws a few years ago, street prostitution in the vicinity of schools, kindergarten, churches and public buildings was drastically stopped. However, big-time speculators in real estate bought whole blocks of houses along the Gürtel and put them to professional use for prostitutes and clients alike.

Even if the Vienna red-light district is one of the safest in the world, nevertheless it means a further decline in living standards along the Gürtel.

When Austria joined the European Union at the beginning of 1995 one of the first endeavors of the city planners was to fight for European funds to increase the value of this "fallow land" within the city.

The urban planners had to fight because the chances seemed pretty hopeless that the forth richest European city

209

im Immobilienbereich ganze Häuserblöcke aufgekauft und einschlägig genützt.

Wenn trotz allem selbst das Wiener Rotlichtmilieu zu den sichersten in der Welt gehört, bedeutet es eine weitere Abwertung für die Wohngegend Gürtel.

Als Österreich Anfang 1995 der EU beitrat, war daher eine der ersten Anstrengungen der Stadtplanung, europäische Fördermittel zur Aufwertung dieser städtischen „Brachenlandschaft" zu erkämpfen. Erkämpfen deshalb, weil es fast aussichtslos erschien, daß die viertreichste europäische Stadtregion Wien überhaupt Fördermittel bekommen würde. Ist doch das Regionalförderungssystem der EU nach wie vor vorwiegend auf ländliche Gebiete ausgerichtet. In Österreich schaffte lediglich das östlichste Bundesland Burgenland die „Ziel-1-Kategorie", was freilich auch ein wenig den Geruch des Armenhauses Europas vermittelt. Im Falle des Burgenlandes kann man aber davon ausgehen, daß die EU an die beitrittswilligen Länder im Osten, wie das benachbarte Ungarn, ein Signal hatte setzen wollen.

Wien kam schließlich das URBAN-Programm zugute, von dem es heute in Europa insgesamt 43 Projekte gibt. Wien hatte dabei das umfassendste Projekt, sowohl flächenmäßig wie auch inhaltlich, anzubieten und so gelang es in der Rekordzeit von 4 Monaten, ein Programm zu entwickeln, das die Zustimmung der Union erzielte.

Ausschlaggebend ist dabei die kombinierte Finanzierung zwischen der Stadt Wien, der Republik Österreich und der EU, wobei Privatinitiativen ebenso gefragt sind.

Caroline, die mit Wehmut an die jahrelange Aushungerung der US-Städte durch ihre Bundesregierung dachte, läßt sich die Ziele des Wiener URBAN-Projektes erklären:

Die Schaffung neuer und innovativer Arbeitsplätze vor allem für Langzeitarbeitslose, Frauen und ausländische Mit-

region would get financial aid at all. The financial aid system of the EU is primarily concentrated on helping rural areas. In Austria, the most eastern province Burgenland, managed to attain "1st category" which quite naturally gives the impression of being the poor-house of Europe. In the case of Burgenland one can assume that the EU wished to give a signal to the surrounding neighboring countries in the East, such as Hungary which is eager to join the EU.

Vienna eventually benefited from the URBAN program, which has given rise to a total of 43 projects in Europe so far. Vienna had the most extensive project, not only from the size, but also in substance, to offer and succeeded in the record-time of 4 months to develop a project which was accepted by the EU.

The decisive factor was the combined financing of the project between the City of Vienna, the Republic of Austria and the EU, whereby private initiatives are also asked for.

Caroline who is reminded of how the American government has allowed the various cities to starve in this respect has the goal of the Vienna URBAN project explained to her:

The creation of new and innovative jobs especially for people who have been unemployed for a long time, for women and for foreign citizens is the first priority. New forms of integration through cultural and educational centers and above all the revitalizing of the Gürtel, and especially the old metropolitan railway bridges as a youth and cultural mile is the aim of the project. Furthermore, a general improvement of the living standards and the quality of life.

Caroline discovers that a project management has already started on the work for a quick and efficient realization of the various projects. In the first phase around 60 projects have been secured.

Ten projects as an example of the desired variety of ideas were chosen. Ranging from the street work of the

bürger steht dabei an erster Stelle. Neue Formen der Integration durch eigene Kultur- und Bildungseinrichtungen und die Revitalisierung des Gürtels und insbesondere der alten Stadtbahnbögen stehen im Mittelpunkt. Dazu kommt die generelle Verbesserung der Wohn- bzw. der Wohnumweltqualität.

Bereits an der Arbeit, erfährt Caroline, ist ein Projektmanagement zur raschen und effizienten Umsetzung der einzelnen Projekte. In einer ersten Phase wurden rund 60 Projekte gesichtet und bewertet.

Die zehn herausgefilterten Vorhaben spiegeln die gewünschte Vielfalt der Ideen wieder: Von der „Grätzelarbeit" des Wilhelmsdorfer Vereins „Kugel" über die Neugestaltung des Yppenmarktes in Ottakring, eine „Kunstmeile Gürtel" vor den Stadtbahnbögen, ein Internet-Café für Jugendliche und ein Telematikzentrum bis hin zur Förderung von Klein- und Mittelunternehmen reicht die Palette.

Wilhelmsdorf club 'Kugel', to the redesign of the Yppen market in Ottakring, an 'Gürtel art-mile' in front of the old metropolitan line arches, an Internet coffee-house for young people and a telematic center, to provide support for small and medium-sized businesses.

212

213

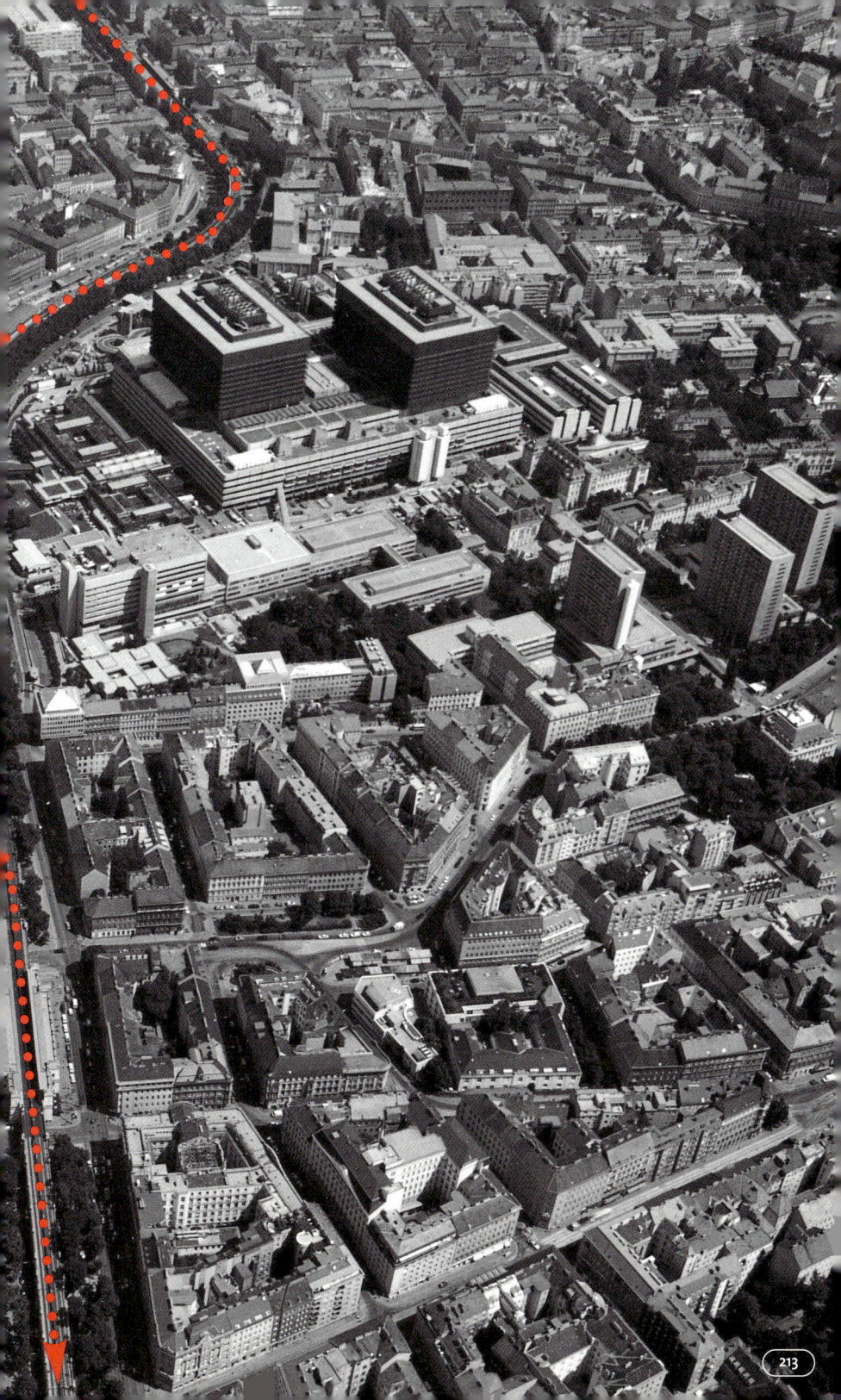

Alte Bögen – Neues Leben

Zusammen mit den Wiener Stadtwerken, denen die Stadtbahnbögen gehören, wurde für die kilometerlange Stadtlandschaft der Stadtbahnbögen eine neue Nutzung im Sinne des Gesamtprojektes ausgearbeitet. Als Caroline die schier endlos lange Front der markanten, von Otto Wagner geplanten Bögen entlangspaziert, fällt ihr eine Passage aus Elias Canettis „Augenspiel" ein, das sie zur Einstimmung auf Wien gelesen hatte. Canetti beschrieb darin sein Leben in den Wiener Ateliers, Cafés und intellektuellen Zirkeln der dreißiger Jahre: „Ich besuchte Wotruba in seinem Atelier. Zwei Bögen unter dem Viadukt der Stadtbahn waren ihm von der Gemeinde Wien als Atelier zugewiesen worden. In einem – oder bei gutem Wetter davor – schlug er auf seinen Stein los ... Im anderen standen Figuren, die ihn bei der Arbeit gestört hätten. Am liebsten, wenn das Wetter nicht zu schlecht war, arbeitete er draußen. Anfangs fühlte ich mich von der Nüchternheit der Lokalität und dem Lärm der Züge abgestoßen, aber da es nichts Überflüssiges zu sehen gab, da alles, was immer hier vorhanden war, einen anzog und zählte, fand man rasch in den Ort und spürte, daß er richtig war, er hätte nicht geeigneter sein können." Auch an Berlin fühlte sich Caroline erinnert, wo die alten S-Bahn-Bögen sich zu einem Biotop für Kultur, Handwerk und Gastronomie entwickelt hatten, nach dem Fall der Mauer. Selbst die weltweit berühmte Architekturgalerie Aedes hatte sich dort eingenistet. Hier sollte also die neue Jugend- und Kulturmeile entstehen. Caroline war dringend empfohlen worden, am Abend das „Chelsea" zu besuchen, eines jener unzähligen Wiener Szenelokale, in dem die beste Live-Musik der Rock-Avantgarde zu hören war. Das „Chelsea" war nach heftigen Auseinandersetzungen mit den Anrainern von seinem früheren Standort übersiedelt worden. Hier am Gürtel stör-

Old Arches – New Life

In collaboration with the Vienna public transport authorities who own the bridges along the Gürtel a new usage for the arches under the bridges has been worked out for this kilometer-long city region.

As Caroline walks by the endless frontage of the bridges planned by Otto Wagner, a passage from Elias Canetti's book "Play of the Eyes" comes to mind. She had read the book prior to her trip to Vienna in which Canetti describes his life in the artist studios, cafes and intellectual circles of Vienna in the 1930s." I visited Wotruba in his studio. Two arches under the viaduct of the metropolitan railway were placed at his disposal by the Vienna council. In one of them, or before them by good weather, he chiseled away at his stone. In the other stood figures which would have disturbed him at his work. Preferably, when the weather allowed, he worked outside. In the beginning I felt disturbed by the insipidness of the locality and the noise of the trains, but the fact that there was nothing superfluous to be seen, and everything I saw attracted me, I soon felt the place was right and could not have been better."

Caroline was also reminded of Berlin after the fall of the wall where the arches of the old railway bridges have been turned into a biotope for culture, handicrafts and restaurants. Even the worldwide famous architectural gallery Aedes has settled there. Here a new youth and cultural mile will come into being. Caroline had been recommended to visit the "Chelsea" at night, one of Vienna's many night-life venues, in which the best avant-garde rock music could be heard. The "Chelsea" transferred to its present spot after many problems with local inhabitants. Here, on the Gürtel, the loud music doesn't disturb anyone.

"We built this city on rock'n'roll" – it seemed that rock music even in the classical music City of Vienna could have its

te die zugegebenermaßen laute Musik niemanden. „We built this city on rock'n' roll" – Rockmusik schien also auch in der klassischen Musikstadt Wien noch etwas bewegen zu können. Caroline, die unbedingt noch den Brunnenmarkt, Europas längsten Straßenmarkt, besuchen hatte müssen, der sich parallel zum Gürtel erstreckt, und dort die bunte Mischung von Menschen aus aller Herren Länder genossen hatte, dachte nochmals über das Ausländerproblem nach: Komisch, daß auf Märkten von den Spannungen zwischen den einzelnen Nationalitäten und Kulturen nichts zu merken war. Vielleicht würde auch das Projekt des multikulturellen Jugendzentrums in den Gürtelbögen ein wenig beitragen zum Abbau der Vorurteile. Gerade bei Jugendlichen müßte das ja noch am ehesten funktionieren. Und Straßen-Gangs hatte sie in Wien bisher noch nicht gesehen, wenngleich es dieses Phänomen sicherlich auch in Wien gab, auch wenige Spuren einer städtischen Drogenszene gesehen.

say. Caroline definitely wanted to visit Europe's longest street market, namely the Brunnenmarkt. This market runs parallel to the Gürtel and is a colorful mixture of people from many countries. She thought once again about the problems with foreigners. It was strange that on the market there was no notice of the tension between the different personalities and cultures. Perhaps, the multicultural youth center project in the arches of the Gürtel bridges would contribute something towards the gradual collapse of prejudices. Surely, this should be the case, especially with youth. Until now she hadn't seen any street-gangs in Vienna although this phenomenon must exist even here. In comparison she had seen elements of a city drug scenes.

Schmelztiegel Wien ?

War Wien nun ein Schmelztiegel der europäischen Kulturen?

War es wie New York ein Platz, an dem die Menschen verschiedener Herkunft getrennt voneinander in ihren Quartieren lebten oder mischte sich hier die Bevölkerung? Als Besucherin konnte sie sich keinen wirklichen Eindruck davon verschaffen, aber wie sie hörte, neigten die Zuwanderer aus den Gebieten des ehemaligen Jugoslawiens dazu, sich rasch zu integrieren, während etwa die Türken ihre Identität sehr lange bewahrten und auch zur Schau trugen.

Einen eigenen Integrationsfonds hatte die Stadt Wien da eingerichtet, der sich um das Zusammenleben der eingesessenen Wiener mit den Zuwanderern kümmern sollte. Bei allen Problemen, von denen ihr berichtet wurde, schien sich der Wiener Weg der Integration offenbar wesentlich besser zu bewähren, als sie es aus amerikanischen Städten kannte oder aus den französischen und britischen Großstädten mit den Jugend- und Rassenkrawallen.

Caroline war mittlerweile bei der Station Burggasse angelangt und versuchte sich vorzustellen, wie jenes merkwürdige „Wolkenspangen"-Projekt des Wiener Architekten Krischanitz aussehen würde, der auch die Kunsthalle am Karlsplatz, die Beleuchtung der Mariahilfer Straße oder jenes vielbeachtete Wohnbauprojekt in der Donaustadt geplant hatte.

Die „Wolkenspange" sollte ein Einkaufszentrum mit der U6-Station verbinden und ein Jugendzentrum beherbergen. Motor des Projektes war ein landesweit bekannter Baumeister namens Lugner, der nicht nur in seinem angestammten Metier tätig war, sondern sich den PR-wirksamen Spaß leistete, alljährlich zum Opernball mehr oder weniger bekannte bis nicht mehr ganz taufrische Hollywood-Stars einzuladen. Heftig umstritten war das Projekt, hatte

Melting pot Vienna?

Was Vienna then a melting pot of European cultures?

Was it like New York, a place in which people from different backgrounds live apart from one another in their own quarters, or did the different nations mix together here? As a visitor she couldn't really gain an impression of the situation, but as she heard, the immigrants from former Yugoslavia tended to integrate much more quickly, whereas the Turks for example retain their identity much longer. A special integration fund has been set up to help with the problems of integration between those born and bred in Vienna and the immigrants. Despite all the problems that had been explained to her, it seemed the Viennese way of dealing with integration was proving much better, as far as she knew, than in the American States or in the French and British cities where quite often it came to youth and racial riots.

Caroline by now had arrived at the Burggasse station and tried to imagine how the curious "Wolkenspangen Project" by the Viennese architect, Krischanitz would look. Krischanitz was responsible for the Kunsthalle in Karlsplatz, the street lighting in Mariahilferstrasse and a much respected building project in Donaustadt.

The "Wolkenspangen" project will combine a shopping mall with the U6 station and a young people`s drop-in center. The driving force behind this project has been a Viennese building constructor by the name of Richard Lugner. A master of many trades, not only his own, Lugner – by now a household name – treats the nation to the PR stunt of inviting, every year, famous, not-so-famous and not-so-young-any-more Hollywood stars to the Vienna Opera Ball.

Caroline had heard that the project was hotly disputed, even a reputable advisor for urban planning and layout had looked at the project and found it negative. Nonetheless, the urban planning

Caroline gehört, selbst der hochwohllöbliche Beirat für Stadtgestaltung hatte sich damit auseinandergesetzt und es abschlägig beurteilt. Dennoch war die Stadtplanung massiv dafür eingetreten, handelte es sich dabei doch um genau jene Art von privaten Initiativen, die im URBAN-Projekt gefordert waren. Und außerdem brauchte der Gürtel wohl jene Fußgängerverbindungen über den Verkehrsstrom, die es ja auch in der Vergangenheit gegeben hatte. Apropos Fußgänger: Lange Zeit hatte der Mittelbereich des Gürtels als unsicher für Fußgänger gegolten. Eine neue Beleuchtung, die die Gürtel-Designerin Tillner angeregt hatte, war nun im Testbetrieb und sollte auch in den Nachtstunden mehr Sicherheitsgefühl vermitteln. So wie übrigens auch jenes Projekt am Urban-Loritz-Platz, den Caroline jetzt querte: Hier sollte in den kommenden Jahren ein neuer Park entstehen, mit viel sichtbarem Wasser, einem überdachten Übergang und vor allem mit einer neuen Lichtgestaltung. Apropos Sicherheit: Caroline war aufgefallen, daß man auch als Frau zu fast allen Tages- und Nachtzeiten in Wien unterwegs sein konnte, selbst in der U-Bahn. Schienen recht viel Wert auf Sicherheit im öffentlichen Raum zu legen, die Wiener!

Caroline hatte nun bereits den Europaplatz in Sichtweite, den sie auf ihrer Tour bereits einmal besucht hatte. Ihr Wien-Besuch neigte sich dem Ende zu, und sie war voller Eindrücke über diese alte und doch so neue europäische Stadt. Und irgendwie erinnerte sie sich an eine Passage aus Richard Sennetts Buch „Civitas – Die Großstadt und die Kultur des Unterschieds", in der dieser große Stadttheoretiker gemeint hatte:

„Es ist ein Merkmal unseres Städtebaus, daß er die Unterschiede zwischen Menschen verstellt, ausgehend von der Annahme, diese Unterschiede würden vor allem als gegenseitige Bedrohung und nicht als gegenseitige Anregung empfunden. Deshalb schaffen wir in der

authority was very much in favor of the project because private initiatives were called for in the URBAN Project.

Besides, pedestrian bridges across the heavily-trafficked Gürtel were needed. In fact, such crossings had existed in the past.

By the way, on the subject of pedestrians: for a long time the middle part of the Gürtel was considered unsafe for pedestrians. New street lighting by the Gürtel designer, Tillner has been tested and found excellent, providing a stronger feeling of safety at night.

Likewise, the project in Urban Loritz Platz which Caroline now crosses: here in the coming years a new park will be built with lots of water, a covered-over crossing and above all a new lighting system.

On the subject of safety: it had occurred to Caroline that a women could be out day or night and feel quite safe, even in the subway. The Viennese seemed to attach great importance to safety in open places.

Caroline could now see the Europaplatz which she had already visited on her tour. Her visit to Vienna was drawing to its close and she was full of impressions of this old and yet so new European city. Somehow she was reminded of a passage from Richard Sennett's book "Civitas – The city and differences of culture", in which the great city theorist says:

"It is a feature of city building that it obscures the differences between people starting from the assumption that these differences above all would be a threat against each other rather than a source of inspiration for each other. Therefore in city spheres we create neutral buildings that have nothing to say and rooms that cut out the threat of social contact. Facades made out of mirror glass, highways which separate the poor part of the city from the rest of the city. Housing estates which are only suitable as 'sleeping' cities". Sennett also says "The cultural problem of the modern city is how to bring an impersonal surrounding to life,

städtischen Sphäre nichtssagende, neutralisierende Räume, Räume, die die Bedrohung durch sozialen Kontakt ausschalten: Straßenfronten aus Spiegelglas, Autobahnen, die arme Stadtviertel vom Rest der Stadt abtrennen, Siedlungen, die nur als Schlafstädte taugen."
Und Sennett hatte weiter gemeint: „Das kulturelle Problem der modernen Stadt besteht darin, wie man diese unpersönliche Umgebung zum Sprechen bringen kann, wie man ihr ihre Ödnis, ihre Neutralität nimmt, deren Ursprünge an die Überzeugung geknüpft sind, daß die Außenwelt der Dinge nicht die eigentliche wirkliche Welt ist ... Unterschiede sind nicht dazu da, daß man sie überwindet."

Dieses Gürtelgebiet stellt für Wien neben der Stadterweiterung sicherlich die größte Herausforderung der kommenden Jahre dar, vor allem, weil es eben die zweifelsohne brisanteste Bevölkerungsmischung der Stadt beherbergt.

Euro-Stadt

Caroline hatte in Wien mehrmals den Vergleich mit den amerikanischen Städten erlebt: Er war seitens der Wiener immer recht negativ ausgefallen. Von „Wien darf nicht Chicago werden" bis zur „Manhattanisierung", wenn es um Hochhäuser ging, reichten die Slogans.

Wie hatte ein Wiener Gesprächspartner gemeint? „Der Vergleich mit amerikanischen Städten kann dort gezogen werden, wo es um allgemeine Tendenzen geht. Und hier müßte Wien seine Fähigkeiten und Möglichkeiten voll ausschöpfen. Wie kann Wien Wachstumsprozesse und Strukturänderungen im kleinräumigen und europäischen Kontext so verarbeiten, daß die Identität dieser Stadt gewahrt wird und gleichzeitig ein neuer „Gesellschaftsvertrag" zwischen verschiedenen Gruppierungen und Anschauungen geschlossen wird? Wie kann Offenheit und Liberalität bewahrt bzw. wiederhergestellt werden

taking away its neutrality, its monotony whose origins are tied to the conviction that the things of the outside world are not really the real world ... Differences do not exist that one overcomes them" .

This area, apart from the extension of the city, definitely presents the biggest challenge for Vienna in the coming years, above all, because it accommodates the most explosive mixture of population in the city.

Euro-City

Caroline more than once came across a comparison between Vienna and the American cities on account of the political slogans which turned out negatively for America. "Vienna must not become Chicago" or "Manhattan" in connection with high-rise buildings.

What was it that a Viennese said to her? The comparison with American States can only be made when it deals with general tendencies. Vienna must make full use of its possibilities and capabilities. How can Vienna's expansion and structural change in the European context take place so that the identity of the city is maintained and at the same time a new "social contract" is made between the different groups and views? How can openness and liberalness be preserved, and the longing for home, security and well-being fulfilled? The question which we are dealing with is: is there a model for the development of our cities, the great achievement? as Julian Green demands when he says "Which future young architect will give us the city of the future, a beautiful city which is as seductive for future generations as Paris is, which has developed over hundreds of years and still enchants us?" What are the results? Many cities of this earth, let us only consider the industrialized cities, are brought into disruption through the migration of people. Investors are looking for optimal locations, more and more people suffer from the consequences of

und dennoch die berechtigte Sehnsucht nach Heimat, Geborgenheit und Wohlbefinden erfüllt werden? Die Frage, die sich uns stellt ist: Gibt es ein Modell für die Entwicklung unserer Städte, den großen Wurf, wie ihn Julian Green verlangt, wenn er sagt „Welcher junge Architekt wird uns endlich die Stadt der Zukunft geben, eine schöne Stadt, die ebenso verführerisch auf die Generation der Zukunft wirken wird, wie das allmählich aus den Jahrhunderten entstandene Paris uns verzaubert?"

Was folgt daraus? Viele Städte dieser Erde – und betrachten wir vergleichshalber nur die Städte der industrialisierten bzw. tertiärisierten Welt – werden durch Migrationsbewegungen in Unruhe gebracht, Investoren suchen nach optimalen Standorten, immer mehr Menschen leiden unter den Auswirkungen ihrer Kaufentscheidungen. Die Trends sind ähnlich, ob in Los Angeles, Miami, Paris oder Wien. Die Antworten jedoch sind je nach Geschichte und Gegenwart der Städte spezifisch zu geben. Was Wien anbelangt, fand Caroline, befand es sich ganz offensichtlich auf dem richtigen Weg. Es war eben ein europäischer Weg.

Caroline befand sich nach einem abschließenden abendlichen Besuch im „Chelsea", wo sie junge europäische Rockmusik gehört (auch nicht schlecht, diese jungen Europäer, dachte sie sich) und mit ihrer Begleitung noch über die alternative Wiener Kulturszene geplaudert hatte, auf dem Heimweg in ihr Hotel am Stadtpark.

Für heute war Caroline zu müde, um noch durch weitere einschlägige Lokale zu ziehen, aber fürs nächste Mal hatte sie schon einige heiße Tips: Von der „Arena" bis zum „Flex", dem wohl derzeit schrägsten Jugendtreff am Donaukanal. Also doch nicht nur alles Walzer in Wien, dachte Caroline noch kurz vor dem Einschlafen.

their purchases. The trends are similar whether in Los Angeles, Miami, Paris or Vienna. However, the answers can only be specifically given according to the past and the present of each individual city. Concerning Vienna, Caroline found it obviously developing the right "European" way.

After her late-night visit in "Chelsea" where she had listened to young European rock music and generally talked to her friends about the Viennese alternative cultural scene, Caroline made her way back to her hotel, situated at the Stadtpark.

For today, Caroline was far too tired to make her way through any further clubs and bars, but for the next time she had a few good tips: starting from the "Arena" to "Flex" which is the hottest meeting place for youngsters along the Danube canal. Shortly before she fell asleep Caroline thought – so it is not just waltzes in Vienna!

Der Weg nach Europa
The Way to Europe

221

Ein bißchen wehmütig packte Caroline ihre Sachen. Die drei Tage Wien waren um. So viel hätte es noch zu sehen, zu fragen gegeben. Aber sie mußte weiter nach Brüssel, wo sie ja noch einen Hauch von Wien verspüren sollte. Nicht nur weil die Habsburger einst hier wie dort regiert hatten, sondern weil die Stadt Wien vor kurzem dort ein eigenes Wien-Haus eingerichtet hatte. Weil Wien, das auch in Tokyo und Hong Kong eigene Vertretungen hat, als Land, als Mittelpunkt der Vienna Region auch in der Zentrale der europäischen Macht entsprechendes Lobbying betreiben muß, hatte man ihr erklärt.

Auf dem Weg zum Flugplatz, den sie mit dem Taxi fahren würde, wollte sich Caroline noch einige Eindrücke neuer Wiener Entwicklungen mitnehmen. Und ein Besuch in der Heimatstadt Sigmund Freuds wäre ohne das Erlebnis eines Besuches am Zentralfriedhof ja unkomplett.

Stichwort Freud: Beim nächsten Besuch mußte sie unbedingt das Freud-Museum in der Berggasse 19 anschauen. Denn auch wenn derzeit vor allem in den USA eine pseudowissenschaftliche Debatte über die Wertigkeit der Freudschen Erkenntnisse lief, die ihn vielleicht nicht gut aussehen ließ – dieser Dr. Freud hatte unser Jahrhundert doch entscheidend mitgeprägt. Und Caroline schien, daß die Diskussion über Freud zumindest ein wenig auch von der neokonservativen politischen Entwicklung geprägt war.

Das legendär merkwürdige Verhältnis der Wiener zum Tod war ja auch etwas, das wenigstens das Image dieser Stadt mitprägte. „Es lebe der Zentralfriedhof" hatte Wolfgang Ambros, erster Interpret des Austropop, vor Jahren gesungen und dabei die ambivalente Beziehung der Stadt zum Jenseits ironisierend beschrieben. Caroline interessierte freilich vor allem die Otto-Wagner-beeinflußte Lueger-Kirche, die erst

---

Caroline was somewhat sad as she packed her suitcase. Her three days in Vienna had ended and there was still so much to be seen. However, she had to make her way to Brussels where she would still feel a touch of Vienna. This had nothing to do with the fact that the Hapsburgs had once ruled here as well as there, but because the City of Vienna a short while ago built a Vienna-House there. Vienna, that is also represented in Tokyo and Hong Kong as a state and as center of the Vienna region, is also represented in the center of European power and has built these cultural centers for lobbying purposes.

In the taxi on her way to the airport Caroline wanted to take a few more impressions of Viennese development with her. What would a visit to the home country of Freud be without the experience of a visit to Vienna's central cemetery?

Keyword Freud: on her next trip to Vienna she would definitely have to visit the Freud Museum in Berggasse, number 19. Even though debates are taking place in the States at the moment about the actual value of Freud's theories, it is beyond doubt, that Dr. Freud had played a part in the shaping of ideas in the last century. It seemed to Caroline that the discussions about Freud were at least slightly influenced by the neo-conservative political development.

The unusual legendary relationship of the Viennese towards death was also something that influenced the image of the city. "Long live the central cemetery" was the title of a song sung by the Austrian pop star, Wolfgang Ambros describing ironically the ambivalent relation the Viennese have to next world.

Above all, Caroline was naturally interested in the Otto Wagner influenced Lueger church that had been completely renovated shortly before. On my next visit to Vienna ... but the taxi had already arrived.

vor kurzem aufwendig renoviert worden war. Bei ihrem nächsten Wien-Besuch mußte sie unbedingt noch … aber da war das Taxi schon vorgefahren.

Auf der Landstraße

Sie ließ sich durch die Landstraßer Hauptstraße führen, eine jener Wiener Straßen, die wie die Mariahilfer Straße oder die Meidlinger Hauptstraße nach dem U-Bahn-Bau zu urbanen Einkaufsstraßen wurden. Wie eng in Wien alt und neu zusammenliegen, empfand Caroline hier besonders deutlich: Unter der Straße fährt die hochmoderne U3, oben laden die liebevoll revitalisierten Biedermeierhäuser zu einem Spaziergang ins alte Wien ein.

Wien-Reisende, die Zeit genug haben, können Carolines Fahrt übrigens mit der Buslinie 74 A ab Wien Mitte nachvollziehen, um dann in die Straßenbahnlinie 71 umzusteigen, die seit kurzem bis Kaiser-Ebersdorf fährt.

Am oberen Ende der Landstraßer Hauptstraße, dort, wo sie einen „Zwickel" mit dem Rennweg bildet, findet sich ein besonders interessantes städtebauliches Projekt: Jahrzehntelang hatte Wien mit dem Bund verhandelt, bis es die alte Rennwegkaserne nutzen konnte. In einem Wettbewerbsverfahren wurde dann der Wohnpark Rennweg erarbeitet. Rund 550 Wohnungen mit zugehöriger Infrastruktur wurden dabei so in die bestehende denkmalgeschützte Bausubstanz integriert, daß eine der typisch Wienerischen „Schnittstellen" zwischen Geschichte, Gegenwart und Zukunft des Städtischen entstand. Hinter der modernen Architektur der Wohnbauten findet sich ein altes Kloster, mittendrin ein kleiner Park. Moderne Fassaden und alte Gemäuer gehen eine faszinierende Symbiose ein. Für die Wiener Stadtplanung, hat sich Caroline vor ihrer Abfahrt zum Flughafen noch sagen lassen, ist die Rennwegkaserne ein Musterbeispiel einer gelungenen Durchmischung der

Along Landstrasse

The taxi drove her along Landstrasser Hauptstrasse, one of those Viennese streets – like Mariahilferstrasse or Meidlinger Hauptstrasse – which, after the construction of the subway, has been turned into an urban shopping street. Caroline felt how close the old and the new are to each other in Vienna. Below the streets there is the highly modern subway and at ground level beautifully restored houses of the Biedermeier period, which beg to be visited.

Visitors to Vienna who have enough time at their disposal, can start Caroline's trip on the 74A bus, which leaves from the station Wien -Mitte, and then change to the no. 71 tram, which now goes right to Kaiser-Ebersdorf.

At the upper end of Landstrasser Hauptstrasse where it forms a junction with Rennweg one finds a particularly interesting municipal building project: for more than ten years Vienna negotiated with the federal government until it could use the old Rennweg barracks. Consequently, the residential park Rennweg was built. Around 550 apartments with all the necessary infrastructure were integrated into this building which stands under protection order, creating a typical Viennese mixture between past, present and future of the city. Behind the modern architecture of the residential park there is an old cloister, in the middle a small park. Modern facades and old walls make for a fascinating symbiosis.

Before Caroline left for the airport she had been told that from the point of view of the Vienna urban planning authorities the Rennweg barracks are a prime example of a successful mixture of functions: apartments, shops, offices, kindergarten, a primary school, a technical high school complete with gym, a senior citizens' home and various official buildings all creating a harmonious, urban building. With this enormous mixture a district was created which is filled with

Funktionen: Wohnungen, Geschäfte, Büros, Kindergarten, Volksschule, eine technische Mittelschule mit Sporthalle, ein Seniorenheim und verschiedene Amtsgebäude fügen sich zu einer städtebaulichen Einheit zusammen. Mit dieser Durchmischung der einzelnen Lebensbereiche wurde ein Quartier geschaffen, das bis in die Abendstunden mit Leben erfüllt ist. Von diesem Stadterneuerungsprojekt profitiert der gesamte Bezirk, weil durch die Schleifung der alten Kasernenteile ein durchgängiges Areal entstanden ist, das auch die Verbindung zwischen den einzelnen Bezirksteilen erleichtert.

Fast fertig ist, als Caroline am Rennweg vorbeischaut, die neue Gestaltung der Landstraßer Hauptstraße mit breiten Gehsteigen und Bäumen.

Apropos Kasernen: Wien wartet seit langem darauf, daß die weitestgehend ungenutzten oder untergenutzten Kasernen auf Wiener Boden, die allesamt an die Niederschlagung der Revolution

life and where activity abounds well into the evening. The whole district has profited from this city redevelopment project. Through the rebuilding of the old barracks an accessible area has been created which makes the moving between the different parts of the district much easier.

The new layout of Landstrasse Hauptstrasse with broad sidewalks and rows of trees is almost complete, as Caroline notices driving past in the taxi.

Concerning barracks: Vienna waited for a long time before it could use the various barracks within the city which for the most part were unused or hardly used. The old barracks are a reminder of the suppression of the revolution in 1848 and offer tremendous potential for inner city development.

Traveling along Simmeringer Hauptstrasse in the outbound direction, Caroline sees the high buildings of old gasometers. These monuments of 19th century industrial architecture have been standing unused for years. In a competi-

von 1848 gemahnen, endlich städtisch genutzt werden können. Die innere Stadterweiterung hätte hier noch ein beträchtliches Potential.

Auf der Simmeringer Hauptstraße stadtauswärts fahrend, sieht Caroline die hochragenden Gebäude der alten Gasometer. Diese Denkmäler der Industriearchitektur des 19. Jahrhunderts stehen seit Jahren fast ungenutzt. In einem Wettbewerbsverfahren wurde nun entschieden, daß je eines der Gebäude von folgenden Architekten gestaltet werden soll: COOP-Himmelblau, die dem alten Gemäuer einen ihrer dekonstruktivistischen „Rucksäcke" verpassen, Jean Nouvel (der in Floridsdorf bereits an einem Wohnprojekt arbeitet), Denkmalschutzexperte Manfred Wehdorn und Wilhelm Holzbauer. In jedem der Gasometer sollen Wohnungen entstehen. Zu erschwinglichen Preisen, die dem sozialen Wohnbau in Wien entsprechen. Und drunter soll Wien endlich seine Rockhalle bekommen. „We built this city on rock'n'roll". Also doch!

Noch liegen die Gasometer im Dornröschenschlaf – vor wenigen Jahren kurz unterbrochen durch die Ausstellung anläßlich des hundertsten Geburtstages der österreichischen Sozialdemokratie. Hin und wieder zieht es auch die „Raver" hierher. „Teccno" in der Ziegel-Steinzeit ist dann angesagt. Spätestens wenn die U3, die bis Simmering verlängert wird, hier eine Station bekommt, werden die Ziegelbauten aber wieder mit neuem Leben erfüllt sein.

Die Fahrt durch Simmering führt durch eine sich entwickelnde Vorstadt. Ohne große Gestaltungspläne ist hier städtisches Leben entstanden, wie es am Rande aller Großstädte zu finden ist.

Zauberberg

Beim Zentralfriedhof angelangt, muß sich Caroline entscheiden, ob sie sich die Kirche ansehen oder einen kurzen Abstecher zum Schloß Neugebäude ma-

tion it was decided that each of the following architects should re-design these buildings. COOP-Himmelbau, Jean Nouvel (who is working on a residential project in Floridsdorf), the expert on protected buildings, Manfred Wehdorn and Wilhelm Holzbauer. Into each of the gasometers an apartment house will be built at prices laid down by council policy. Underneath one of these gasometers Vienna will get a hall for rock music, so perhaps it's true after all "We built this city on rock'n'roll".

The gasometers are still lying in their "sleeping beauty" sleep that was disturbed a few years ago by an exhibition commemorating the 100th birthday of the Austrian Social Democratic Movement. At the latest, when the U3 is extended to Simmering and a new station is built, the old walls will be filled with new life. The ride through Simmering takes Caroline through a developing suburb. Here without a great deal of planning, city life has come, about which is typical for the periphery of every major city.

Zauberberg – Mystery Mountain

Having arrived at the central cemetery Caroline has to decide whether to take a look at the Lueger church, or make a short detour to take a look at Schloss (palace) Neugebäude that is situated behind the crematorium.

This renaissance palace, the only one of its kind north of the Alps built in the Italian style, is, so to speak, the greatest unfinished construction in Austrian building history. The construction was started in the 16th century by the Emperor Maximilian, continued, but never completed. The impressive structure has fallen into decay over the past years. A renaissance garden of which there are exact plans is crying out for resurrection. However, the Neugebäude sleeps the "sleep of the dead" of the area. Plans for revitalizing and putting the house into use have been

chen will, das sich hinter dem Krematorium verbirgt. Dieses einzige Renaissanceschloß im italienischen Stil nördlich der Alpen ist sozusagen die große Unvollendete österreichischer Baugeschichte. Begonnen von Kaiser Maximilian im 16. Jahrhundert, wurde es immer weiter-, aber nie fertiggebaut. Seine beachtliche Bausubstanz ist über die letzten Jahrzehnte verfallen, ein Renaissancegarten, von dem genaue Beschreibungen existieren, harrt der Auferstehung. Doch das Neugebäude schläft den Totenschlaf der Umgebung. Pläne zur Revitalisierung und Neunutzung wurden zwar entwickelt, nicht gefunden wurden bisher aber die Geldgeber, die sensibel genug in die Geschichte Österreichs investieren wollen. Auch das Millenium ist am Neugebäude spurlos vorübergegangen.

Neues Leben blüht dagegen unmittelbar vor der Wiener Stadtgrenze: Den „Simmeringer Zauberberg" nannte eine österreichische Tageszeitung das Stadt-

developed but sponsors who are sensitive enough to invest in Austria's history have not been found. Even the celebration of Austria's millennium has failed to include the palace's potential.

In contrast, new life blossoms just outside the city limits. The urban development area at Leberberg was christened "Simmeringer Zauberberg" (Simmering's magic mountain) by an Austrian newspaper. The route of the no.71 tram has been extended to reach the area. Around 10,000 people will find a new home here. The first plans for the 90 hectare area were already developed in 1972 but it was the urgent need for apartments over the last few years that brought the project to life. In 1991 the contracts for the building of 4,000 apartments were given to 11 different building constructors and architects. Quite interesting is the 28,000 square meter park in the middle of the area that contributes to the area's identity. The relatively high density makes possible the necessary infrastructure for the

erweiterungsgebiet am Leberberg, zu dem die Straßenbahnlinie 71 verlängert wurde. Rund 10.000 Menschen finden hier eine neue Heimat. Bereits 1972 wurden erste Planungen für das 90-Hektar-Areal entwickelt, aber erst der dringende Wohnbaubedarf der vergangenen Jahre erweckte das Projekt zum Leben. 1991 wurde der Auftrag für 4.000 Wohnungen erteilt, die nach den 1980 entwickelten Grundgedanken von 11 verschiedenen Bauträgern und Architekten weiterbearbeitet wurden. Markant dabei der 28.000 Quadratmeter große Park in der Mitte des Areals, der mit zur eigenen Identität des neuen Stadtteils beiträgt. Die relativ hohe Dichte ermöglicht auch die nötige Infrastruktur von der bereits begonnenen Besiedlung an. Wien stößt hier an seine Grenze. Und Carolines Reise durch Wien geht zu Ende. Die Wegweiser an der Straße signalisieren ihr, wie nahe der ehemalige Eiserne Vorhang ist: Knapp 60 Kilometer sind es bis Bratislava, der Hauptstadt der Slowakei. Nirgends in Europa liegen zwei Hauptstädte so nahe beieinander, die allerdings über ein halbes Jahrhundert voneinander abgeschnitten waren. Daß die Beziehungen dennoch sehr rasch wieder aufgebaut werden konnten, lag vielleicht auch an den vielen familiären Beziehungen zwischen den Menschen in den beiden Städten. Heute beginnt die Region wieder zusammenzuwachsen, gefördert von der EU, die ja mit ihren Interreg-Programmen vor allem das EU-grenzübergreifende Element stärken will. Die Region zwischen Wien und Bratislava mit ihren kleinen, aber lebendigen Städten wie Hainburg oder Bad Deutsch Altenburg ist dafür besonders prädestiniert. Zusammenarbeit bietet sich auch zwischen den beiden Flughäfen und den Donau-Häfen an.

Gerne wäre Caroline noch die wenigen Kilometer bis nach Carnuntum gefahren, das „Pompeij vor den Toren Wiens", wo ein neugestalteter Archäologischer Park das römische Leben an der

population which has already begun to move in.

Here we have reached the borders of Vienna and Caroline's journey through Vienna is coming to its end.

The road signs along the street indicate to her how near the former iron curtain actually is: it is just about 60 kilometers to Bratislava, the capital of Slovakia. Nowhere in Europe do two capital cities lie so close to each other and yet, for more than 50 years they were cut off from one another. That the relationship between the two cities could be re-established very quickly lies possibly in the many close family relationships between the people of both cities. Today the regions are beginning to grow together, supported by the EU with its EU-border Interreg program that aims to increase relationships with neighboring regions. The regions between Vienna and Bratislava with their small but lively towns, such as Hainburg or Bad Deutsch Altenburg are predestined for such development. The two airports and the Danube harbors also offer a possibility of working together.

Caroline would have liked to travel a few kilometers further to Carnuntum, the "Pompeii at the gates of Vienna" where a new archeological park, depicting Roman life along the Danube is situated. Oh well, the next time perhaps ...

By the way: Caroline had hardly seen the "classical Vienna" promoted by the tourist industry, but on the other hand the face of a city approaching the turn of the century. The face of an old European city. A face almost without wrinkles! A city looking forward to the future.

Donau dokumentiert. Na ja, beim nächsten Mal ...

Übrigens: das Wien, das ihr die klassische Tourismus-Werbung vermitteln wollte, hat sie diesmal kaum gesehen. Aber dafür das Gesicht einer Stadt an der Jahrtausendwende. Das Gesicht einer alten europäischen Stadt. Ein Gesicht fast ohne Falten. Im Outfit der Zukunft.

Im Städtesternenhaufen

Caroline steht vor der Anzeigentafel für die Abflüge. Ihr Flug nach Brüssel, einer von mehr als zehn pro Tag, wird pünktlich sein. Der Flughafen Wien ist ja noch nicht so ausgelastet wie andere Metropolen-Airports.

Caroline studiert die Flugziele: Belgrad, Budapest, Prag, Zagreb, Krakau, Laibach, Tirana und alle anderen mittel- und osteuropäischen Städte sind es. Wien liegt tatsächlich in jenem „mitteleuropäischen Städtesternenhaufen",

In the Milky Way of European Cities

Caroline is standing before the indicator board at the airport. Her flight to Brussels, one of ten per day will depart on time. Vienna's airport is not as busy as those of other major cities.
Caroline studies the indicator board: Belgrade, Budapest, Prague, Zagreb, Krakow, Ljubljana, Tirana and all the other middle and east European cities. Vienna really does lie in this middle European "milky way of cities" as once formulated by a Hungarian poet. Sarajevo is the only city missing which is not served by a direct flight. Sarajevo, the city that was once so branded in the consciousness of Vienna as it is today in the consciousness of many Americans.
It was in Sarajevo that one gun shot started World War I, led to the destruction of the Austro-Hungarian Empire and changed the destiny of Europe.
Sarajevo today is the breaking point of inner European relationships as well as

wie es ein ungarischer Dichter einmal formuliert hat. Nur Sarajewo fehlt noch bei den Direktflügen. Sarajewo, jene Stadt, die sich einst in das Bewußtsein Wiens so eingebrannt hat wie heute in jenes auch vieler Amerikaner.

Sarajewo war es, wo der entscheidende Funke für den Ausbruch des Ersten Weltkrieges übersprang, der letztlich zum Ende Österreich-Ungarns und zur Neuordnung Europas führen sollte.

Sarajewo ist heute der Knackpunkt innereuropäischer Beziehungen ebenso wie der Beziehungen zwischen Europa und den USA. Ohne Übertreibung: Die Zukunft des Friedens wird dort entschieden.

Die Österreicher waren massiv dabei, als es darum ging, den Menschen in Bosnien zu helfen, weiß Caroline. Über eine Milliarde Schilling haben sie in einer beispiellosen Spendenaktion aufgebracht. Fast so etwas wie die Care-Hilfspakete der Nachkriegszeit, für die sich die Stadt Wien bei den Amerikanern übrigens eindrucksvoll bedankt hatte: Aus Anlaß der 50jährigen Wiederkehr Österreichs durch die Alliierten lud Wien je einen behinderten Jugendlichen aus jedem US-Bundesstaat für zwei Wochen nach Wien ein. Eine Aktion, die Caroline in den US-Zeitungen mitverfolgt hatte.

Wien hilft in Sarajewo als Stadt, in materiell vielleicht bescheidenerem Rahmen – einige Autobusse hat es erst unlängst zum Wiederaufbau des Verkehrssystems in die bosnische Hauptstadt gebracht. Es will beim Wiederaufbau vor allem durch Know-how und die Beteiligung Wiener Unternehmen mitwirken. Wie übrigens auch in Beirut, jener schicksalhaften Schwesterstadt Sarajewos im Nahen Osten.

Denn auch zum Nahen Osten hatte und hat Wien gute Beziehungen. Bruno Kreisky war es schließlich, der als einer der ersten die Lösungsansätze für einen Frieden in dieser Krisenregion erkannt hatte. Lange nach seinem Tode wird er

between Europe and the USA. Without exaggeration: the future of peace will be decided here.

Caroline knew that the population of Austria offered tremendous support to the people of Bosnia. More than one billion Austrian schillings were donated by the people of Austria. The situation was somewhat similar many years before when Austria received help in the form of Care-packets from America. On the occasion of the 50th anniversary of the liberation of Austria by the allies, Vienna invited two handicapped youths from the exact state in America that had supplied these Care packets for a two weeks' vacation. Caroline had followed this in American newspapers.

As far as possible, Vienna is trying to help the City of Sarajevo. Recently, buses were sent to the capital for the rebuilding of a public transport system. As far as reconstruction of the capital goes, Vienna hopes to help with its know-how and the involvement of Austrian firms – just as in the case of Beirut in the Middle East, which, like Sarajevo, has also been badly struck by fate.

Then Vienna had, and still has, quite a good relationship to the Near East. It was Bruno Kreisky who was one of the first people to recognize a solution for peace is this crisis region. Long after his death, even when there are set-backs, his ideas are confirmed through the progress being made at the end of this century.

Vienna, the natural center of the middle European "milky way of cities" wishes to cultivate its relationships both in the East and West. Caroline remembers that Austrian foreign policy wishes to contribute towards new European integration. From experience, through the building up of traditional relationships; not burdened by belonging to any block; Austria is neutral and many Austrians wish it to remain so even when the country takes on and fulfills its new tasks within the new Europe.

In Europe? Caroline thinks "Where is this new Europe really?" Somehow it

durch die – wenn auch immer wieder rückschlagsbehafteten – Fortschritte am Ende dieses Jahrhunderts bestätigt. Wien, das natürliche Zentrum des mitteleuropäischen Städtesternenhaufens, will seine Beziehungen in Ost und West gleichermaßen ausbauen. Wiener Außenpolitik, erinnert sich Caroline, will zur neuen europäischen Integration beitragen. Aus Erfahrung, aufbauend auf traditionellen Beziehungen. Unbelastet von Blockzugehörigkeit. Denn das kleine Österreich ist nach wie vor neutral. Und die meisten Österreicher wollen es auch bleiben, auch wenn Österreich seine Aufgaben im neuen Europa ernst nimmt und erfüllen wird.

In Europa? Wo ist denn dieses Europa eigentlich wirklich?", denkt sich Caroline. Irgendwie scheint ihr, hat sie hier in Wien einen Querschnitt durch das erlebt, was Europa ausmacht. Vor allem die mitteleuropäischen Städte sind ja oft so etwas wie kleinere Abbilder Wiens, jedenfalls durch die jahrhundertelange gemeinsame Geschichte von der Donau-Metropole geprägt. Wie gesagt: Auch in Brüssel wird Caroline wieder Wiener Spuren finden.

Auf Wiedersehen in Wien

Wann „Metropolis TV" Wirklichkeit wird, wann es Carolines Wien-Feature anbieten wird, wissen wir heute noch nicht. Aber alle Mitreisenden haben sich ihr Wien-Bild ohnehin bereits selbst machen können. Und wer sich Wien noch nicht selbst hat ansehen können, dem haben hoffentlich die Bilder in diesem Buch einen sehr lebendigen Eindruck vermittelt.

Auf Wiedersehen!
Bei einer Reise durch Wien.

seems that here in Vienna she had experienced a cross- section of that which constitutes this Europe. Above all the central European cities are often something like copies of Vienna, in any case they are influenced through their shared history by the Danube metropolis. As already mentioned: even in Brussels Caroline will again find traces of Vienna.

Auf Wiedersehen in Vienna!

When "Metropolis TV" will become reality we do not know, nor when Caroline's Vienna feature will be shown but anyhow, all fellow travelers have been able to gain their own impression of the city. For those who have not been able to see Vienna for themselves, hopefully, the pictures in this book will have made a vivid impression.

Auf Wiedersehen – See you in Vienna!

In der Wiesen, Wien 23
Franziska Ullmann

Osramgründe, Wien 23
Bauteil/*Project section*: Eric Steiner
Leitprojekt/*Master project*:
Martin Treberspurg

Wiener Projekte – Eine Auswahl
Viennese Projects – A Selection

Museumsquartier, Wien 7
Ortner & Ortner, Manfred Wehdorn

Versicherungsgebäude/
Insurance Company Building
Taborstraße, Wien 2
Hans Hollein

Bebauung/*Highrise Buildings* **Wienerberg**, Wien 10
Massimiliano Fuksas

Bebauungsstudie/*Building covering* **Gaudenzdorfer Knoten**, Wien 15, Ortner & Ortner

Wohnpark Neue Donau/*New Danube Residential Park*, Wien 22, Harry Seidler

Andromeda-Tower
Donau-City, Wien 22
Hans Hollein

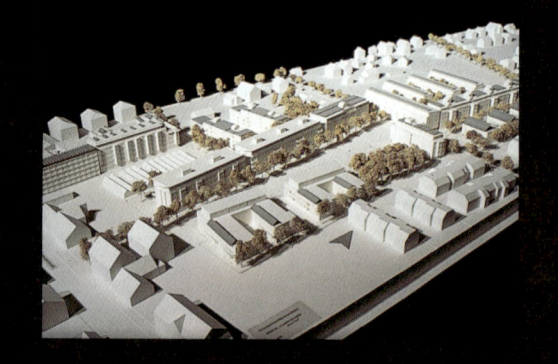

Sun-City, Wien 22
Atelier 4

„Wolkenspange" über den Gürtel, Wien 15
Adolf Krischanitz

Wohnbau Stadtbahnbögen/*Residential Building – Railway Bridges*,
Spittelau, Wien 9, Zaha Hadid

Wohnbau/*Residential Building* **Thürnlhofstraße**,
Wien 11, Regina Pizzinini

Erlebniswelt
Öffentlicher Raum.
Rund um den Spittelberg
wird zeitgenössische Kunst
auf Litfaßsäulen präsentiert.
Kunst als Konfrontation
im Alltag,
im Vorübergehen.

gewista

Bank Austria

SDG

Blue Danube Schiffahrt GmbH

Donaukraft

Ein schnell wachsender Kreis von Erdenbürgern verschreibt sich einer sehr billigen, kleinen und technisch geheimnisvollen russischen Photokamera namens Lomo Kompakt Automat und versucht sich mit dem „unmäßigen Experiment": möglichst viele Photos - genannt Lomographien - aus möglichst unmöglichen Positionen und in möglichst unmöglichen Situationen schießen und das Ganze möglichst billig beim Supermarkt entwickeln lassen. Resultat ist eine unmenge von unmöglichen Lomographien, die - zu Phototableaus mit tausenden Photos zusammengefügt - durch ihr Farb- und Ausdruckskraft regelmäßig die Betrachter begeistern. Eine Doppelausstellung in Moskau und New York im Oktober 1994, bei der jeweils 10.000 Lomographien der jeweils anderen Stadt gezeigt wurden, hat die Lomographie erstmals international bekannt gemacht. Seither werden nach einem neuartigen Kunst – Franchising-System im In- und Ausland Lomo-Botschaft gegründet, eigens inaugurierte Lomo-Botschafter bauen auf dem lomographischen Basiskonzept selbständige Lomographen-Vereine auf und führen mit den Hundertschaften ihrer Mitglieder – den Lomographen eben – eigene Aktionen durch; Ausstellungen, lomographische Streifzüge und Reisen, Aktionen mit Massenmedien, Feste, Publikationen, Aktionen in Zusammenarbeit mit anderen Lomo-Botschaften und der Zentrale usw.; Lomo-Botschaften bestehen bereits in Berlin, Innsbruck, Bregenz, München, Pforzheim, Detmold, Moskau, New York, Zürich, Winterthur, Hanoi und Göteburg. Und Botschaftsgründungen in Lausanne, Paris, Graz, Köln, Kapstadt, Tokio und Toronto stehen vor der Tür.

Seit dem Frühjahr 1996 wird an der Lomo-Weltaktion gebastelt; Eine noch intensivere internationale Vernetzung der Mitglieder mit den lomographischen Organisationen und grenzüberschreitenden Projekte sollen das Rad der Lomographie beschleunigen. So soll ein

A rapidly growing circle of earthlings is prescribing to a cheap and technically baffling little Russian camera that goes by the name of the "Lomo-Compact-Automatic". This rapidly growing circle of earthlings is having a stab at experimenting with a brand of excess by taking as many photographs as possible - called "lomographs", here – from the most impossible of bodily positions and in the most unlikely of situations. These are then developed as cheaply as humanly possible in the next supermarket.

The result is a vast quantity of thoroughly impossible lomographs which are then mounted to form tableaus comprised of thousands of pictures. These tableaus never fail to enthrall the viewer by means of their sheer colorfulness and power expression. In October 1994„ two exhibitions held simultaneously in Moscow and in New York City, each showing 10.000 lomographs of the other sity (Moscow in New York and vice versa), first drew international attention to the existence of lomography. Since then in an innovative from of art-franchising system at home, in Austria, and abroad, Lomo Embassies have been established. Based on the basic lomographic concept, specially inaugurated Lomo Ambassadors have been working to establish independent Lomopher's clubs and, with their own members – hundret of keen lomographers – they have been taking their own initiatives: organizing exhibitions, lomographic outings and tours, project involving the mass media, parties, publications, and events for their own areas and in conjunctions with other Lomo embassies and the Central Office. There are already Lomo embassies in Berlin, Innsbruck, Munich, Pforzheim, Detmold, Moscow, Sankt Petersburg, New York City, Zurich, Winterthur, Hanoi and Göteburg. Further embassies are just about to open in Lausanne, Paris, Graz, Cologne, Capetown, Tokyo and Toronto.

lomographisches Gesamtwerk geschaffen werden, ein lomographischer Bilder-Globus, ein dokumentarisches Lomo-Weltarchiv, eine umfassende Bestandsaufnahme der sichtbaren Weltoberfläche mit all ihren kleinen und feinen Fältchen und Grübchen aus der Perspektive der Lomo-Linse. Jeder ist eingeladen, mit lomographischen Materialien an der Gesamtaktion mitzubauen. Spezielle Fundstücke werden im Lomo-Magazin veröffentlicht.
   Wir freuen uns auf weitere Projekte und Mitglieder!

Lomographische Gesellschaft International
Ungargasse 37, 1030 Wien
tel+fax: +43-1-71 53 834
lomo
blackbox.at, http://www.wien.at/lomo

We have been working on the Lomo Global Event since Spring 1996: An intensification of the organization of an international network of Lomo members in project which cut clear across the boundaries, speeding-up the course of lomographic progression. It is designed to create one massive complete Lomo oeuvre, a lomographic globe, an archive of the world in lomographic documentation, an all-embracing stocktake of the visible surface of the world all ist wonderful little tics, seen from the Lomo lens perspective. Everybody is invited to contribute Lomo material to add to the progress of the project itself. Selected material acquired is to be published in the Lomo-Magazine.
   We are looking forward to new projects und new members:
Lomographische Gesellschaft International, Ungargasse 37, 1030 Wien, tel+fax: +43-1-71 53 834
lomo
blackbox.at, http://www.wien.at/lomo

Liste der Fotografen/
List of the photographers

Verena Örley
Nina
Helmut Pokornig
Ricardo Ignazi
Jugendzentrum Strebersdorf
Jugendzentrum Floridsdorf
Amira Bibawy
Caroline Sherins
Peter Lohmann
Regina Schuler
Simeon Bläsi
Markus Johst
Andrea Neuwirth
Christina Bibawy
Wolfgang Stranzinger
Michael Mignon
„Didi" Merker
„Smoky" Robert Stinauer
„Luvi" Reinhard Radislovich
„Hömerl" Helmut Dobscha
Ciccio Lembotti + friends
Sally Bibawy
Mathias Fiegl
Rolf Leitenbor
Markus Zahradnik
Georg Zahradnik
Julia
Bernhard Winkler
Stefanie Wilhelm
Arne Hettrich
Veronika Szücs

Wien von A-Z
Ein Service der Stadtplanung Wien

Adressen

Wiener Planungswerkstatt
1,Friedrich-Schmidt-Platz 9, A–1082 Wien
Telefon: +43-1-408 80 70
Telefax: +43-1-4000 7271
e-mail: foea@ma18.magwien.gv.at
WWW-Server-Adresse:
http://www.adv.magwien.gv.at:8080/
Öffnungszeiten: Montag bis Freitag von
9 bis 16 Uhr, Donnerstag bis 19 Uhr
Samstag, Sonn- und Feiertag geschlossen

In der Wiener Planungswerkstatt (betreut von der Gruppe Öffentlichkeitsarbeit der Stadtplanung Wien) werden Ausstellungen zum Stand der Dinge unterschiedlicher Themen gezeigt (Architektur, Stadtmöbel, Stadterhaltung/ Stadterneuerung, Grün/Umwelt, regionale Beziehungen oder die internationale Position Wiens). Dazu gibt es meist Kataloge. Einzelne dieser Ausstellungen werden auch im Ausland präsentiert. Die Wiener Planungswerkstatt verfügt über einen Medienraum mit TV, Video und den „Neuen Medien" (Portfolio-CD, interaktive CD, CD-ROM, Internet). In der Wiener Planungswerkstatt können die hier angeführten Bücher und Broschüren erworben werden.

Architekturzentrum Wien
Museumsquartier (Messepalast)
Burggasse 1, A-1070 Wien
Telefon: +43-1-522 31 15
Telefax: +43-1-522 31 17
e-mail: azw@magnet.at
Öffnungszeiten: Montag bis Freitag 9 bis 17 Uhr, Ausstellungsbesichtigung (falls nicht anders angekündigt) täglich von 11 bis 19 Uhr

EuropaForum Wien
Rahlgasse 3/2, A-1060 Wien
Telefon: +43-1-5858510-0
Telefax: +43-1-5858510-30
eMail: institut.efw@europaforum.or.at
http://www.europaforum.or.at/wien/

Konzeption, Organisation und Durchführung von öffentlichen Informations- und Diskussionsveranstaltungen, Studienprojekten, internationalen Tagungen und Städtekooperationen zu Themen der gesamteuropäischen und internationalen Politik und Zusammenarbeit.

Vienna from A-Z
A Service by the Urban Planning Department of the City of Vienna

Addresses

Wiener Planungswerkstatt
(Vienna Planning Workshop)
Friedrich-Schmidt-Platz 9, A-1082 Vienna
Tel: +43 1 408 80 70
Fax: +43 1 4000 7271
e-mail: foea@ma18.magwien.gv.at
WWW server address:
http://www.adv.magwien.gv.at:8080/
Office hours: Monday to Friday, 9 a.m. – 4 p.m.
Thursday, 9 a.m. – 7 p.m., Closed on Saturdays, Sundays and Public Holidays

The Planning Workshop features exhibitions on a variety of subjects, attempting to highlight the state of the art in such fields as architecture, street furniture, preservation and renewal of the urban environment, ecology/the environment, regional relations or Vienna's position in the world. Catalogues tie in with most of the exhibitions, many of which are also shown abroad. The Planning Workshop has a small auditorium, complete with TV, video and such new technologies as portfolio Cds, CD-ROMs and the Internet. The books and brochures listed below may be purchased at the Planning Workshop.

Architekturzentrum Wien
(Vienna Architectural Center)
Museumsquartier (Messepalast)
Burggasse 1, A-1070 Vienna
Tel: +43-1-522 31 15
Fax: +43-1-522 31 17
e-mail: azw@magnet.at
Office hours: Monday to Friday, 9 a.m. – 5 p.m.
Exhibitions may be visited daily
from 11 a.m. – 7 p.m.
(unless otherwise specified)

Europaforum Wien
Rahlgasse 3/2, A-1060 Vienna
Tel: +43-1-5858510-0
Fax: +43-1-5858510-30
e-mail: institut.efw@europaforum.or.at
http://www.europaforum.or.at/wien/

Planning and organization of panel discussions and public information events, study projects, international meetings and collaboration projects between cities focussing on European and international politics and cooperation.

Kunstraum Wien
Messeplatz 1, A-1070 Wien (Museumsquartier)
Telefon +43-1-522 76 13
Telefax +43-1-522 66 42
e-mail: kunstraum@thing.or.at
Öffnungszeiten: Dienstag bis Freitag von 14 bis 19 Uhr, Samstag von 11 bis 19 Uhr

Ausstellungen, Reflexionen, Ausstellungsgespräche

MAK
(Österreichisches Museum
für angewandte Kunst)
Stubenring 5, A-1010 Wien
Telefon: +43-1-711 36-0
Telefax: +43-1-713 10 26
Öffnungszeiten MAK, MAK-Design Service Terminal, MAK-Bibliothek, MAK-Designshop, Buchhandlung Minerva im MAK: täglich 10 bis 18 Uhr, Donnerstag bis 21 Uhr, Montag geschlossen
MAK-Cafe täglich 10 bis 24 Uhr,
Montag geschlossen

Wien Tourismus
Obere Augartenstraße 40, A-1020 Wien
Telefon: +43-1-211 14-0
Telefax: +43-1-216 84 92
Wien-Prospekte und -Informationen

Wiener Linien
Wiener Stadtwerke-Verkehrsbetriebe
Erdbergstraße 202 (U3-Station Erdberg),
A-1030 Wien
Telefon: +43-1-79 09-105
Öffnungszeiten: Montag bis Freitag (werktags) von 8 bis 15 Uhr

Informationsstellen in den U-Bahnstationen Karlsplatz, Stephansplatz, Westbahnhof, Praterstern, Philadelphiabrücke, Landstraße, Volkstheater

Wiener Wirtschaftsförderungsfonds
1., Ebendorferstraße 2, A-1082 Wien
Telefon: +43-1-4000-86794
Telefax: +43-1-4000-7070

Nur als östlichste Metropole Mitteleuropas in der EU eröffnet Wien einem Investor neue Perspektiven. Viele Unternehmen machen sich das gute Angebot an Fachkräften, die ausgezeichnete Infrastruktur sowie das internationale Renommee der Donaustadt zunutze. Ansprechpartner für alle, die sich für den Standort Wien interessieren, ist der Wiener Wirtschaftsförderungsfonds (WWFF). Der kostenlose Beratungsservice hilft bei der Erstellung von Finanzierungskonzepten und bei der Klärung aller bau-

Kunstraum Wien
Messeplatz 1, A 1070 Vienna (Museumsquartier)
Tel: +43-1-522 76 13
Fax: +43-1-522 66 42
e-mail: kunstraum@thing.or.at
Opening hours: Tuesday to Friday, 2 p.m. – 7 p.m., Saturday 11 a.m. – 7 p.m.
Exhibitions, interpretative programmes

MAK
(Österreichisches Museum für angewandte Kunst/Museum of Applied Arts)
Stubenring 5, A-1010 Vienna
Tel: +43-1-711 36-0
Fax: +43-1-713 10 26
Opening hours: MAK, MAK Design Service Terminal, MAK Library, MAK Design Shop, Minerva Bookshop in the MAK: daily, from 10 a.m. – 6 p.m., Thursday from 10 a.m. – 9 p.m., closed on Mondays
MAK Cafe open daily from 10 a.m. to midnight, closed on Mondays

Wien Tourismus (Vienna Tourist Board)
Obere Augartenstraße 40, A-1020 Vienna
Tel: +43 1 211 14-0
Fax: +43 1 216 84 92
Brochures and information on Vienna

Wiener Linien (Vienna Transport Board)
Vienna Public Enterprises: Transport Board
Erdbergstraße 202 (U3 subway station Erdberg), A-1030 Vienna
Tel: +43-1-79 09 105
Office hours: Monday to Friday (working days) from 8 a.m. to 3 p.m.

Information offices located in the subway stations Karlsplatz, Stephansplatz, Westbahnhof, Praterstern, Philadelphiabrücke, Landstrasse, Volksteather

Wiener Wirtschaftsförderungsfonds
(Vienna Business Promotion Fund)
Ebendorferstrasse 2, A-1082 Vienna
Tel: +43-1-4000-86794
Fax: +43-1-4000-7070

Vienna offers investors new perspectives, not only as the easternmost metropolis of the European Union. Many enterprises have taken advantage of the broad gamut of specialized staff and excellent infrastructure as well as of the international renown of this capital city on the Danube. The best contact address for all those interested in Vienna as a business location is the Wiener Wirtschaftsförderungsfonds (WWFF), which offers a free advisory service in preparing

und gewerberechtlichen Fragen. Weiters informiert er über Förderungsmöglichkeiten, unterstützt bei Behördenwegen und bietet Hilfe bei der Suche nach geeigneten Geschäftsräumlichkeiten oder Grundstücken.

Zukunfts.Station Wien
Rahlgasse 3, A–1060 Wien
Telefon: +43-1-586 10 11
Telefax: +43-1-586 10 11-33
e-mail: zukunfts.station@adis.at

Beschäftigt sich mit Fragen der nachhaltigen ökonomisch/ökologischen Stadtentwicklung auf Basis interdisziplinär erarbeiteter wissenschaftlicher Erkenntnisse (Wiener Internationale Zukunftskonferenz).

Wien-Haus in Brüssel
Maison de Vienne, Avenue de Tervuren 58,
B–1040 Brüssel
Verbindungsbüro der Stadt Wien
Telefon: +43-322-734 10 17
Telefax: +43-322-733 70 58

Bücher, Broschüren
Auszug aus den in der Wiener Planungswerkstatt erhältlichen Publikationen im Rahmen der Schriftenreihe „Beiträge zur Stadtforschung, Stadtentwicklung und Stadtgestaltung":

Band 33
Orte des Spiels
Loidl-Reisch C., 1992, öS 190,-
(A4, 184 S., Skizzen, Pläne, Photos)

Band 36
Behindertengerechte Städtische Freiräume
Drexel A., Feuerstein B., Licka L., Proksch T., 1992, öS 120,- (A4, 128 S. plus Zusammenfassung in Brailleschrift, Pläne, Skizzen, Photos)

Band 41
Klaus Novy
Beiträge zum Planungs- und Wohnungswesen
Förster W., 1993, öS 150,- (A4, 58 S., Photos)

Band 52
Verkehrskonzept Wien – Generelles Maßnahmenprogramm
Heft 9 – Hiess H., Rosinak W., Sedlmayer H., Snizek S., 1994, öS 180,- (A4, 172 S., Graphiken, Pläne)

---

financing plans and resolving legal questions relating to building activities as well as trade and industry. WWFF also provides information on the financial assistance available, gives help in dealing with all administrative matters and offers support in locating suitable office space or business premises.

Zukunfts.Station Wien (Future.Base Vienna)
Rahlgasse 3, A-1060 Vienna
Tel: +43-1-586 10 11
Fax: +43-1-586 10 11-33
e-mail: zukunfts.station@adis.at

Focusses on all aspects of sustainable economic/ecological urban development on the basis of insights developed within the context of interdisciplinary scientific projects (Vienna International Conference on the Future).

Vienna House in Brussels
Maison de Vienne
Avenue de Tervuren 58, B-1040 Brussels
Liaison office of the City of Vienna
Tel: +32 2-734 10 17
Fax: +32 2-733 70 58

Books and Brochures
A selection of the publications available from the Vienna Planning Workshop within the series "Contributions to Urban Research, Urban Development and Urban Design"
(The English titles given in brackets are literal renderings of the German titles; most of the brochures are not available in English).

Volume 33
Orte des Spiels (Places for Play)
Loidl- Reisch C., 1992, ATS 190,- (A4, 184 pages, drawings, maps, photos)

Volume 36
Behindertengerechte Städtische Freiräume (Urban Public Space Accessible for the Disabled)
Drexel A., Feuerstein B., Licka L., Proksch T., 1992, ATS 120,- (A4, 128 pages, plus summary in Braille; maps, drawings, photos)

Volume 41
Klaus Novy
Beiträge zum Planungs- und Wohnungswesen (Contributions to Planning and Housing)
Förster W., 1993, ATS 150,- (A4, 58 pages, photos)

In den letzten Jahren wurden vom Wiener Gemeinderat in zwei Schritten die „Leitlinien" und das „Maßnahmenprogramm" zum Wiener Verkehrskonzept, das unter Einbeziehung einer breiten Öffentlichkeit (Bürgerinitiativen) erarbeitet worden war, beschlossen. Hauptziele sind die Erhöhung der Verkehrssicherheit aller Verkehrsteilnehmer und die Attraktivierung der öffentlichen Verkehrsmittel. Im Jahr 2010 soll ein wesentlicher Anteil der Wege – konkret rund 45% – mit öffentlichen Verkehrsmitteln zurückgelegt werden (1990 waren es noch 37%). Daher ist vor allem eine Attraktivierung und Erweiterung des öffentlichen Verkehrs vorgesehen.

Im März 1993 wurden die Leitlinien zum neuen Wiener Verkehrskonzept vom Wiener Gemeinderat beschlossen. Sie sollen als grobe Zielrichtung und als strategischer Handlungsrahmen für den verkehrspolitischen Weg ins nächste Jahrhundert dienen.

Folgende allgemeinen, verkehrspolitischen und verkehrsplanerischen Grundsätze waren demgemäß bei der Entwicklung von konkreten Maßnahmenprogrammen einzuhalten.
• Die Menschen in der Stadt haben Vorrang,
• Verkehr muß umweltschonender werden,
• Verkehr muß sozial verträglicher werden,
• Verkehr muß sicherer werden,
• mehr Platz für FußgängerInnen und RadfahrerInnen,
• Verkehr hat der Wirtschaft zu dienen,
• Verkehrsbewältigung erfordert Kooperation,
• Verkehr ist in der gesamten Region zu vernetzen.
• Der Erfolg des neuen Verkehrskonzeptes ist wesentlich von den neuen Qualitätsansprüchen bei der Umsetzung und der Überwachung sowie von der Erfolgskontrolle abhängig.

Band 53
Stadtentwicklungsplan Wien 1994
Wien 1994, öS 320,- (Format 23,0 x 30,0 cm, 362 S., Graphiken, Photos, Pläne)

Ein „Drehbuch für Wien" erfordert langfristige und kontinuierliche Arbeit. Die Stadtplanung Wien hat in den letzten Jahren eine Fülle von Grundsatz- und Detailplanungen erarbeitet, aus der hier nur beispielsweise einige wenige angeführt sind.

Zur Neudefinierung der gesamtstädtischen Entwicklung und der Rolle Wiens in einem neuen Europa wurde 1991 mit der Vorlage der „Leitlinien für die Stadtentwicklung Wiens" an den Wiener Gemeinderat die Überarbeitung des Stadtentwicklungsplanes aus dem Jahr 1984 eingeleitet. Das Ziel einer umweltgerech-

Volume 52
Verkehrskonzept Wien –
Generelles Maßnahmenprogramm
(A Traffic Concept for Vienna – General Program)
No.9 – Hiess H., Rosinak W., Sedlmayer H., Snizek S., 1994, ATS 180,- (A4, 172 pages, charts, maps)

Over the past few years, the Vienna City Council adopted in two stages, a "master plan" and a "general program" for the Vienna Traffic Concept, which had been drawn up with strong public participation (citizens' initiatives).
The main objectives of the Traffic Concept consist in increasing traffic safety for all and enhancing the attractiveness of public transport.
By the year 2010 the public transport system should account for a substantial proportion – more specifically around 45% – of all transport activities in Vienna. (In 1990 ist share was 37%).
For this reason, the City of Vienna is endeavouring to make public transport more attractive and expand the system accordingly. In March 1993 the master plan for the New Traffic Concept for Vienna was adopted by the City Council. The master plan is to serve as a rough outline and as a strategic basis for defining an appropriate transport policy for the 21st century.

Therefore, the following general principles of transport and planning policies have had to be taken into account in establishing a specific program of measures:
• In a city, people have priority.
• Transport must become more environmentally-friendly.
• The social aspects of transport must increasingly be taken into account.
• Transport must become safer.
• More space must be made available for pedestrians and cyclists.
• Transport must serve the interests of the business sector.
• Traffic management calls for cooperation.
• Consolidated efforts must be made to link up public transport troughout the region.
• The success of the New Traffic Concept is largely dependent on the new demands on quality we see manifesting themselves when it comes to implementing an monitoring the concept as well as checking ist progress.

Volume 53
Stadtentwicklungsplan Wien 1994
(1994 Vienna Urban Development Plan)
Vienna 1994, ATS 320,- (230 mm x 300 mm, 362 pages, charts, photos, maps)

A scenario (as embodied in "A Film-Script for Vienna") requires long-term and consistent

ten Verkehrspolitik sollte auf Basis eines „Neuen Wiener Verkehrskonzeptes" forciert umgesetzt werden. Für die vier wichtigen Stadtentwicklungsgebiete wurde die Erstellung von städtebaulichen Leitprogrammen begonnen, um ausgehend von den gesamtstädtischen Konzepten klare Vorgaben über die Bebauungsstruktur, die Verkehrserschließung, die freizuhaltenden und auszugestaltenden Grünflächen und für die Umsetzung einzelner Projekte in diesen Gebieten rechtzeitig zur Verfügung zu haben. Dieses beispiellose Planungsprogramm bedurfte sowohl zur inhaltlichen Inspiration wie auch hinsichtlich des Ablaufes spezieller organisatorischer Vorkehrungen. Zur Erstellung des Leitprogrammes und des Verkehrskonzeptes wurde eine straffe Organisationsform unter der Leitung der „Gruppe Planung" eingerichtet. Weiters wurde, insbesondere im Hinblick auf die neue Aufgabe der Stadterweiterung, ein internationaler „Beirat für die Stadtentwicklungsbereiche", bestehend aus Experten unterschiedlicher Wissensdisziplinen eingesetzt. Gemeinsam mit den magistratsinternen Planern wurden Visionen für die Stadtentwicklung unter besonderer Berücksichtigung sozialer, ökologischer und gestalterischer Aspekte entworfen. Besonders hervorzuheben war die Rolle des Beirates als Diskussionsplattform für Fachleute und Politiker sowie engagierte Bürger. Der „Stadtentwicklungsplan 1994" legt die Richtlinien für das stadtplanerische Handeln der nächsten Jahre fest. Die Schwerpunkte der Aussagen beziehen sich vor allem auf die zukünftige Rolle Wiens im europäischen Wettstreit der Städte, auf die Frage, wo und wie der große Bedarf an Wohnungen und Arbeitsplätzen in den nächsten 20 Jahren abgedeckt werden kann, auf die Zielvorstellungen eines sparsamen Umgangs mit Grund und Boden durch kompakte Bebauungsformen und, als ein sehr wesentlicher Punkt, auf ein ehrgeiziges Programm zur Sicherung des übergeordneten Grünsystems im Nordosten von Wien und in der Folge im Süden, als Beitrag zur Schließung des Wald- und Wiesengürtels, etwa vergleichbar mit der Initiative der Unterschutzstellung des Wienerwaldes vor ca. 90 Jahren. In diesem Sinne sind zukünftig neben den neuentwickelten Optionen für die Stadtentwicklung im Norden, Nordosten und Süden Wiens entlang der Entwicklungsachsen gezielt untergenutzte Flächen innerhalb des dicht verbauten Stadtgebietes für die Wohnraumbeschaffung einzubeziehen. Der Stadtenwicklungsplan 1994 kann in der Planungswerkstatt erworben werden. Die Zeitschrift „Perspektiven", Heft 10/1994 enthält eine Kurzfassung.

work. Over the past few years the Urban Planning Department of the City of Vienna has drawn up a host of basic and detailed plans, of which only a few are listed here as examples. With a view to refining the overall urban development strategy and the role of Vienna in a new Europe, a "Master Plan for the Urban Development of Vienna" was submitted to the Vienna City Council in 1991, which initiated a revision of the 1984 Urban Development Plan. The goal of an environmentally-friendly transport concept was to be strengthened on the basis of a "New Traffic Concept for Vienna". Planning guidelines were drawn up for the four major urban development regions, in order to define, well ahead of time and on the basis of the overall Master Plan for Vienna, unequivocal directives for zoning, development in terms of transport, the green areas that are to be left untouched and those that are to be laid out as parks and gardens, as well as for the implementation of individual projects in these areas. This unprecedented planning program required special organizational measures, both regarding the substance and the schedule of implementation.

For the purpose of preparing the Master Plan and the Traffic Concept, a specialized organizational unit was set up within the context of the City Planner's office. Furthermore, an international "Advisory Board for Urban Development Areas" was established, particularly with regard to the new challenge of urban expansion. The Advisory Board consisted of experts from different specialized fields. Together with the city's own team of planners, visions for urban development were conceived, with particular regard for social and ecological soundness as well as overall urban design. The role of the Advisory Board as a discussion platform for experts, politicians and citizens with a high level of commitment deserves special mention.

The "1994 Urban Development Plan" defines the context for the urban planning activities of the next years. The Plan focusses on the role Vienna will play among the other European cities, on how (and where) the massive need for housing and jobs can be met during the next 20 years, on the goal of compact building techniques to ensure economical land-use and, importantly, on an ambitious program for preserving the large expanse of forests and meadows in the north-east and also in the south of Vienna in order to gloce the green belt. The latter endeavour is similar in scope to the initiative of approximately 90 years ago to place the Vienna Woods under protection. Consequently, efforts should be made in future to use underutilized areas along the development axes in the high-

Band 54
Planung initiativ
Bürgerbeteiligung in Wien
Antalovsky E., König I., 1994, öS 180,-
(A4, 196 S., Photos)

Stadtplanung wird oftmals als eine überwiegend technische und planerische Aufgabe betrachtet. Sie ist selbstverständlich weit mehr, insbesondere ist Stadtplanung eine gesellschaftliche Aufgabe und damit auch ein zentrales Element des politischen Meinungsbildungs- und Entscheidungsprozesses. Anliegen einer modernen Stadtpolitik muß es sein, das Handeln der in den Stadtplanungsprozeß involvierten öffentlichen und privaten Akteure für die Bevölkerung transparent und nachvollziehbar zu machen. Ein nächster und demokratiepolitisch noch wichtigerer Schritt ist aber, der Bevölkerung Möglichkeiten und Angebote zu schaffen, die ihr erlauben, aus der Rolle der Konsumenten von Stadtplanungsprodukten in die Rolle der Mitgestalter zu schlüpfen und sich dadurch ihre Stadt aktiv anzueignen. Wien hat sehr früh begonnen solche Möglichkeiten zu entwickeln. Der Stadt Wien ist es gelungen, aus dem Spannungsfeld von eigenem Anspruch nach verbesserten Partizipationsmöglichkeiten einerseits und Forderungen von Interessierten und Bürgeraktivisten andererseits heraus kontinuierlich innovative Schritte zur Bürgerbeteiligung zu setzen. Wien kann im internationalen Vergleich betrachtet auf eine breite Erfahrungspalette an Bürgerbeteiligungsverfahren zurückgreifen. Um auf Basis eines möglichst vielfältigen Meinungsspektrums Antworten finden zu können, hat die Stadtplanung Wien den Band „Planung initiativ" herausgegeben. In den einzelnen Diskussionsbeiträgen setzen sich Planungsexperten, Meinungsforscher, Sozialwissenschafter und Journalisten sehr kritisch mit der Bürgerbeteiligung in Wien, ihren Erfolgen und Zukunftsperspektiven auseinander.

Für die Bürgerbeteiligung in Wien liefert dieser Band eine umfassende Zusammenschau, was in den letzten Jahren wo und vor allem wie erfolgreich gelaufen ist und er ist eine gute Diskussionsgrundlage für die Entwicklung neuer, besserer Kommunikationsformen zwischen Bürger, Experten und Politiker.

Band 55
Typen öffentlicher Freiräume in Wien
Ansätze zu einer Kategorisierung
Loidl-Reisch C., 1995, öS 120,-
(A4, 80 S., Pläne, Photos)

density metropolitan area for the express purpose of creating new housing – in addition to the new urban development options proposed for the north, northeast and south of Vienna.

The 1994 Urban Development Plan may be purchased at the Planning Workshop. The periodical "Perspektiven"No. 10/1994 features a short summary.

Volume 54
Planung Initiativ (Citizens' Initiatives in Vienna)
Antalovsky E., König I., 1994, ATS 180,-
(A4, 196 pages, photos)

Urban planning is often regarded as a largely technical task. It is of course much more; urban planning is, first and foremost, a social responsibility and therefore forms a core element in the political and decision-making process. Urban development policies must ensure that the activities of the public and private actors involved in the urban planning process are made transparent and comprehensible. However, another step – even more important from the democratic point of view – is to afford the public the possibility to change from being mere consumers of urban planning "products" to being co-designers and thus becoming actively involved in their city. Vienna began to develop such options very early on. The city administration has continuously succeeded in making innovative strides toward the increased involvement of the general public, responding both to ist own claim for an increased participation of citizens and to demands made by interested parties and civil activists. By international comparison, Vienna can look back on rich experience in citizens' participation in urban development processes. In order to find solutions based on as wide a range as possible of the public opinion, the Urban Planning Department of the City of Vienna has published the volume "Planung Initiativ". The individual contributions, written by planning experts, opinion pollsters, sociologists and journalists, explore very closely popular participation in Vienna, ist success and future perspectives.

This volume provides a comprehensive survey of citizens' initiatives in Vienna, the latest developments and, above all, their achievements. It also provides a good basis for establishing new forms of communication between citizens, experts and politicians.

Volume 55
Typen öffentlicher Freiräume in Wien
(Types of Public Space in Vienna: Attempts at classification) Loidl-Reisch C., 1995, ATS 120,-
(A4, 80 pages, maps, photos)

Band 58
Step by Step
Vienna, Urban Development Plan/
The New Traffic Concept
Stadtplanung Wien, 1995, öS 150,- (englisch)
(A4, 134 S., Pläne und Graphiken)

Band 60
Neue Wege der Öffentlichkeitsarbeit
Stadtplanung Wien, 1996, öS 350,-
Broschüre und CD-ROM
(A4, 124 S., Photos)

Sonstige Publikationen

Wiener Schutzzonen
Bestandsaufnahme und Grundlagensammlung
MA 19, Wien 1992, öS 300,- (A3, Abb. und Pläne)
(Ergänzungsblätter je öS 80,-)

Wien – verkehrt ?!
(deutsche Ausgabe)
Verkehrspolitik für ein Wien auf dem Weg
ins 21. Jahrhundert
Traffic in Vienna/Les Transports à Vienne
(engl./franz. Ausgabe)
Stadtplanung Wien, 1994, öS 110,-
(A4, 72 S., Abb., Pläne und Photos)

Projekte und Konzepte der Schulen Wiens
Hefte 1–8
Stadtplanung Wien, 1994–1996, je öS 80,-
(195 x 240 mm, 24S.–36 S., Photos)

Lernen fürs Leben
Das Schulbauprogramm 2000
Heute, in einer neuen Wachstumsperiode der Stadt, in der wir von einer Bauerfordernis von 10.000 geförderten Wohnungen jährlich ausgehen, neue Stadtteile entstehen, ist auch der Schulbau wieder zu einem zentralen Thema geworden. Quantitativ – weil wir jetzt dringend mehr Schulen brauchen – und qualitativ – weil die öffentliche Hand gefordert ist, in der Stadtentwicklung auch architektonische Akzente zu setzen. Daß es dabei nicht bloß um die äußerlich sichtbare Qualität geht, liegt auf der Hand. Die Schule ist – Stichwort Ganztagsschule – nicht nur Unterrichts- sondern zunehmend Lebensraum – ihre Gestaltung muß sich daher in erster Linie an den Bedürfnissen der Kinder und Jugendlichen orientierten. Künftige Generationen sollen sich wenigstens an eine angenehme Lernumgebung erinnern können. Je angenehmer, je freier und heller, je farbenfroher, kreativer dieser Raum gestaltet ist, umso eher werden die Schülerinnen und Schüler ihren Lernalltag nicht unter Zwang, sondern mit einer positiven Ein-

Volume 58
Step by Step
Vienna, Urban Development Plan/
The New Traffic Concept
Urban Planning Vienna, 1995, ATS 150,- (A4, 134 pages, maps and charts; available in English)

Volume 60
Neue Wege der Öffentlichkeitsarbeit
(available in English as **"New Approaches in Public Relations"**) Urban Planning Vienna, 1996, ATS 250,- Brochure and CD-ROM (A4, 124 pages, photos)

Other publications

Wiener Schutzzonen (Protection Zones in Vienna)
Inventory and descriptions
Municipal Department 19 (Architecture and Urban Design), Vienna 1992, ATS 300,-
(A3, illustrations and maps)
(Supplementary sheets ATS 80,- each)

Traffic in Vienna/Les Transports à Vienne
(English/French): Defining a transport policy for Vienna in the 21st century, Urban Planning Vienna, 1994, ATS 110,- (A4, 72 pages, illustrations, maps and photos)

Projekte und Konzepte Hefte 1-8
(Projects and Concepts Nos. 1-8)
Focus on schools
Urban Planning Vienna 1994-1996, ATS 80,- each
(195 x 240 mm, 24–36 pages, photos)

Lernen fürs Leben (Learning for Life)
School Construction Program 2000
Today, in a new period of Vienna's growth, in which we envision a construction volume of around 10,000 subsidized apartments per year and in which entirely new urban areas are being created, the building of new schools has again become a key issue. This refers both to quantity – because Vienna now urgently needs more schools – and to quality – because the public authorities are being called upon to impart architectural stimuli to urban development. It goes without saying that what we mean by quality is not just the outward appearance of buildings. Schools are increasingly becoming not only places of learning but also complete living evironments – just think of the growing demand for alls-day schooling. Their design must therefore primarily take into accounmt the need of the children and young people attending them. Future generations should at least be able to look back on a relaxed learning atmosphere. The more pleasant, attractive and bright the environment and the more

stellung bewältigen. Die städtebauliche und architektonische Gestaltung mß demnach in Einklang mit den aktuellen schulpädagogischen Anforderungen stehen. Deshalb wurden die besten arrivierten, aber auch viele junge Architekten eingeladen, Schulen für Wien zu planen und eine neue Qualität der Lernumgebung zu schaffen.

Wien, Architektur
Der Stand der Dinge
Stadtplanung Wien 1991, öS 150,-, Ausgabe 1991
(318 x 222 mm, 72 S., Abb. und Pläne,
deutsch/englisch)

Wien, Architektur
Der Stand der Dinge
Stadtplanung Wien 1995, öS 150,-, Ausgabe 1995
(318 x 222 mm, 72 S., Abb. und Pläne,
deutsch/englisch)

Wien, Stadterhaltung/Stadterneuerung
Der Stand der Dinge
Stadtplanung Wien, 1995, öS 150,-
(318 x 222mm, 96 S., Abb. und Pläne,
deutsch/englisch)

Wien, Stadtmöbel
Der Stand der Dinge
Stadtplanung Wien 1995, öS 150,-
(318 x 222 mm, 56 S., Abb. und Pläne,
deutsch/englisch)

Wien, Grünes Netzwerk
Der Stand der Dinge
Stadtplanung Wien 1996, öS 150,-
(318 x 222 mm, 72 S., Abb. und Pläne,
deutsch/englisch)

Erhältlich in Buchhandlungen oder direkt bei den Verlagen:

Michael Häupl (Hg.)
Zukunft Stadt
Europas Metropolen im Wandel
ISBN 3-85371-109-X
176 Seiten, br., öS 198,-, Edition Forschung
Promedia, Wickenburggasse 5/12, A-1080 Wien,
Telefon: +43-1-405 27 02

„Zukunft Stadt" enthält einen grundsätzlichen Diskurs über die Perspektiven der Stadtentwicklung. Auf Basis der sozialdemokratischen „Wiener Sommerakademie" präsentiert das vorliegende Buch Beiträge über den aktuellen Wandel urbaner Großräume, der aus unterschiedli-

---

colorful and creative the interior, the more likely pupils are to regard their daily lives at school in a positive way, instead of as something that has been forced upon them.

For this reason, the architectural and urban planning aspects of new school buildings must be in harmony with modern educational needs. Therefore, many of the best established architects, but also numerous up-and-coming ones, have been invited to plan schools for Vienna and create an evironment that affords a new quality of learning.

Wien, Architektur – Der Stand der Dinge (Vienna, Architecture – The State of the Art) German/English, Urban Planning Vienna, 1991, ATS 150,-, 1991 edition (318 x 222 mm, 72 pages, illustrations and maps)

Wien, Architektur – Der Stand der Dinge (Vienna, Architecture – The State of the Art) German/English, Urban Planning Vienna, 1995, ATS 150,-, 1995 edition (318 x 222 mm, 72 pages, illustrations and maps)

Wien, Stadterhaltung/Stadterneuerung – Der Stand der Dinge (Vienna, Preservation and Renewal of the Urban Environment: A Report on the Current State of Affairs) German/English

Urban Planning Vienna, 1995, ATS 150,- (318 x 222 mm, 96 pages, illustrations and maps)

Wien, Stadtmöbel – Der Stand der Dinge (Vienna, Urban Furniture – The State of the Art) German/English, Urban Planning Vienna, 1995, ATS 150,- (318 x 222 mm, 56 pages, illustrations and maps)

Wien, Grünes Netzwerk – Der Stand der Dinge (Vienna, Green Network: The State of the Art) German/English, Urban Planning Vienna, 1996, ATS 150,- (318 x 222 mm, 72 pages, illustrations and maps)

Available in bookshops or directly from the publishers:

Michael Häupl (ed.)
Zukunft Stadt *(Europe's major cities in the winds of change), ISBN 3-85371-109-X, 176 pages, brochure, ATS 198,- Published by: Edition Forschung Promedia, Wickenburggasse 5/12, A-1080 Vienna, tel.: +43-1-405 27 02*

"Zukunft Stadt" explores the perspectives of urban development. Based on the Social Democratic Party's "Vienna Summer Academy", the book features contributions focussing on the current

cher Sicht beleuchtet wird. Die Autoren dieses vom Wiener Bürgermeister mitherausgegebenen Bandes sind Mathias Horx, Wolfgang Nahrstedt, Reinhold Popp, Bernd Marin, Hannes Swoboda, Lore Hostasch, Michael Häupl u.a.

Michael Häupl, Hannes Swoboda (Hg.)
Bleibt Wien Wien?
Spielräume 2020
ISBN 3-85439-155-2
1995 Falter Verlagsgesellschaft,
Marc-Aurel-Straße 9, A-1011 Wien,
Telefon: +43-1-536 60-0,
Telefax: +43-1-536 60-12

„Es gibt viele Möglichkeiten, sich mit Wien zu beschäftigen. Als Insider reizt es einen immer wieder zu überprüfen, wie facettenreich und damit entwicklungs- und konkurrenzfähig denn die Stadt wirklich ist. Wiens Affinität zur Gemütlichkeit zum Beispiel, die auch ein gewisses Maß an Wurschtigkeit und Schlampigkeit impliziert, ist bekannt, in Wiener Liedern besungen, im Wirtschaftsleben aber wohl nicht als Qualitätsmerkmal geschätzt. Der Hang der Wienerinnen und Wiener zur Überhöhung und damit zur Selbstüberschätzung ist in der Geburtsstadt der Psychoanalyse legendär, aber nicht unbedingt konstruktiv und verstellt oftmals den Blick auf naheliegend Originelleres. Wien ist punktuell spektakulär, nicht gerade ein Eldorado der Innovation, in der Summe aber gediegen und europäisch modern: ein Donauwalzer zwischen ‚muddling through' und ‚lean management'?" schrieben die Herausgeber Bürgermeister Michael Häupl und Planungsstadtrat Hannes Swoboda im Vorwort. „Super.visn.vienna 2010" lautete daher die Chiffre für die Arbeit an diesem Buchprojekt, die sowohl die inhaltliche Orientierung als auch die Ambivalenzen zu kennzeichnen sowie die Koketterie durchscheinen zu lassen schien, die die Wienerinnen und Wiener sich selbst, ihrer Stadt und der Zukunft entgegenbringen. Bewußt wurden Fachleute verschiedener Professionen aus dem In- und Ausland ausgesucht. Sie arbeiteten nicht in Form von wissenschaftlichen Abhandlungen, sondern in Form von Essays, Impressionen, Thesen, Kommentaren, Vermutungen und Irritationen. Auch in der Planungswerkstatt erhältlich, öS 280,- (279 x 240mm, 152 S., Abb. und Skizzen)

changes affecting large urban areas and tries to highlight them from different angles.

The authors of this volume include the Mayor of Vienna as well as, inter alia, Mathias Horx, Wolfgang Nahrstedt, Reinhold Popp, Bernd Marin, Hannes Swoboda and Lore Hostasch.

Michael Häupl, Hannes Swoboda (eds.)
Bleibt Wien Wien? Spielräume 2020
(Will Vienna Remain Vienna?)
ISBN 3-85439-155-2
Published in 1995 by Falter Verlagsgesellschaft,
Marc-Aurel-Strasse 9, A-1011 Vienna,
tel.: +43-1-536 60-0, Fax: +43-1-536 60-12

"There are many different ways of getting to know Vienna. As an insider it is fascinating to review how many layers there are to this city and what its potential is for development and for holding its own in the face of competition. There is, for example, Vienna's affinity for conviviality, which also implies a certain measure of sloppiness and a 'don't care' attitude; this aspect is well-known and has been much sung about in Viennese folk-songs, but in the business world it is not exactly valued as a quality. Then there is the tendency of the Viennese toward exaggeration and, consequently, toward an overestimation of their own abilities; in the birthplace of psychoanalysis this is a legendary but not necessarily constructive aspect, and it often clouds the view for more characteristic and original features. Vienna is spectacular in a few aspects, though not exactly an eldorado on innovation; but, all in all, it is a modern, high-quality European city: a waltz composed of 'muddling through' and 'lean management'.", Michael Häupl, Mayor of Vienna, and Hannes Swoboda, City Councillor for Urban Planning, write in the foreword of the book. "Super.visn.vienna 2010" was the code for work on this book project, which seemed to reflect both the thrust of its contents and the ambivalence, as well as the coquettishness, with which the Viennese view themselves, their city and the future. Experts from different professional fields were brought in, both from Austria and outside. Their contributions are not in the shape of scholarly treatises but rather in the form of essays, impressions, theses, commentaries, suppositions and irritations.

Also available from the Planning Workshop, ATS 280,- (279 x 240 mm, 152 pages, illustrations and drawings)

Weitere Wien-Bücher aus dem Falter-Verlag

Grün in Wien
Maria Auböck/Gisa Ruland
öS 320,- (325 S., 290 Fotos)

„Grün in Wien" weiht Wien-Bewohner und -Besucher in die Geheimnisse des Wiener Stadtgrüns ein und stellt – vom Burggarten bis zum Wienerwald – 42 ausgewählte Gärten und Parkanlagen vor. Jede Grünfläche wird nach Geschichte und Gegenwart, Vegetation und Raumerlebnis, Bauten und Denkmälern beschrieben.

Wiener Museumsführer
Berndt Anwander
öS 348,- (400 S., 130 Fotos)

Wiener Märkte
Werner T. Bauer
öS 348,- (300 S., zahlr. Fotos)

Kaffeehäuser in Wien
Thomas Martinek
öS 348,- (264 S., zahlr. Fotos)

Andere Publikationen

Donauatlas Wien
Geschichte der Donauregulierung mit Karten und Plänen aus vier Jahrhunderten
Peter Mohilla(†) und Franz Michlmayr
ISBN 3-85437-105-5
öS 4.300,- (450 x 600 mm, deutsch/englisch, 117 Tafeln, davon 34 ausklappbar, 440 Abb., Karten, Pläne, Grafiken, Luftbilder, Fotos), Österreichischer Kunst- und Kulturverlag P.O.Box 17, A-1016 Wien, Telefon: +43-1-587 85 51

Zeitmaschine U-Bahn
Eine Reise durch Jahrtausende Kulturerfahrungen und Kunstgeschichte(n) mit der „Zeitmaschine U-Bahn". Archäologische Funde und zeitgenössische Werke der bildenden Kunst in den Wiener U-Bahn-Stationen.
öS 120,-, erhältlich im „Wiener Linien-Shop" (Informationsstellen Karlsplatz, Stephansplatz, Westbahnhof, Erdberg)

Wiener Küche 96
Welche Restaurants, Cafes und Konditoreien Ihre Gourmetträume erfüllen, erfahren Sie aus der Broschüre, die Sie gratis in Ihrem Hotel und in den Wien Tourist-Infos erhalten.

Other Books on Vienna published by Falter-Verlag:

Grün in Wien (Green in Vienna)
Maria Auböck/Gisa Ruland
ATS 320,- (325 pages, 290 photos)

"Grün in Wien" opens up to Vienna's residents and visitors the secrets of the city's green areas and introduces – from Burggarten to Vienna Woods – 42 gardens and parks. The past and present, vegetation and visual impact, buildings and monuments of each area are described in this book.

Wiener Museumsführer (Vienna Museum Guide)
Berndt Anwander
ATS 348,- (400 pages, 130 photos)

Wiener Märkte (Viennese Markets)
Werner T. Bauer
ATS 348,- (300 pages, numerous photos)

Kaffeehäuser in Wien (Viennese Cafés)
Thomas Martinek
ATS 348,- (264 pages, numerous photos)

Other Publications

Donauatlas Wien (Vienna Danube Atlas)
History of the Danube regulation, with maps and plans from four centuries (German/English)
Peter Mohilla (+) and Franz Michlmayr
ISBN 3-85437-105-5
ATS 4,300,- (450x600mm, 117 full-page illustrations, of which 34 can be folded out, 440 illustrations, maps, plans, charts, aerial photos, photos) Published by Österreichischer Kunst- und Kulturverlag, P.O. Box 17, A-1016 Vienna, tel.: +43 1 587 85 51

Zeitmaschine U-Bahn (Subway Time Machine:
A journey through thousands of years) Cultural experiences and art from the past and present, with the "subway time machine". Archeological finds and contemporary fine arts in Vienna's subway stations. ATS 120,- Available at the "Wiener Linien Shop" (information offices located at Karlsplatz, Stephansplatz, Westbahnhof, Erdberg)

Wiener Küche 96 (Viennese Cuisine 96)
A list of restaurants, cafés and pastry-shops to tempt your palate. Avaiolable free of charge from your hotel and at the Vienna Tourist Information Offices.

Wien von A–Z
Das kleine Wien-Lexikon hilft bei 200 Sehenswürdigkeiten: Vom Alten Rathaus bis zum Zentralfriedhof. Wenn Sie sich schon daheim informieren möchten: öS 60-Euroscheck an Wien Tourismus, A -1025 Wien, schicken.
Mit der Wien-Karte günstiger bei den Wien Tourist-Infos erhältlich.

Empfehlenswerte Reiseführer

Wien
Stephen Brook (Hauptautor)
RV-Verlag, München 1995
DM 48,- (287 S., viele Farb- und s/w-Abb., Schnittzeichnungen und Grundrisse)
ISBN 3-89480-905-1.

Wien
Karl Unger
DuMont Buchverlag, Köln
DM 39,80, (296 S., zahlr. Farbfotos, Stadtpläne und Karten)
ISBN 3-7701-3609-8

„Der Leser, der über das vorliegende Buch nachdenkt, kann vielleicht die Tiefen und Untiefen der schillernden Wiener Seele erahnen. Ihre Komplexität und existentielle Unruhe liegt hauptsächlich in der zwiespältigen Lage zwischen West und Ost, Europa und Asien" (Frankfurter Allgemeine Zeitung, Jänner 1996)

News

Informationen über das aktuelle Geschehen in Wien erhalten Sie im Rundfunk
Das Neue Radio Wien (UKW 89,9 und 95,5)
Blue Danube Radio (englisch – Nachrichten auch in französisch; UKW 103,8)

Wien-Programme bieten unter anderem die Stadtzeitungen „Falter" und „City" (an Kiosken und in Trafiken).

Perspektiven
heißt eine Fachzeitschrift, die im Auftrag der Stadtbaudirektion der Stadt Wien vom Compress-Verlag herausgegeben wird. Die Zeitschrift beschäftigt sich auf fachlich anspruchsvoller, aber auch für den „Normalverbraucher" lesbarer Ebene mit Fragen der Stadtentwicklung im weitesten Sinn.
Auswahl relevanter Titel:
Die Wiener Bauordnung (8-9/92), Das regulierte Wachstum (10/92), Raum-Bildung (8/93), Ein neues Verkehrskonzept für Wien (8/94), Stadtentwicklungsplan für Wien (8/94)

Vienna from A–Z
This small booklet contains an alphabetical listing of 200 city sights. If you would like to plan your trip to Vienna, just send a Eurocheque for ATS 60,- to "Wien Tourismus" (Vienna Tourist Board), A-1025 Vienna. If you own a Vienna Card, you can get the booklet at a reduced price from the "Vienna Tourist Information Offices".

Recommended travel guides

Wien
Stephen Brook
Published by RV-Verlag, Munich 1995
DM 48,- (287 pages, numerous illustrations in color and black-and-white, sectional drawings and ground plans) ISBN 3-89480-905-1

Wien
Karl Unger
Published by DuMont Buchverlag, Cologne
DM 39,80 (296 pages, numerous color photos, maps) ISBN 3-7701-3609-8

"The reader who takes the time to reflect on this book is perhaps in a better position to plumb the depths of the fascinating Viennese soul, whose complexity and existential unrest can be explained primarily by its ambivalent situation, nestling between West and East, Europe and Asia" (Frankfurter Allgemeine Zeitung, January 1996).

News

Information about topical events in Vienna can be heard on the radio:
Das Neue Radio Wien (FM 89.9 and 95.5)
Blue Danube Radio (broadcasts in English; news in English and French; FM 103.8)

Programs of events in Vienna are found in the newspaper "Falter" and "City" (available at newsstands and "Tabak Trafik" shops).

Perspektiven
is a technical journal that is published by Compress-Verlag at the initiatve of the City Planner's Department. This journal, written both for building experts and for laypersons, deals with urban development issues in their widest sense.
Selection of relevant titles:
Die Wiener Bauordnung (The Viennese Building Code (8-9/92), Das regulierte Wachstum (Regulated Growth) (10/92), Raum-Bildung (Development of Space) (8/93), Ein Neues Verkehrskonzept für Wien (A New Traffic Concept for Vienna) (8/94), Stadtentwicklungsplan für Wien (Vienna Urban Development Plan) (8/94)

Compress-Verlag, Jenullgasse 4, A-1140 Wien
Telefon: +43-1-894 64 49
Telefax: +43-1-894 65 23

Wien Karte/Vienna Card

Die „Reise durch Wien", die in diesem Buch beschrieben wird, läßt sich am besten mit den öffentlichen Verkehrsmitteln und zu Fuß bestreiten. Man kann sie in drei Tagen absolvieren. So lange gilt auch die Wien Karte/Vienna Card der Wiener Linien. Sie ist zum Preis von öS 180,- in über 200 Wiener Hotels, in den Wien Tourist-Infos und den wichtigen Verkaufsstellen der Wiener Linien erhältlich.
Bestellung per Telefon und Kreditkarte:
+43-1-798 44 00-28
Mit der Wien Karte/Vienna Card können Sie 72 Stunden lang die öffentlichen Verkehrsmittel Tram, Bus (ausgenommen Nacht-Busse) und U-Bahn (und S-Bahn in der Zone 100) benützen, bei über 70 Museen, Sehenswürdigkeiten, Theatern, Konzertveranstaltungen, Geschäften, Restaurants, Cafes und Heurigen gibt es damit Ermäßigungen.

Wanderungen

Wenn Sie auf unserer Tour noch nicht genug gewandert sind, Wien hat mehr: Über die Wiener Stadtwanderwege und den neuen Rund-um Wien-Wanderweg informiert der Presse- und Informationsdienst der Stadt Wien, Broschürenservice, Telefon +43-1-4000-8080.

Stadtspaziergänge

Über geführte Stadtspaziergänge informiert: Telefon +43-1-894 53 63, 489 42 63
Regelmäßig stattfindende Spaziergänge führen unter anderem jeden Mittwoch in das „Unbekannte unterirdische Wien" (deutsch, englisch, Treffpunkt Michaelerplatz vor der Kirche, 13 Uhr).

Wien erfahren

kann man auch mit dem Fahrrad. Das Radwegenetz bietet Verbindungen in der ganzen Stadt, private Radverleihe finden sich insbesondere auf der Donauinsel.
Geführte Radtouren bietet Vienna Bike, Wasagasse 28/2/5, A-1090 Wien,
Telefon und Telefax: +43-1-319 12 58.

Stadtrundfahrten abseits der touristische Wege
Neben den privaten Rundfahrten zu den touristischen Highlights bietet die Stadt Wien über das Wiener Rundfahrtenbüro
Rundfahrten zu bestimmten Terminen und Themen in das „neue Wien" an.
A-1082 Rathaus, Telefon +43-1-4000-81050

Published by Compress-Verlag,
Jenullgasse 4, A-1140 Vienna
tel: +43 1 894 64 49, fax: +43 1 894 65 23

Vienna Card

The "tour of Vienna" described in this book can best be undertaken by public transport and on foot. It can be done in three days, using the "Vienna Card" issued by the Vienna Public Transport Board ("Wiener Linien").The Card costs ATS 180,- and is available in over 200 hotels, from the "Vienna Tourist Information Offices" and the major ticket offices of the „Vienna Public Transport Board". It can be ordered by credit card on the following telephone number:
+43-1-798 44 00-28. The "Vienna Card" enables you, for a period of 72 hours, to travel on all public transportation services – trams, buses (with the exception of night-buses) and the subway (also S-Bahn in Zone 100). It also entitles you to a discount in over 70 museums, sites of public interest, theaters, concerts, shops, restaurants, cafés and "Heuriger" wine taverns.

Walks

If you feel you have not done enough walking on our tour, then Vienna still has more to offer. The Press and Information Service of the City of Vienna (Broschürenservice, tel.: +4-1-4000-8080) provides information on "Wiener Stadtwanderwege" (Walks through Vienna) and the new "Rund-um-Wien-Wanderweg" (Walks in the Environs of Vienna).

City walks

Information on guides walks through the city can be obtained on tel.: +43-1-894 53 63 or +43-1-489 42 63. One such guided walk visits "Unknown Subterranean Vienna" and takes place every Wednesday (German/English, meeting point in front of St. Michael's church, 1.30 p.m.).

Experiencing Vienna

is also possible by bicycle. There is a large network of cacle tracks troughout the city and bicycles can be hired in many places, especially on the Danube Island. Guided cacle rides are offered by Vienna Bike, Wasagasse 28/2/5, A-1090 Vienna,
tel./Fax: +43-1-319 12 58.

City tours with a difference

Over and above sightseeing tours to the tourist highlights offered by private companies, the City of Vienna runs a program of tours visiting "modern Vienna". Information on the dates, times and types of tours available can be obtained from the Wiener Rundfahrtenbüro, A-1082 Rathaus, tel.: +43-1-4000 81050.

Wien in Zahlen
Alle Angaben 1994/1995

Wiener Stadtfläche	15 km²
davon Grünfläche	205 km²
EW/m² Grünfläche	
(dichtbes. Stadtgebiet)	133/4,8
höchster/tiefster Punkt	
(Hermannskogel/Lobau)	543 m/151 m
Östliche Länge/Nördliche Breite	16°/48°
Wohnbevölkerung	1,636.000
weiblich	861.000
männlich	775.000
Ausländer	301.000
ehem. Jugoslawen	128.000
Türken	52.000
Polen	19.000
BRD	12.000
Bevölkerungsdichte (EW/km²)	3.944
Wirtschaft	
Beschäftigte (Erwerbstätige)	780.000
Erwerbsquote (Beschäftigte/EW)	48 %
Arbeitslosenrate	7 %
Dichte je 1.000 EW	
KFZ	427
TV	355
Telefon	613
Verbrauch je EW/Jahr	
Gas	1.060 m³
Strom	5.574 kWh
Wasser	94 m³
Müllaufkommen	317 kg
Fremdenverkehr	
Bettenzahl	39.670
Nächtigungen	7,050.000
BRD	1,593.000
Italien	541.000
USA	551.000
Österreich	850.000
Verkehr	
Straßennetz (in km)	2.776
ÖV-Netz (in km)	1.560
Straßenbahn (34 Linien)	240
U-Bahn (5 Linien)	57
Autobus (87 Linien)	658
Schnellbahn (11 Linien)	179
Beförderungen	687,500.000
Flugverkehr PAX an	4,180.000
ab	4,192.000
Budget der Stadt Wien (in Mrd. S)	
Stand: Juni 1996	
Gesamtsumme	146,449

Vienna in Figures
Data from 1994/1995

Total Surface Area of Vienna	*415 km²*
of which green areas	*205 km²*
m² of green space per inhabitant in	
high-density urban area	*33/4.8*
highest/lowest point	
(Hermannskogel/Lobau)	*543m/151m*
Longitude/Latitude	*16°/48°*
Population	*1,636,000*
Female	*861,000*
Male	*775,000*
Foreigners	*301,000*
from former Yugoslavia	*128,000*
Turks	*52,000*
Poles	*19,000*
Germans	*12,000*
Population density	
(per inhabitant/km2)	*3,944*
Economy	
Employed (gainfully employed)	*780,000*
Employment quota	
(employed/per inhabitant)	*48 %*
Unemployed	*7 %*
Per 1,000 inhabitants	
Cars	*427*
TV sets	*355*
Telephones	*613*
Consumption per inhabitant/year	
Gas	*1,060 m3*
Electricity	*5,574 kWh*
Water	*94 m3*
Volume of refuse generated per	
inhabitant/year	*317 kg*
Tourism	
No. of beds	*39,670*
No. of overnight stays	*7,050,000*
Germany	*1,593,000*
Italy	*541,000*
USA	*551,000*
Austria	*850,000*
Transport	
Road network (in km)	*2,776*
Public transport network (in km)	*1,560*
Trams (34 lines)	*240*
Subway (5 lines)	*57*
Bus (87 lines)	*658*
S-Bahn	*179*
Rides	*687,500,000*

- Vertretungskörper und
  allgemeine Verwaltung　10,193
- Öffentliche Ordnung
  und Sicherheit　1,736
- Unterricht, Erziehung, Sport
  und Wissenschaft　13,653
- Kunst, Kultur, Kultus　2,175
- Soziale Wohlfahrt und
  Wohnbauförderung　23,551
- Gesundheit　27,240
- Straßen- und Wasserbau,
  Verkehr　1,668
- Wirtschaftsförderung　1,286
- Dienstleistungen　43,026
- Finanzwirtschaft　21,926

Air transport PAX
　arr.　4,180,000
　dep.　4,192,000

Municipal Budget
(in ATS billion)
As per: June 1996
Total　146.449
Representative bodies
and adminstration　10.193
Public safety and order　1.736
Education, sport and science　13.653
Art, culture, religion　2.175

Social welfare and
housing assistance　23.551
Health　27.240
Road construction,
river engineering, transport　1.668
Business development　1.286
Services　43.026
Financial management　21.926

Impressum

Herausgeber: Hannes Swoboda, Arnold Klotz, Lothar Fischmann
Text: Lothar Fischmann
Gestaltung und Bildredaktion: Andrea Neuwirth
Photographien: Lomographische Gesellschaft Wien
Abbildungen: Landesbildstelle Wien, Freigabezahl: 13.088/93-1.1.1996
Projektabbildungen: Atelier Hollein/Sina Baniahmad, Alfred Schmid und Architekten
Koordination: Susanne Debelak
Übersetzung: MDP – Übersetzungsdienst, Bettina Klötzl, Susan Siegle
Produktion: Druckhaus Grasl, Bad Vöslau

Das Werk ist urheberrechtlich geschützt. Die dadurch begründeten Rechte, insbesondere die der Übersetzung, des Nachdruckes, der Entnahme von Abbildungen, der Funksendung, der Wiedergabe auf photomechanischem oder ähnlichem Wege und die Speicherung in Datenverarbeitungsanlagen, bleiben, auch bei nur auszugsweiser Verwertung, vorbehalten.

© 1996 Springer-Verlag/Wien
Printed in Austria
ISBN 3-211-82881-8
Springer-Verlag Wien New York

Imprint

Publisher: Hannes Swoboda, Arnold Klotz, Lothar Fischmann
Text: Lothar Fischmann
Graphic design and photographic editor: Andrea Neuwirth
Photographs: Lomographische Gesellschaft Wien
Aerial photographs: Landesbildstelle Wien, Freigabezahl: 13.088/93-1.1.1996
Project illustrations: Atelier Hollein/Sina Baniahmad, Alfred Schmid and architects
Coordination: Susanne Debelak
Translations: MDP-Übersetzungsdienst, Bettina Klötzl, Susan Siegle
Production: Druckhaus Grasl, Bad Vöslau

This work ist subject to copyright. All rights are reserved, whether the whole or part of the material is concerned, specifically those of translation, reprinting, re-use of illustrations, broadcasting, reproduction by photocopying machines or similar means, and storage in data banks.

© 1996 Springer-Verlag/Wien
Printed in Austria
ISBN 3-211-82881-8
Springer-Verlag Wien New York